VERDICT ON EREBUS

PETER MAHON

W0013755

COLLINS

First published 1984. Reprinted 1984.
First issued in Fontana Paperbacks 1985. Reprinted 1987.
William Collins Publishers Ltd
P.O. Box 1, Auckland

ISBN 0 00 636976 6,
Typeset by Saba Graphics Ltd, Christchurch
Printed in Hong Kong

CONTENTS

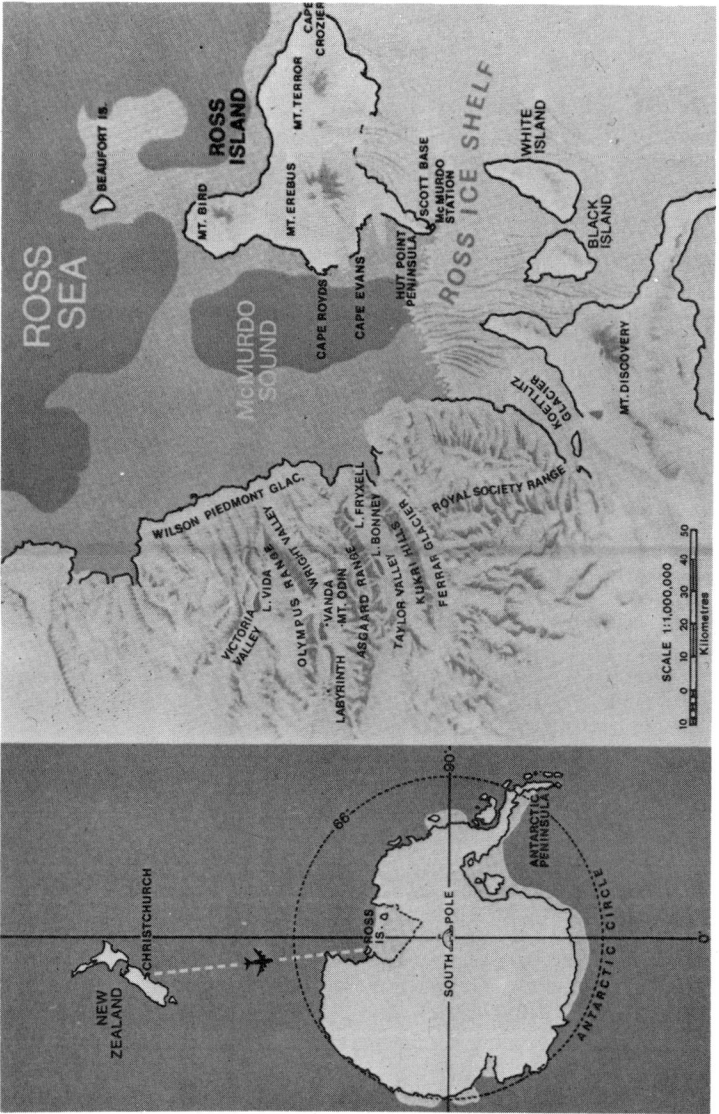

Scale map of the McMurdo area (Courtesy D.S.I.R.)

LIST OF ILLUSTRATIONS

This book is dedicated to W.D. Baragwanath Q.C. and G.M. Harrison, who were counsel assisting the Royal Commission into the Mount Erebus air disaster, and without whose industry and perception the full story of the tragedy might never have been disclosed.

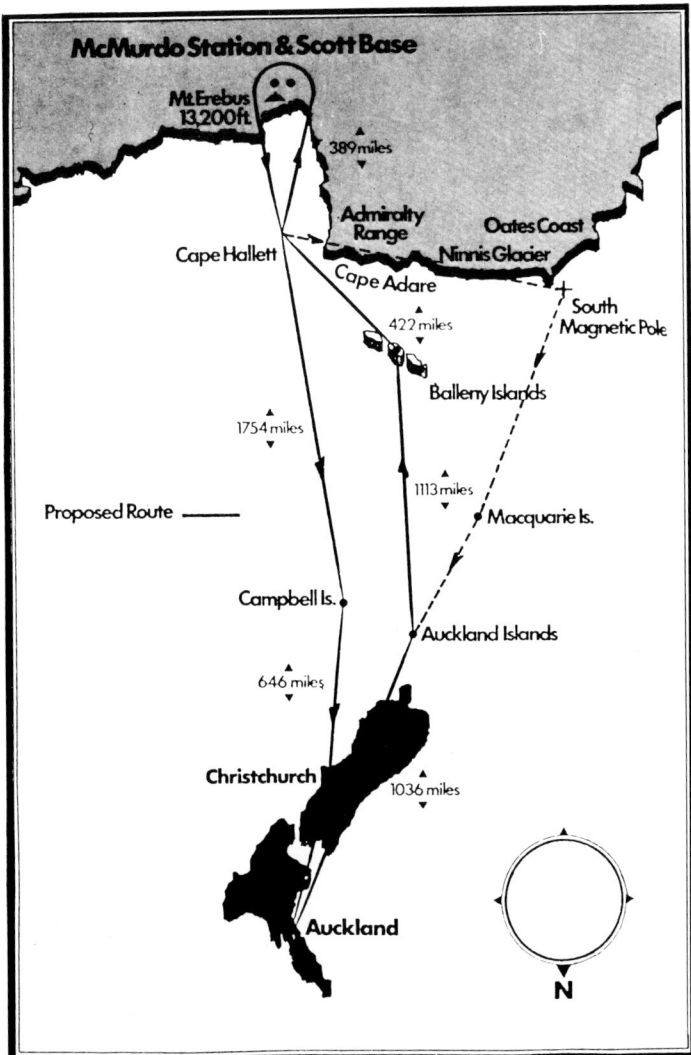

This diagram was printed in passenger brochures and also displayed as a slide at the briefing of Antarctic crews. It shows the approximate standard flight track to Antarctica together with the alternative route to the South Magnetic Pole. The track depicted from Cape Hallett to McMurdo was altered by the airline on the eve of the fatal flight.

The crash site   Photo: Sergeant S.J. Gilpin

About to leave for the crash site. From left to right: The author, W.D. Baragwanath, Air Marshal Sir Rochford Hughes, J.E. Davies (Air New Zealand)

Three photographs, taken at 30-second intervals, from the helicopter approaching the crash site, show the rapidity of the partial then total development of Mount Erebus in cloud   Photo: R.B. Thomson

Three men whose evidence about flying hazards had a significant effect at the inquiry
Left: Captain A.G. Vette, former senior Air New Zealand pilot who produced the vital whiteout evidence
Centre: First Officer P.M. Rhodes, the Air Accident Investigator for the Airline Pilots' Association
Right: Antarctic expert R.B. Thomson, Superintendent of the Antarctic Division of D.S.I.R.

FOREWORD

On 28 November 1979 a DC10 passenger jet airliner owned by Air New Zealand, carrying out a tourist flight from New Zealand to Antarctica and back, flew in broad daylight into the lower slopes of Mount Erebus in Antarctica. There were no survivors of the crash and 257 people lost their lives.

The New Zealand Government appointed me to be a Royal Commissioner of Inquiry to investigate the disaster and to report to the Government my opinion as to its cause. In due course I conducted an open hearing in Auckland which occupied a total of seventy-five sitting days. Fifty-two witnesses were examined and cross-examined, I had to make various investigations overseas, and 284 documentary exhibits were produced and studied. This book is my own account of the inquiry.

Many investigations into air disasters are complicated by engineering or aeronautical questions involving technical expertise. This is almost invariably so when the crash has been caused by some gross malfunction of the aircraft in flight. In the case of the Mount Erebus disaster, no such difficulties arose. The electronic recording systems in the aircraft reproduced every aspect of its flight up to the moment of impact, and all the aircraft's systems were found to have been functioning perfectly. The questions to be answered consisted almost entirely of the inferences to be drawn from known facts. Why was the aircraft on that course? Why was it flying at that altitude? Above all, why had no one on the flight deck seen the mountainside?

There was one supervening factor which dominated all these questions and many others. The aircraft was navigated by the inertial navigation system which has for many years dispensed with the need for human navigators on commercial flights. An aircraft fitted with this equipment records its own progress through the air, and a digital readout tells the crew second by second exactly where the aircraft is. The INS on this DC10 was found to have been operating accurately during the flight, so the aircrew had always known where they were. But following the disaster there were many senior pilots in Air New Zealand who suspected that the standard flight track to Antarctica had not been the flight track which had been typed into the aircraft computer on the morning of the flight. They believed that the standard flight track had been changed without the knowledge of the crew. As things turned out this theory proved to be correct, and a considerable time was spent at the inquiry in ascertaining how and why this appalling mistake came to be committed by the airline's Flight Operations Divison.

Another difficulty which overshadowed the inquiry was the attitude of the airline management. They had decided to reject each and every suggestion of culpability on the part of the airline and they steadfastly maintained the allegation, right throughout the inquiry, that the aircrew was alone to blame. In order to support this proposition there were witnesses from the Flight Operations Division who gave evidence which I was compelled to reject, and the company's conduct at the inquiry created deep resentment on the part of the Airline Pilots' Association and on the part of all those who were familiar with the long experience and dedicated skills of the dead aircrew.

Air New Zealand is a very small airline but its reputation as an international carrier is outstanding, and in my opinion its status should not be and has not been undermined merely because in the wake of this tragedy and during the inquiry a group of individuals within the airline foolishly attempted to conceal the company's negligence. And after all, the credibility of the airline's witnesses was in the last resort only a side issue. The real issue was the question of causation. How and why had the disaster occurred?

At the time of its occurrence this was the fourth worst disaster in aviation history. The location of the crash and its surrounding circumstances combine to make the tragedy unique in the annals of the air. In this book I describe my investigation and the conclusions which I formed as to how and why this modern passenger jet aircraft with its sophisticated electronic systems carried 257 people to their deaths in the vast white wilderness of Antarctica.

GLOSSARY OF TERMS

AINS	Area Inertial Navigation System
ALPA	Airline Pilots' Association (NZ)
ASR	Airport Surveillance Radar (mode)
CAM	Cockpit Area Microphone
CDU	Computer Display Unit
CVR	Cockpit Voice Recorder
DFDR	Digital Flight Data Recorder ("Black Box")
DME	Distance Measuring Equipment
DSIR	Dept. of Scientific & Industrial Research
GPWS	Ground Proximity Warning System
HDG SEL	Heading Select
HF	High Frequency
ICAO	International Civil Aviation Organization
IFF	Identify Friend/Foe
IMC	Instrument Meteorological Conditions
INS	Inertial Navigation System
MSA	Minimum Safe Altitude
NCU	Navigation Computer Unit
NDB	Non-Directional Beacon
QNH	Local atmospheric pressure
RCU	Route Clearance Unit
RNC	Route Navigation Chart
TACAN	Tactical Air Navigation System
VHF	Very High Frequency
VMC	Visual Meteorological Conditions

I

THE DAY OF THE DISASTER

It was November 28, 1979, and I was carrying out my ordinary judicial duties in Auckland — at that time I had been a Judge of the Supreme Court of New Zealand for eight years. At 10 a.m. I had begun the hearing of a jury trial in the No. 1 Courtroom in the Auckland Supreme Court. A young man was claiming damages for injuries sustained in a road accident. The defendant did not contest the right of the plaintiff to recover damages but his insurers contested the amount of the claim. So, the jury had only to fix the amount of damages.

On that same day something else was taking place which was to take up a great deal of my time in the following year. A DC10 aircraft, operated by Air New Zealand and officially recorded as ZK-NZP, was on its way from Auckland to Antarctica. It had left Auckland Airport at 8.17 a.m., carrying 237 passengers on a scenic flight planned to fly over the McMurdo Sound area in Antarctica and then to return to New Zealand, landing at Christchurch. The round trip would be about 5,000 miles and would occupy about eleven hours. The aircraft carried a crew of twenty, so there were 257 people on board. These scenic flights to Antarctica had been going on since February 1977, but there had not been many of them. This was the fourteenth flight, Flight TE901.

As I sat in the courtroom that day, listening to the evidence, I was not, of course, aware of the departure of the DC10. I had never taken much notice of these Antarctic flights, although I had heard them referred to very favourably by some people who had been sightseeing passengers. To me, it seemed a very long time to be in the air but the scenery at McMurdo was said to be magnificent and, after all, it was something to be able to say that one had flown over part of the Antarctic Continent and been fairly close to the South Pole.

The court case dragged on. Conflicting medical evidence was given and there were disputed questions as to the extent to which the plaintiff might have sustained some permanent disability. Finally the evidence was concluded, counsel addressed the jury and I summed up. At 12.28 p.m. the jury retired to consider its verdict, which was not returned until 3 p.m. The jury awarded the plaintiff $21,274.50 and I entered judgment for that amount. I spent the rest of the afternoon writing a reserved judgment in another case.

I drove home at about 6 p.m. On the way I turned on the car radio and heard a news item referring to radio silence from the Air New Zealand DC10 which had flown to Antarctica that day. It appeared that there had been previous announcements to the same effect earlier in the evening. There was some reference to the uncertainty of radio transmissions in the polar region.

I continued listening at home and it was soon apparent that deep anxieties were felt as to the safety of the aircraft and those on board. There were references to the aircraft's being nearly out of fuel. Then the news broadcasts began to be more specific.

By about 7 p.m., it was being alleged that the aircraft had not been heard of for some hours. It appeared that the crew were required to report their position at regular intervals. One commentator suggested that these were thirty-minute intervals but no one seemed to know exactly when it was that the aircraft had missed its first reporting call.

Time moved on. By 8 p.m. it was announced that the aircraft was probably out of fuel and there could be no doubt that a massive disaster must have occurred. The aircraft should have landed at Christchurch at 7.05 p.m. There were only two sources of information available to the public and to the Press. One was the radio centre at Auckland known as Oceanic Control, the reporting centre for the aircraft once it was north of 60°S latitude; the other the radio traffic from the U.S. Navy Base at McMurdo Sound. This is a scientific base situated close to New Zealand's Scott Base. Each of these scientific stations is maintained all the year round with the headquarters of the American Base being situated at Christchurch. The American name for the whole system of maintaining and supporting their McMurdo Base is 'Operation Deep Freeze'.

By 8 p.m. no information had been received from either Oceanic Control or Deep Freeze Headquarters as to the whereabouts of the missing aircraft. There had been an unusual silence on the part of Air New Zealand, and public anxiety was mounting through the night. It was not until after 11 p.m. that the airline made any statement. The Chief Executive, Mr M.R. Davis, held a press conference at Air New Zealand's head office in

Auckland. A large group of press, radio and television reporters were present. The Chief Executive said that there was little chance of finding the aircraft and its passengers safe. For the news media people, there was nothing novel in that statement. They all knew that the aircraft had been out of fuel for hours. Either it had made a forced landing somewhere on the Antarctic Continent, or it had crashed in Antarctica or gone down in the sea. The only conceivable hope that could have existed after 8 p.m. was the possibility of a forced landing in Antarctica but if that had taken place, then obviously the people at the American Base and at Scott Base knew nothing about it. It was clear enough that there had been no message from the aircraft announcing that it was in difficulties or that it was intending to make a landing.

Air and sea rescue procedures had been put into operation during the late afternoon. As it transpired later, the U.S. Navy at McMurdo had placed its sea and air rescue organisation on standby at about 3 p.m. New Zealand time, and not long afterwards the Americans had despatched aircraft to search the approaches to McMurdo.

At about 10 p.m. a U.S. Navy four-engine jet Starlifter aircraft arrived at Christchurch from Antarctica. It was piloted by Major B.L. Gumble. He had flown the Starlifter to Antarctica that morning; on the route to the south, he had been about forty minutes behind the DC10, and from time to time, he had been talking to the Air New Zealand crew.

As the Starlifter began to get close to McMurdo, Major Gumble attempted to contact Flight 901 again. He wanted to determine its flight path, as he needed to know just where the DC10 would be when he began his approach to the ice runway at McMurdo. But he got no reply. The radio operator in the Starlifter kept calling the DC10 but there was still no reply.

At about forty miles from McMurdo Station, the Starlifter had been picked up by the McMurdo radar and Major Gumble had descended under radar control and landed on the ice runway. It was then he heard that the DC10 had missed a reporting call. After refuelling, the Starlifter took off again to return to Christchurch. By the time his aircraft left, the McMurdo authorities had become even more anxious about the radio silence from the DC10 and Major Gumble was therefore instructed to keep a careful lookout on his return flight to the north.

Major Gumble took the big jet past Cape Royds on the western coast of Ross Island and reduced altitude to 2,000 feet, and later to 1,500 feet, as he turned east towards the northern aspect of Ross Island. Neither he nor the crew could see any sign of wreckage but there was heavy cloud in the area. As the big Starlifter jet was unsuitable for low altitude search missions in the mountains, Major Gumble gave up a search of Ross Island, turned the aircraft to the left and flew away in a northerly direction towards New Zealand. On the journey north up McMurdo Sound, in broad daylight, the crew of the Starlifter saw no sign of the DC10. On arrival at Christchurch, Major Gumble was naturally besieged by reporters, but he could tell them only what I have just described. The big passenger jet with its 257 people on board had vanished.

At 1 a.m. New Zealand time the fate of the missing DC10 was revealed. A U.S. Navy Hercules aircraft, which had been systematically searching the McMurdo area, had seen wreckage on the northern slopes of Mount Erebus, and on close observation, it became clear that this was the wreckage of the missing airliner. The crew of the Hercules were astounded at the sight below them. Here was the white snow-covered rising ground of the mountain with the wreckage looking like nothing more than a long black smear extending hundreds of yards up the ice slope. Some large pieces of wreckage could be seen near the top of the disaster track but, from the air, it was difficult to see anything else of substantial size. The impact point was about 1,500 feet above sea level.

The Hercules circled the wreckage and reported the latitude and longitude of the crash site. The crew looked intently for any sign of movement on the ground, but there was nothing. There seemed to be no survivors.

The radio message from the U.S. Navy Hercules notifying discovery of the wreckage reached New Zealand in time to be published in the morning papers and in the afternoon editions of newspapers on the other side of the world. So, on November 29 it was known throughout the world that this air disaster had occurred with a loss of 257 lives. It was, at the time, the fourth worst air disaster in aviation history.

In New Zealand, these sightseeing flights to Antarctica were well enough known, but the northern hemisphere news agencies were at first mystified as to what a passenger jet was doing in that far-off wilderness of snow and ice, and there were millions of people, no doubt, who had to rely upon newspaper maps to ascertain exactly where New Zealand was.

Like everyone else in New Zealand, I read with close attention the morning newspaper in Auckland, and the first of the afternoon editions of the evening newspapers. Even at that early stage, theories were being propounded. What could have happened? I could not foretell that four months later the New

Zealand Government would appoint me as a one-man Commission of Inquiry to answer, if I could, that very question. Nor could I anticipate, even after I was appointed as Commissioner, the strange and tortuous evidential journey on which I would be conducted as I sought to ascertain the true causes of this massive air disaster. And I could not foresee the obdurate and implacable series of obstructions and evasions which were to be created by the airline itself in a bold attempt to thwart the discovery of the truth.

II

AT THE CRASH SITE

The most urgent question was how to recover the bodies from the crash site. In addition, there was an obvious necessity for investigators to go to Antarctica and find out what they could about the circumstances of the crash.

The New Zealand Police Force had a standard plan — known as their Disaster Victim Identification Procedure (DVI) — for use in the case of major disasters. This plan involved a command structure and the delegation from that level of specific tasks to groups of personnel. The people who would be in charge of the operation were pre-selected. But the DVI procedure was created for a disaster like a major urban fire, an earthquake, or an airport crash. It was certainly never considered that it would need to be brought into operation in a snow-clad polar wilderness 2,500 miles south of New Zealand. But as things turned out, the police system withstood every strain imposed upon it and the success of the body recovery and identification procedures pointed significantly to the great merit of having advance plans ready to cope with dire emergencies.

It was the responsibility of the police to recover the bodies and all personal property from the mountainside, and inquiries as to the cause of the disaster were for the time being regarded as of secondary importance. So, at Police Headquarters in Wellington, arrangements were immediately put in hand to convey the police party to McMurdo. In the meantime, the authorities at Scott Base were taking every possible step to inspect the scene and to notify Police Headquarters in Wellington by radio telephone of all the problems which might arise in getting access to the crash site.

It happened that among the people working at Scott Base were three New Zealand mountaineers — Daryll Thompson, Hugh Logan and Keith Woodford. These three men were dropped into the crash area by helicopter in the early hours of November 29, fortunately a time of the year when there is perpetual daylight in

Antarctica. The task of the mountaineers was to locate any survivors and to report by radio as to the possibility of a large party being flown in. They satisfied themselves that there were no survivors and after two hours they were picked up by helicopter. It was arranged that they would return later to set up a camp with polar tents and basic survival equipment which could be used by a large party. The slope of the mountainside in this area was about 15° and helicopters could not land safely on the sloping snow, bearing in mind the unpredictable winds which arise without warning in Antarctica. Therefore it was decided that a helicopter launching pad would have to be constructed on the mountainside.

Meanwhile, in New Zealand, preparations had been completed for the carriage by air to Antarctica of the key personnel who would be required at the crash site. A Hercules aircraft left Christchurch at 5.15 p.m. It carried the head of the police party, Inspector Bob Mitchell, together with ten other police officers, five New Zealand mountaineers, two representatives of Air New Zealand, namely Mr Ian Wood and Captain Ian Gemmell, Mr Ron Chippindale, Chief Inspector of Air Accidents, together with Mr David Graham, an inspector on his staff, two journalists and a television cameraman. Last, but certainly not least, was Bob Thomson, Superintendent of the Antarctic Division of the New Zealand Department of Scientific and Industrial Research.

Bob Thomson had been in control of Scott Base for many years and was a veteran of the Antarctic region. He would be required to play a leading part in the organisation of the recovery procedures as a great deal would turn upon matters of accommodation and availability of supplies, both from Scott Base and McMurdo Station and, in general, his task would be to use his special knowledge of the environment and the conditions to facilitate the operations of the police recovery party. While the Hercules was on its way south, the mountaineers who had first been dropped at the site went back there by helicopter and established a base camp with tents, radios, and food and equipment for twenty people.

On November 30 the weather began to deteriorate, but the next day work began at the crash site and the two electronic recorder boxes (which might contain the only evidence as to what had happened over the last few minutes of the flight) were recovered. These two vital pieces of equipment were flown back to McMurdo.

About this time another Hercules arrived with a group of American personnel who had flown down from the United States. There were representatives of the Federal Aviation

Administration and the National Transportation Safety Board and three technical people from McDonnell Douglas and a representative of the General Electric Corporation which had manufactured the engines used on DC10 aircraft. Also on this flight were Mr Milton Wylie, another New Zealand accident inspector and Captain Tony Foley and First Officer Rhodes who were there in their capacities of air accident investigators for the New Zealand Airline Pilots' Association.

But Mr Dennis Grossi, the National Transportation Safety Board representative, and Milton Wylie did not remain long at McMurdo. Some hours after their arrival they returned by air to New Zealand taking with them the electronic recorder equipment, namely the cockpit voice recorder and the 'black box'.

The technical name for the 'black box' is the Digital Flight Data Recorder (DFDR). It is certainly a remarkable piece of equipment and is yet a further example of the development of computer technology. Located in the centre of this very strong metal box, with its multiple shock-absorbing equipment, is a data recording system which monitors and stores in its memory every mechanical function of the aircraft. In order to retrieve the information, the air accident investigators merely connect the 'black box' to a computer printout mechanism and the printout will then record every function of the aircraft, including its course, altitude, speed, separate engine output, and the setting of all controls at every second of its progress through the air. As a result, providing that the 'black box' is recovered from the site of the crash of an aircraft, which it almost always is, then there can never be any doubt as to the exact functioning of the aircraft in every respect right up to the time of impact.

From New Zealand the two 'black box' couriers proceeded in due course to the Sunstrand Corporation in Seattle, where the instruments are made. There a copy of the 'black box' material was made, together with a recording of what was on the voice recorder tape. They then took these tapes and the recorders to the headquarters of the National Transportation Safety Board in Washington and, within a matter of two or three days, the board's experts had derived considerable information from the two recorders and shortly afterwards prepared official transcriptions of that information.

Up until now, I have been repeating the official course of events, as presented later at the Royal Commission hearings. The two electronic recorders were located in the snow among the wreckage, and sent to Washington. But that is not quite a complete account. Upon arrival at Wellington the voice tapes were played at the offices of Civil Aviation Division and copies were made. And then, though I was never told about it, Civil Aviation undoubtedly spoke to the Chief Inspector by radiotelephone and told him that the aircrew appeared to have been lost, and flying in cloud.

In the meantime, at the crash site, the police were carrying out their DVI procedures. The site had been divided into a series of rectangular grids all marked by long sticks with black flags. All visible bodies and parts of bodies were marked with green flags, and attached to each green flag was a number. This number was allocated to that body alone, and where there was personal property found on a body or sufficiently identifiable as having belonged to that victim, then it was placed in a bag which bore that same number. The location of every body or part of a body was fixed in relation to the grid pattern and each body was photographed before being removed.

But here, I will leave this part of the story, and look at what was happening in quite a different area. I have referred to the three experts from McDonnell Douglas and the expert from General Electric. They had certainly gone to Antarctica with great expedition, having arrived on December 1. Their presence at the crash site was understandable. They were representatives of the manufacturers of the aircraft and they would no doubt be able to give invaluable assistance in identifying various parts of the widely scattered wreckage. But they had another concern and it was something which they did not reveal publicly. They all thought that the disaster had been caused by a gross malfunction of the aircraft.

These experts had known before their arrival that the operational altitude on these sightseeing flights ranged between 1,000 and 4,000 feet. They knew that there had been a sudden radio silence from the DC10. There had not been one transmission from the aircraft indicating an emergency. They thought that something had disabled the aircraft at low altitude and without warning, so as to plunge it into the ground. They had reason for suspecting that one of two things had happened — either one of the wing engines had fallen off the aircraft, or one of its cargo doors had blown open and the depressurisation had thrown the aircraft out of control. These apprehensions had their origin in a very unfortunate sequence of previous aircraft incidents and accidents involving DC10 aircraft in which similar malfunctions had occurred.

From a marketing viewpoint, it was essential for the manufacturer to attribute the crash to human error. Any evidence suggesting a malfunction in the aircraft would surely have spelt the doom of future DC10 manufacture and sales. As the McDonnell Douglas personnel clambered through the wreckage on the frozen mountainside their employers in California must have been anxiously awaiting the information which the 'black box' and the cockpit voice recorder would reveal.

But, in the end, the anxieties of the manufacturer were laid to rest. The read-out from the 'black box' eventually confirmed that the aircraft was functioning perfectly in all respects until the moment when it collided with the mountain. But it was not until about mid-December that this was known for certain. In fact, when the Chief Inspector returned from Antarctica on about December 13, he was reported by an air magazine as indicating that the investigators were still concerned about the 'airworthiness' of the DC10.

In the meantime the police had been proceeding with the task of flying the bodies of the victims to McMurdo Station where arrangements had been completed for their transport by air to Auckland. There was only one possible way of transferring the bodies and human remains to McMurdo, twenty miles away from the northern slopes of Mount Erebus, and that was by helicopter. Each body, with its identification number attached, was, of course, in a frozen state and it was loaded into a long open-ended, polythene bag which was then tied at each end. The bodies were loaded into a net which was picked up by the helicopter which then flew to McMurdo Station. In addition, there were the multiple remnants of disintegrated bodies which lay all along the crash site, and all that could be done was to load these remnants into polythene bags in the same way as the intact bodies.

The first bodies were flown out on December 4 and the last arrived at McMurdo Station six days later. On December 7 the first of the Hercules aircraft carrying the dead victims arrived at Auckland and the police plans for body identification were put into operation. Autopsies were conducted by five teams of pathologists at the Auckland Medical School, and they were assisted by dentists and by police fingerprint experts and photographers, as well as police officers from the DVI Squad. Each body or part body which arrived from Antarctica was accompanied by a partially completed DVI form which had the same number as the body number, and as each autopsy was carried out, the DVI form was completed. Then the form went to Police Records where identifiable clothing, jewellery and other personal property had been recorded on a property sheet bearing the same number as the DVI form. As bodies were progressively identified, the property sheets had the names recorded. Finally 213 recovered bodies were identified. The bodies of the 44 other persons on the aircraft could not be identified.

The conduct of the Police DVI Team was beyond praise. The hostile terrain in that polar wilderness provided every difficulty which could be imagined. Bodies and parts of bodies were buried in snow, and the unpredictable winds of Antarctica were responsible for many delays and frustrations. All the work was done in frozen conditions on sloping terrain covered in soft snow.

To add to the hardships inherent in the operation, there was the unwelcome presence of the scavenging skua gulls of Antarctica. These dark brown birds, large and powerful, are found in their hundreds in the vicinity of Scott Base and McMurdo Station. They are fearless predators. They attack penguin rookeries so as to seize and devour penguin chicks. When the chained husky dogs at Scott Base are fed their allowance of seal meat, the skua gulls are always in attendance ready to dispute the possession of a piece of meat with an ill-tempered husky.

When the three mountaineers were first dropped at the crash site some fifteen hours or so after the disaster had occurred, they saw that the skua gulls were already arriving and right through the process of body recovery on the mountainside, policemen and their assistants had to do what they could to beat off the gulls. Even after the bodies had been securely wrapped inside the polythene bags, the gulls continued to attack. The hard-working team on the mountainside then had to cover the bags with ice and snow to protect them until their removal by helicopter. Even upon arrival at McMurdo Station, the skua gulls took a close interest in the body bags which were being unloaded, and had to be frightened off with shotguns.

The second phase of the police DVI procedure was carried out at the Auckland Mortuary, for it was the responsibility of the police to identify the bodies. No identification was held to be complete until two independent and positive forms of identification had been established. In completing the identification task, the police teams, in their work at the mortuary and in consequential inquiries, put in a total of 15,000 working hours. In due course an inquest of considerable length and complexity was completed. The identified bodies were returned to next-of-kin for burial or cremation, and on February 22, 1980 an interdenominational burial service was held in Auckland and the unidentifiable body bags were buried in a common grave.

III

THE CHIEF EXECUTIVE SPEAKS TO THE PRESS

From the date of the disaster its occurrence had been the subject of investigation by the Chief Inspector of Air Accidents, but I must now go forward in time to record an event which later became of considerable significance. Air New Zealand had put a complete embargo on any attempt by employees to give information to the public or to the Press. This was a natural reaction in a situation where inquiries were being made as to the cause of the disaster. In particular, it might be said that grounds suggested, or opinions given, by the company's operational pilots could possibly prejudice the position of Air New Zealand's passenger liability insurance.

In any case, the company had always been very wary of the Press. The veiling of its commercial operations from public scrutiny had been a continuing pre-occupation of the company's Chief Executive, for the airline flew internationally in strong competition with other carriers. The fact that the airline was publicly owned did not seem to make any difference. This position, taken by the airline in relation to any information about its affairs, was well known to all employees. But, in spite of this, a piece of information had become public in February 1980 and public curiosity had been aroused.

A weekend newspaper had stated that the computer track of the aircraft had been changed just before the DC10 left Auckland, and it was alleged that the crew of the DC10 had not been told of the alteration. It was explained in the newspaper that a DC10 aircraft is guided not by a human navigator but by typing into a computer system on the aircraft a list of co-ordinates of latitude and longitude. After take-off, the aircraft is then locked on to the course represented by the list of co-ordinates and will fly itself over each and every co-ordinate until it reaches the co-ordinates representing the aircraft's destination. The newspaper reported that there were some pilots who claimed that the final co-ordinates of the flight — that is, those located at McMurdo — had been altered just before the aircraft left Auckland, that the crew had not been told of the alteration, and that the undisclosed alteration had played a major part in the tragedy because the aircraft's computer track had been altered by many miles on the approach to McMurdo.

On February 19, 1980 Air New Zealand made a public denial that incorrect data had been fed into the navigation computer of the DC10. The Chief Executive said that the computer had been fed the correct information. But the *Auckland Star* began making further inquiries and on February 25 the newspaper's aviation reporter put to the Chief Executive the specific suggestion that the navigation co-ordinates had been changed without the knowledge of the crew of the crashed DC10. In reply, the Chief Executive said, 'You are moving into a very highly speculative area and I cannot go further than to say that the navigation information and flight plan for the aircraft which crashed was accurate and entirely in order.' Mr Davis went on to say that he could not comment further. 'To do so,' he said, 'would be completely improper in view of the investigation still proceeding.'

I should make it clear that I was paying only limited attention to the very large number of news items which appeared from time to time in the New Zealand newspapers during the course of the Chief Inspector's investigation, but the incident to which I have just referred did catch my eye because one of my friends was a retired navigator and he had explained to me long before the occurrence of the Antarctic disaster the way in which modern jets were now navigated by computer, and how human navigators were not carried. I did not at that time profess to follow the technical details of the operation of an aircraft navigation computer but I knew that it held the aircraft on a predetermined track without the slightest deviation, and that the crew, if they wanted to find out exactly where they were, had only to look at an instrument panel which gave a continuous digital readout of the number of miles to the next waypoint marked on the map supplied to the crew. These waypoints, as I understood it, were about 300 miles apart and were marked in stages on the flight track plotted on the map. I was also aware that aircrews throughout the world relied implicitly upon the computer printout in the cockpit in fixing their position.

So when I read these newspaper items about the destination co-ordinates of the flight track having been changed, and when I saw it was alleged that the crew had not been told of the change, I could not help but wonder whether this had been the reason that the aircraft had flown into the mountainside. Had the aircraft been flying in cloud? Was the crew relying, with cloud all around them, upon a computer track which had been changed without their knowledge?

However, there had been an authoritative statement by the Chief Executive that the correct information had been fed into the computer on the aircraft before it left Auckland. So far as I could see, that was the end of the matter. If the aircraft was flying on this computer track when it struck the mountain, and if the correct co-ordinates establishing that track had been fed into the aircraft computer, then the crew must have known the exact track of the aircraft. Therefore, like most other people, I disregarded the newspaper suggestions that there had been an altered flight track not revealed to the crew which may have played its part in deceiving the crew as to where they were as they approached McMurdo.

There had apparently been no computer mistake. This was one of those speculative rumours which so often proliferate from a tragedy or disaster with an unknown cause.

IV

THE CHIEF INSPECTOR'S INQUIRIES

As at the time the investigators finally left McMurdo, any information as to the cause of the disaster had necessarily been scarce. The vital factor had been the recovery of the cockpit voice recorder and the 'black box' and of the modules which were the key component of the sophisticated computer navigation system installed in the aircraft. But there had not been much information discovered concerning the aircraft itself, apart from the recovery of these scientific instruments. One of the investigators had listened to the voice tapes which record all radio transmissions to and from McMurdo base, but the transmissions to and from the DC10 would also be recorded on the cockpit voice recorder which had been recovered from the wreckage. Only limited information was obtainable from the air traffic control personnel. They said the DC10 had not appeared on the radar at McMurdo. They had apparently been unaware of the flight path of the approaching airliner. There was some evidence as to the weather at the time of impact but it was not conclusive because the weather on the north side of Mount Erebus, twenty miles from Scott Base and McMurdo Station, might or might not have been similar to the weather prevailing at the two bases. In the latter area there had been an overcast with a base of 3,000 feet and visibility in all directions had been unlimited.

On the other hand, a helicopter pilot who had flown across the Lewis Bay terrain not long after the disaster, had spoken of poor visibility and very uncertain surface definition, meaning the difficulty of separating the white terrain from the pale overcast of the sky. The Chief Inspector adopted an early opinion that the DC10 had been flying in cloud. How else could the aircraft have flown into the mountain in broad daylight? But in the minds of others there was an insuperable objection to such a theory. It assumed that the highly experienced crew of the airliner, captained by a man known for his meticulous compliance with all flying rules, had flown at low altitude in a mountainous area when they could not see where they were. But the 'flying in cloud' theory persisted, and it seemed from that time onwards to dominate much of the thinking of the Chief Inspector and his staff. Yet, at the crash site, were items of evidence which told a different tale.

Among the debris there were hundreds of personal belongings — watches, handbags, purses, binoculars, necklaces, bracelets, wallets, cheque books, bank notes and indeed all the extensive range of personal property which might be expected to have belonged to the 237 passengers and the crew. But above all, there were the cameras. There must have been at least 200 cameras lying scattered in the snow. A great many were badly damaged or completely broken, but there were many which were relatively intact, and they contained rolls of exposed film recording the photographs which had been taken by passengers on the long flight from New Zealand. A fair proportion of the film was damaged by light, as a result of the cameras breaking open, but the film laboratories at McMurdo were able to produce some hundreds of clear prints.

Most of the prints related to photographs taken when the DC10 was a long way from McMurdo but there were some which showed features of the landscape when the DC10 was very close to Lewis Bay. There were some very clear prints, for example, of Beaufort Island which was only six minutes flying time from the impact position. There were photographs taken when the aircraft was close to the shoreline of Lewis Bay and only seconds from destruction. Most of these latter photographs were to some extent damaged by exposure to light, but the coastline on each side of the aircraft was plainly visible and patches of sunshine could be seen on the ice stretching on either side of the aircraft.

Such was the answer to the 'flying in cloud' theory. At the time of impact, the aircraft had been flying in clear air. But a considerable time went by before the developed prints became available to the investigators, and some weeks elapsed before all the photographs could be carefully examined and appraised, and in this interval the theory had persisted that the aircraft had been flying in cloud. When the photographs proved this to be wrong, there was an understandable reluctance on the part of the investigators to agree that their first conjecture had been premature. In addition, the startling evidence produced by the photographs now made the disaster inexplicable. With the aircraft flying in cloud, the Chief Inspector and his staff had a simple explanation, but with the aircraft flying in clear air, the whole inquiry now took a different direction.

Strange to say, the 'flying in cloud' theory persisted, although not in its original form. In the course of time, it became amended, without the support of any real evidence, to a theory of the aircraft 'flying towards an area of poor visibility', thus ascribing blame to the aircrew on a different basis.

Such were the general results of the investigation in Antarctica. Leaving aside the discovery of the recorders from the aircraft, not very much had been discovered. No doubt it did not occur to anyone at the time, but those days of investigation in Antarctica might more profitably have been spent by the Chief Inspector somewhere else. As later became clear, the investigation should have started on the night of November 28 at the head office of Air New Zealand in Auckland with the Chief Inspector's Auckland branch taking possession of all company files and documents which referred in any manner to the Antarctica flights.

At about the time of these events, the initial steps towards bringing legal claims against Air New Zealand were being taken. Of the 237 passengers 151 had been New Zealanders, and many of the legal representatives of their estates had given notice of claim. An arrangement was made by the Auckland Law Society to construct a register of all claims with particulars of the law firms involved and an ultimate agreement was reached to consolidate as many claims as possible and to have them handled by one group of counsel. The advantages of such a procedure are that it is then not possible for the insurers of an airline to settle claims individually and on terms not known to other claimants. In the latter event many persons might unwittingly recover less by way of compensation than other persons in a similar situation.

The lawyers handling the claims were necessarily dependent upon the information in the hands of the Office of Air Accidents. The vital pieces of information were the 'black box' and the voice recorder tapes, and these were in the possession of the Chief Inspector. They were certainly not likely to be released or their contents revealed in any way until a report was finally prepared.

Another question was what should be the form of the official inquiry which must take place. Everyone was aware that the Chief Inspector was busy with his investigations. The papers reported him as travelling to various parts of the world obtaining information, but his report would be delivered to the Minister of Civil Aviation and it would be for the Minister to determine whether or not the report would be made public. The procedure followed by the Chief Inspector with regard to completion of his report was settled by the terms of the Air Accident Regulations. His duty was first to prepare an interim report and if he ascribed blame to any person or organisation in respect of the disaster, then each such person or personal representative was entitled to receive a copy and was entitled to make a statement in reply which had to be lodged within a period of ninety days.

The newspapers continued to make various predictions as to when the interim report would be delivered to the Minister, but eventually it was announced that the Chief Inspector's interim report had been delivered to the Minister of Civil Aviation on March 4, 1980. It became known that copies had also been delivered to the legal representatives of the two pilots, and to Air New Zealand and to the Civil Aviation Division of the Ministry of Transport. It also became known that the interim report blamed the aircrew for the disaster. The Airline Pilots' Association demanded a copy of the report but their request was rejected. The lawyers representing the passengers' consortium protested that they were not given a copy, but the Civil Aviation authorities merely kept stating that, apart from the Minister himself, the only persons entitled to the interim report were those persons selected by the Chief Inspector as being in some way blameworthy. It was announced that the Attorney General would receive a copy of the report in order to help him decide whether a public inquiry should be held.

Meanwhile, there were many published assertions from various persons, including the Leader of the Parliamentary Opposition, that a public inquiry was essential, and that it would be unthinkable for an official inquiry not to take place. On March 8, 1980, four days after the interim report had been delivered to the Minister of Civil Aviation, it was announced by the Attorney General that it was still too early for a decision as to whether he would order a public inquiry, but on March 10 the Government decided that a Commission of Inquiry would be established to investigate the causes and circumstances of the disaster. But it was also stated that the inquiry was not likely to start for several months — until after the Government had received the final report of the Chief Inspector.

A rather strange revelation then appeared in the newspapers. Under the Accident Investigation Regulations, it is possible for an inquiry to be established into any aircraft incident or accident. This is a procedure essentially devised for minor aircraft crashes and is very close to being an inquiry controlled by the Civil Aviation Division. It was clear that the Attorney General had been pressed by the Civil Aviation Division to authorise an inquiry of this kind because he made a public statement as to why he had rejected a statutory inquiry under the regulations. The principal reason for rejection of the statutory inquiry caused a great many eyebrows to be raised. The Attorney General said that the commencement of a statutory inquiry 'would have prevented the Inspector of Air Accidents from completing his own inquiries into the disaster and reaching conclusions relating to it'. The Attorney General went on to say that the statutory inquiry would have 'taken over the investigation' almost immediately and would have prevented the Chief Inspector 'from making a final report'.

This very unusual statement attracted considerable discussion among lawyers. It almost seemed as if the Government was intent on establishing the cause of the disaster through the medium of the Chief Inspector's final report before any Commission of Inquiry would commence its sittings. It was obvious enough that the interim report already contained the Chief Inspector's view of the cause or causes of the disaster. It seemed a strange thing that the sittings of a Commission were to be postponed until the Chief Inspector's final opinion on the cause of the disaster had been delivered to the Government and no doubt made public.

One of the newspapers looked into this situation, after making inquiries into air accident investigation procedures overseas. They discovered, not surprisingly, that in other countries there was always an open inquiry into an air disaster of any significance where the immediate cause of the disaster was a matter of doubt. It was said that the opinion of a Government investigator could never be accepted as conclusive except where the cause of the disaster was so obvious and undisputed as to make a public inquiry only a mere formality. It was pointed out that where an accident investigator conducted private inquiries of his own, then the detailed evidence on which the investigator relied was seldom, as a matter of practice, fully revealed. There was every opportunity for some interested party privately to influence the investigator's final opinion. So it was said there must always be an open inquiry except in a simple and undisputed case.

In the meantime, there were various newspaper reports as to difficulties in transcribing the voice recorder tapes. After delivery of his interim report, the Chief Inspector had gone to England to have the tapes processed through the equipment at the Farnborough Air Base. The tapes had been transcribed in Washington by the National Transportation Safety Board in early December 1979, but it now appeared that after three months, and after his interim report had been lodged with the

Government, the Chief Inspector was still at work trying to decipher what had been said during the last thirty minutes of flight.

I remember reading these accounts in the newspapers. They suggested that the Ground Proximity Safety Device had sounded on the flight deck warning the crew that the aircraft was too close to the ground. Then it was suggested that the tapes disclosed the final words of the crew 'as they tried to avert disaster'. This information derived by the Press from the Chief Inspector raised the obvious inference that the aircraft must have been flying in low altitude and in cloud. Had the aircraft been flying in clear air then the crew could see for themselves how close they were to the ground, and no warning device would have been necessary.

By such means did the popular opinion first arise that the aircraft was flying in thick cloud at the time of impact in a situation where very plainly the crew could not have known where they were. This latter conclusion was carefully noted by the international pilots flying Air New Zealand aircraft. They regarded it as ludicrous. Captain Jim Collins, the pilot in command, had a total flying time of over 11,000 hours and the co-pilot, First Officer Greg Cassin, a total flying time of about 8,000 hours. They were both well experienced in flying DC10 aircraft, but the vital factor was that Captain Collins was noted right through the Flight Operations Division of the airline as being almost pedantic in his meticulous attention to detail and in his exact compliance with every rule and regulation governing aircraft operations. Yet, it was evidently being seriously suggested that he was flying in cloud at 1,500 feet in mountainous terrain, wholly unaware until the warning system sounded that the ground was rising rapidly beneath him.

The Airline Pilots' Association had obtained from the solicitors representing the estates of Captain Collins and First Officer Cassin a copy of the Chief Inspector's interim report, and they had seen that he had, in effect, blamed Collins and Cassin for the disaster. The aircraft had been flown towards an area of poor visibility and then, although this next conclusion was carefully omitted by the Chief Inspector, the aircraft had entered cloud and was flying in cloud when it struck the mountainside. Not only had this alarming and erratic conduct been engaged in by Captain Collins, but it must have been concurred with by First Officer Cassin. It seemed to the Airline Pilots' Association that the Chief Inspector was treating the aircrew as if they were amateur pilots who had between them crashed a small light aircraft in the hills and who had gone to their deaths through flying recklessly in bad weather or losing their way in cloud, such being the types of aerial misadventure which comprised almost the total investigation experience of the Chief Inspector and his staff.

For the moment, the contents of the interim report were known to few people. The experienced passenger-jet pilots who read the Chief Inspector's interim conclusion considered it to be quite untenable. Still, it was only an interim report. Representations would be received on behalf of the estates of the two dead pilots, and from Air New Zealand and from Civil Aviation Division. Perhaps in the final report a different view of the 'probable cause' would be advanced, but there were senior pilots in the association who did not believe that the Chief Inspector's interim conclusion would be altered. 'He never changes his mind,' they said. As it turned out, these cynics were right.

While the Chief Inspector's final report was in the course of preparation, there was some speculation in the Press regarding the tapes from the cockpit voice recorder. The general function of those tapes had been described in the Press and there had been reference to the Chief Inspector's going to England to have further work done on preparing a written transcription of what the tapes had to say. Then it was announced by the Chief Inspector, when speaking to a newspaper correspondent in London on March 9, 1980, that the attempted analysis of the voice tapes was difficult because they were 'a noisy sort of tapes with a lot of conflicting information on them'. Then, on March 13 there was a full Press Association report from London. The Chief Inspector was reported as saying that the British analysis of the tape was a refinement of the original work done in Washington, but he went on to say that it was unlikely that there would ever be a full transcript of cockpit conversation. The Chief Inspector said that voice tapes are always very noisy and there are a lot of competing noises 'and sometimes a person's voice is not recorded clearly'. Then the Chief Inspector, according to the same Press report, went on to deny that there were 'conflicting reports on the tape'. He said that work on the tape in Britain would add detail and context to his final report. He said that the analysis had helped to fill in data and to qualify some areas.

In New Zealand there were continual expressions of dissatisfaction by the solicitors for the passengers' consortium at not being supplied with a copy of the interim report. They had also asked, without success, for a copy of the voice tapes and a copy of the flight data recorder tape. But the Chief Inspector maintained, and quite correctly, that the only persons entitled to a copy of the interim report were persons whom he claimed to have been blameworthy and that it would be for the Minister of Civil Aviation to decide whether the final report would be made public.

The passengers' consortium, in the course of its demands for the interim report and for the tapes, claimed that overseas experience had shown that reports filed by Government investigators in air crashes had often been found to be wrong when detailed findings were produced in subsequent legal proceedings.

On April 21, 1980 I was appointed to be a one-man Commission of Inquiry into the disaster. A Commission of Inquiry is only another name for a Committee of Inquiry. The Crown may appoint one or more persons to be a Commission, or the Crown may appoint one or more persons to be a Royal Commission. There is no substantial difference between the functions of the two types of Commission.

The Prime Minister made a press statement on the matter. He said that a Commission of more than one person had been considered, but it was difficult to find people with technical experience of big aircraft who had not been associated in some way with Air New Zealand during their careers. He pointed out that technical information would be available through evidence and cross-examination, and would be analysed by the judge, and he emphasised that if technical information were provided by persons who were members of the Commission then such information could not be the subject of cross-examination.

This latter statement was undeniably correct. It is a repetition of the common argument against having a judge accompanied by technical assessors when hearing cases of technical difficulty. The assessors can give opinions to the judge which the parties to the case never hear and, apart from all that, it has been a standard feature of our judicial system for generations that a judge is expected to master, and does in fact master, the details of highly technical evidence.

I was in agreement with the decision that I should be the sole Commissioner. After all, one never knows what private approaches may be made to a member of a Commission appointed for his technical knowledge. Where the matter under consideration is not only technical but controversial, then there is a great temptation for people with an interest in the inquiry to attempt to convey their views privately to one of the technical members of the Commission. But, apart from all this, there was in this particular case another reason which appeared to justify the appointment of a legal expert as the sole Commissioner.

Shortly after my appointment had been announced, I happened to be speaking to a highly placed Government official who, by reason of his particular employment, was familiar in detail with the contents of the Chief Inspector's interim report, and with the general circumstances of the whole matter, and in particular with what he said were 'profound differences of opinion' about the Chief Inspector's interim conclusions. He gave me no details of what he was talking about and I naturally made no enquiry, but later events showed how very well informed this man must have been. He said to me that the essential questions would not involve technical evidence or technical knowledge of aviation. The inquiry would involve, so he said, as its major factor, the determination of a number of substantial disputed factual issues. He said that I was going to be faced with some vital questions of credibility, and this was why, in his opinion, a lawyer — and preferably a judge — should be the sole Commissioner.

The hearings were scheduled to start in Auckland on July 7, but now there came into public contention the question of whether the Chief Inspector's final report should be made public before the hearings of the Commission began. The natural view was to oppose any such procedure. The Chief Inspector's task, so it was suggested, was to produce what evidence he had collected. He should not be permitted to give his opinion on the very issues which the Royal Commission was appointed to resolve. The Government replied with the view that publication of the final report would assist the Royal Commissioner.

Counsel for the Commission, counsel for the estates of the dead pilot, and counsel for Air New Zealand all protested against the decision of the Government to release the final report before the Royal Commission began its hearings. I protested myself. I wrote to the Prime Minister about it. But the Government would not change its mind. I learned that the printing of the Chief Inspector's final report was being given high priority by the Government Printer. It was evident that the Government was insistent on the report being made public before July 7, that is to say before the starting date for the hearings of the Royal Commission. The more I thought about all this, the more it seemed to me that there was something behind the Government's decision which we had not been told. The Chief Inspector would be the first witness called before the Royal Commission. He would describe his inquiries. Why publish his printed opinion as to causation a few days beforehand? There seemed to me to be only one logical explanation — the report was clearly going to follow the lines of the interim report. Although there were some criticisms in that report about Air New Zealand's briefing procedures and one or two technical criticisms of Civil Aviation Division, in substance it blamed the aircrew. The basis of assigning blame to the aircrew was non-compliance with the instruction that they were not to descend below 16,000 feet on the approach to McMurdo. Whatever minor administrative errors or omissions had been committed by Air New Zealand or Civil Aviation, they would have had no effect if the aircraft had kept at this height of 16,000 feet because Mount Erebus is 12,450 feet high.

After considering all these factors, I thought I could see why the Government wanted the report published before the hearings of the Commission commenced. If it were not published when the Commission hearings started, and if the Chief Inspector sought to produce it in evidence, there would be instant objection from counsel for most of the parties. A Royal Commission is not restricted to evidence which is legally admissible. It can receive any evidence, but I would have no option but to uphold the objections against production of the report because it would be expressing conclusions and announcing factual evidence on the very issues which the Crown had directed me to answer.

If my views on the point were so far correct, then there was only one reason for the Government's pressing for publication of the report before the Commission hearings started. If the Government did not publish the report then it would not be published at all. This left the question as to what it was that the Government intended to accomplish by publishing the report. It was clear that the Government had some strong motive. What could that be? I could only think of one explanation: the airline was owned by the State; the Prime Minister was the registered owner of all the shares in the company. The airline and its management had been for a long time the target of steady political attack by the Parliamentary Opposition. The position of the airline and of the Civil Aviation Division, and in general the position of the Government, could all be made safe from political attack if it were to be established that the aircrew were solely to blame, and that no one in the company management was responsible.

I could think of no other explanation for the Government's attitude. In any case, the final report of the Chief Inspector was published on June 20, 1980.

V

THE REPORT IS PUBLISHED

Before discussing the Chief Inspector's report, it is necessary first to say something about the modern computer navigation of aircraft.

It was implicit in planning the Antarctic flights that the method of navigation used to fly to and from Antarctica would be the same as for the airline's ordinary international scheduled flights. In fact, the Area Inertial Navigation System (AINS) was ideal for the purpose of bringing each aircraft to a specific point in the Antarctic wilderness 2,500 miles away. In all the international and domestic flights of Air New Zealand the computer programming of the flight paths to various destinations had been established for some years.

Let us assume that an aircraft is to be programmed to fly from Auckland to Honolulu. First of all, the latitude and longitude co-ordinates of Auckland Airport are fed into the navigation computer on the aircraft; then the latitude and longitude of each one of the waypoints established between Auckland and Honolulu. The waypoints will be about 300 miles apart, the final one being Honolulu Airport. The track thus established will be overprinted on maps covering the distance between Auckland and Honolulu, and the position of each waypoint will be plotted on the maps.

Once the commencing and destination waypoints and all the intervening waypoints have been fed into the aircraft's computer by inserting the successive co-ordinates of latitude and longitude, then the AINS will navigate the aircraft from Auckland to Honolulu via each one of the waypoints. Every movement of the aircraft from the start of its journey to the end is measured and recorded by electronic sensors mounted on delicate gyroscopes, and they continuously register, in terms of the inertial reaction induced by the movement of the aircraft, its changing position right down to split seconds of latitude and longitude. On a DC10, there are three of these inertial sensor platforms. Each measures the progress of the aircraft independently, and the aircraft computer keeps averaging the three results and presenting a continuous printout of the average of the three systems which it calculates five times per second. This is only another example of the new wonders of the microprocessor age.

At all times the pilot has in front of him a digital printout showing the distance to run to the next waypoint. Therefore he can, at any time, compare the distance to run with the flight track printed on his map and see exactly how far he is from the particular waypoint to which his instruments are referring, and the Horizontal Situation Indicator (HSI) on his instrument panel will tell him whether or not the aircraft is flying on its Nav track. So, the aircraft is therefore navigating itself. This is why navigators no longer form part of the crew of a modern commercial jet. The captain need not ask a human navigator where the aircraft is. The aircraft itself is telling him where it is.

The triple inertial system used in DC10 aircraft was the most sophisticated navigation system used in civil aircraft. In theory, the system had a tolerance of error to the extent of one mile per hour of flight. Suppose the aircraft is flying at 600 miles per hour, then at the end of one hour it is possible for the aircraft to be one mile left or right of its computer track, or one mile in front of or behind a specific waypoint. But in their trans-Tasman and trans-Pacific flights the Air New Zealand pilots had found the AINS in the DC10s to be completely accurate. For example, with two aircraft flying respectively to and from Honolulu at different altitudes, it was common for the crew of each aircraft to see the lights of the other passing exactly overhead or underneath as the case might be, and towards the end of the flight from Auckland to Honolulu, the crew would invariably find the aircraft, after its eight-hour journey, flying directly at Honolulu Airport. Then, following instructions from Honolulu Air Traffic Control, the Nav mode would be disengaged and the aircraft would commence its approach at whatever altitude and direction had been directed.

Exactly the same manner of navigation applied to Antarctica. Taking Auckland Airport as the starting point there were nine waypoints on the outward journey including the destination waypoint at McMurdo. The aircraft would fly itself from one waypoint to another. Cape Hallett was the second to last waypoint on the outward journey. After flying over Cape Hallett, the aircraft would roll slightly to its right and then fly straight down the computer track to the destination waypoint. However, because those were sightseeing flights, it was not to be expected that an aircraft would be held on its Nav track all the way from Cape Hallett to McMurdo. At some distance out from McMurdo the Nav mode would normally be disengaged and the aircraft flown by the pilot in the Heading Select mode in whatever direction might be thought most suitable for sightseeing.

When an aircraft is switched from the Nav mode into the Heading Select mode, it will then fly at whatever heading is selected by the crew. They select the heading by turning the Heading Select dial left or right and then fix whatever heading or direction is required. The systems on the aircraft then cause the auto-pilot to obey whatever changes of heading are fixed by the Heading Select dial.

After flying over the McMurdo area to give the passengers a good view of the buildings and other features of interest, including the towering volcano of Mount Erebus, the aircraft would turn to the north and fly away in the vicinity of the coast of Victoria Land. It would then intercept and lock on to the homeward Nav track and climb to its cruising altitude and head for New Zealand.

The remarkable accuracy of the AINS was of particular significance if anywhere between Cape Hallett and McMurdo the aircraft was flying over cloud. The crew had only to look at the distance to run on the instrument panel and check that against the track overprint on their map in order to fix their exact position. When the McMurdo area was covered by a solid overcast, but with the cloud base high enough to permit the aircraft to descend and fly over the area under the cloud base, then the aircraft only needed to let down through the cloud on Nav track and it would emerge into clear air on the same track and at whatever position along that track the captain might select.

This is how the United States Navy aircraft operate on their flights to McMurdo. They are also equipped with the Inertial Navigation System, but being military operational aircraft they also carried navigators. The Navy aircraft approach McMurdo on Nav track until picked up by McMurdo radar about forty miles from the airfield and then they turn left at the Byrd reporting point and make a radar-controlled approach and landing.

It should be noted here, however, that by contrast with the Australian, Far Eastern and American flight routes operated by Air New Zealand, in which maps are supplied with the computer tracks overprinted on them, the Antarctica crews did not have the computer track to and from McMurdo printed on any map supplied by the airline. But Captain Collins, like other pilots, plotted his own flight track on a map so as to portray the computer track to and from McMurdo, and in this manner he and other pilots were able to fix the position of the aircraft at any time as long as it was flying in the Nav mode.

For these reasons, navigation of a DC10 to and from Antarctica presented no problems. When reporting at Flight Despatch Office before a flight departure the pilots would be given the computerised flight plan for Antarctica which contained on the left-hand side the series of latitude and longitude co-ordinates which marked every waypoint to McMurdo and back. The crew would then type these co-ordinates into the aircraft computer on the flight deck. Once the aircraft had cleared the Auckland area it would be switched into the Nav mode and would capture the computer track to McMurdo. It would then fly its way there, from waypoint to waypoint, and could not depart from the computer track unless the pilot in command elected to do so.

The Chief Inspector's report was not an easy document to read. This was due to its format which was as required by the International Civil Aviation Organisation (ICAO). The facts and conclusions regarding any particular incident or accident must be set down under stipulated headings. No doubt this is necessary because of the production over a period of time of many thousands of incident and accident reports which would need to be systematically indexed or computerised under defined headings, but in dealing with the story of a complicated air accident, the system is inappropriate when there is no clear narrative of events and when the investigator is required to state his opinion in one paragraph, as to what was the 'probable cause' of the accident.

Nevertheless, in the present case, the Chief Inspector's report was reasonably comprehensive. The fact that it would be largely unintelligible to members of the public was beside the point within the context of the ICAO requirements. What happened in the present case was that the aviation reporters of the newspapers picked out from the text the pieces of information which seemed to comprise the basis of the Chief Inspector's conclusions, and the paraphrase thus obtained was conveyed to the public as being the gist of the result of the Chief Inspector's inquiries.

The following is a selection of the major newspaper headlines in the New Zealand newspapers:

'CRASH REPORT POINTS TO ERROR BY DC10 CAPTAIN'
'CREW UNCERTAIN AS PLANE NEARED SLOPE'
'FLIGHT THOUSANDS OF FEET TOO LOW'
'THE AIRCRAFT RADAR SHOULD HAVE SEEN MOUNTAIN'

Then there was the following sentence which appeared in one of the top newspapers in Australia, *The Australian*, on June 21, 1980:

> The chilling last seconds in the lives of 257 people who died in the Air New Zealand DC10 that crashed in Antarctica are now known: the pilot bringing his aircraft too low, despite the anxiety of his flight engineers, a last but too late moment in which the danger was recognised, and then disaster.

The same newspaper also criticised the release of the report in advance of the hearings of the Royal Commission. It referred to the fact that the report was released against my advice and went on to say that it surely would have been better to wait, if only for the sake of the friends and relatives of the crew and passengers, 'until all the events connected with the tragedy had come under judicial scrutiny and judgement'.

This, of course, was the view which had been repeatedly pressed on the New Zealand Government but without success and once I had read the Chief Inspector's final report a possible explanation presented itself. Despite its careful catalogue of matters which might be contributing causes, it had very clearly placed the responsibility for the accident upon the aircrew. Certainly no other factor or event was nominated as a cause. There were five specific criticisms against Air New Zealand with regard to the planning of the flights, but these appeared innocuous when carefully analysed and were certainly believed by the Chief Executive, in a press statement which he made on June 24, 1980, to have no validity. The criticisms directed at Civil Aviation Division were also rejected by that division.

So, the paraphrase adopted by the newspapers and presented by the headlines was a correct interpretation.

The alleged 'probable cause' did not say that the flight was being operated in bad visibility. It was the transcript from the cockpit voice recorder (also printed in the newspapers), which created that impression and, of course, it was the overall impression which really counted. That impression could have been dispelled very simply by reproduction in the report of one of the passengers' photographs. There were many such photographs available taken only a matter of seconds before impact. They showed that the aircraft was flying in clear air. They showed the distant shoreline of Cape Bird on the right and of Cape Tennyson on the left. Each was clearly visible under the overcast. There were no photographs showing the view ahead, but there was a movie

41

film which was still running in its camera at the time of impact and the distant shoreline of the Lewis Bay was clearly visible (despite some light damage to the film) and it was quite obvious that the aircraft crashed in perfectly clear air.

The Chief Inspector had indicated this possibility when he had referred to the 'whiteout' phenomenon. The Americans at McMurdo had supplied him with data in relation to 'whiteout' and this was said to consist of loss of depth-perception when there is a uniform snow-covered ground and a low solid pale overcast. He went on to record that in these circumstances undulations of the terrain appear as a flat white surface, and further, that 'whiteout conditions can exist within the normal VMC (Visual Meteorological Conditions) minima'.

In other words, even in visibility so clear that an aircraft is flying and is authorised to fly VMC, the conditions are not VMC at all. Unknown to the pilot, if he is a stranger to polar regions, he is really flying IMC (Instrumental Meteorological Conditions) because he cannot see the true nature of the terrain ahead.

It was, of course, obvious from the voice recorder transcript that the aircraft struck the mountain with no one on the flight deck — and this included Peter Mulgrew, the flight commentator — ever seeing the snow-covered slope right in front of them. They were all looking, as they thought, towards flat, snow-covered terrain stretching far away into the distance. Needless to say, the general public was oblivious to all this. The obvious ultimate cause of the disaster was quite plainly — if one read the Chief Inspector's report in full — the whiteout conditions operating on the approach to Lewis Bay.

But in his announcement of the 'probable cause', the Chief Inspector did not say this. In fact, he departed from what he had said in his interim report about whiteout. The probable cause, so he said, was the decision of the captain to continue the flight at low level 'toward an area of poor surface and horizon definition'. But, by virtue of the Chief Inspector's previous statement based on the information supplied by the United States authorities, the aircrew of TE901 would not have detected that the ground in front of them was rising. The very essence of the whiteout illusion is that the white surface of the snow ahead appears as a uniformly flat surface running far away into the distance. Yet, the Chief Inspector blamed the aircrew on the basis that they plainly saw in front of them 'poor surface and horizon definition', yet elected to fly on and did not detect the rising terrain ahead. This was certainly an ingenious method of attributing the 'probable cause' of the accident to the aircrew.

A close analysis of the whole report also disclosed the following areas of blame attributed by the Chief Inspector to the aircrew:

1. Descent below 16,000 feet on the approach to McMurdo.
2. Disregard by the pilots of the alleged mounting alarm of the flight engineers.
3. The fact that the aircraft radar 'would have detected the mountainous terrain ahead'.
4. The fact that the aircrew were 'uncertain of their position'.

But in reference to all these factors there was in the mind of the Chief Inspector one supervening cause — the aircraft had descended below 16,000 feet which was the limit specified by Civil Aviation and by Air New Zealand. Had it not been for this grave breach of a basic flight rule there could not have been any disaster. The existence of a whiteout would not matter, nor would the availability of the airborne radar, and it would not matter whether or not the crew were 'uncertain' of their position.

So, despite the various contributing factors which were set out by the Chief Inspector as relating to the disaster, it was quite clear when his report was read carefully, that the fundamental mistake of the aircrew was to commence a descent below 16,000 feet.

When I had read the report, which I did on a number of occasions before the hearings of the Commission began, I was naturally inclined to treat the Chief Inspector's conclusions as being quite correct. He seemed to have covered every aspect of the occurrence. A great deal of the technical data concerning the navigation system and the contents of the 'black-box' printout were quite foreign to me, but my view before I began hearing evidence was that the paraphrase of the report as adopted by the newspapers, and in particular the implication of bad visibility appearing to arise from the voice recorder tapes, were probably perfectly sound.

There were only two question marks which cropped up in my mind. The first was the change in the destination co-ordinates which had been reported to the Chief Inspector and which he confirmed had not been conveyed to the crew, but which in his view had not misled the aircrew. I had the impression that there might be a great deal more to this than was admitted on the surface, especially when I recalled the newspaper reports indicating that experienced DC10 pilots had believed that the change in co-ordinates was a cause of the disaster. I suspected that they might know more about this than the Chief Inspector, who had not flown a DC10 with its sophisticated navigation equipment.

The second question mark was an obvious one. How could this flight crew, admittedly highly experienced, have deliberately flown onwards, as the Chief Inspector had decided, towards an area evidently only a short distance in front of the aircraft, in which visibility was so impaired?

I could only suppose that these questions would be inquired into at some length during the hearings of the Royal Commission, and that they would be explained. I had no reason to doubt the Chief Inspector's conclusion. I presumed that the Royal Commission would be to some extent a formal exercise, and that after testing the evidence at first hand, I would probably see no difficulty in confirming the Chief Inspector's opinion.

The Chief Inspector's report contained more than one statement which later came to be clarified (and in one or two cases contradicted) by the long process of cross-examination, but it may safely be said that, despite the Chief Inspector's opinion as to the 'probable cause' of the disaster, he did in the course of his report make reference to virtually all relevant factors which affected the fatal flight. I here set out the quotations from the report to which I have been referring:

(a) In respect of the airborne radar fitted to the aircraft, the Inspector said (para 1.8.9):

Expert opinion from the aircraft manufacturers was that the high ground on Ross Island would have been clearly indicated by the 'shadow effect' had either pilot studied the radar presentation during the aircraft's descent to the north of the island.

(b) In relation to the computer flight plan for McMurdo, the Inspector said (para 1.17.7):

The computer flight plan used at the briefing had been in error for fourteen months in that it showed the destination point for McMurdo as two degrees ten minutes of longitude to the west of the intended turning point. This error was not corrected in the computer until the day before the flight. Although it was intended that it be drawn to the attention of the previous crew immediately prior to their departure this was not done, nor was it mentioned during the pre-flight despatch planning for the crew of the accident flight. The

44

crew was shown a copy of the erroneous flight plan with the incorrect co-ordinates at the route qualification briefing but the flight plan issued on the day of the flight was correct.

(c) In para 1.17.46, the Chief Inspector said:

Whiteout is an atmospheric effect which results in loss of depth perception and is especially common in Polar regions when there is snow cover. Only two conditions are necessary to produce a whiteout, a diffuse shadowless illumination and a mono-coloured white surface. Whiteout, it must be emphasised, is not necessarily associated with precipitation or fog or haze. The condition may occur in a crystal-clear atmosphere or under a cloud ceiling with ample comfortable light and in a visual field filled with trees, huts, oil drums and other small objects.

(d) In a further reference to the altered computer track, the Inspector said (para 2.5):

As all previous flights to McMurdo had approached the area in VMC, earlier crews had not adhered to the flight plan track and hence had not detected the error. In the case of this crew no evidence was found to suggest that they had been misled by this error in the flight plan shown to them at the briefing.

(e) With reference to the descent of the aircraft, the Chief Inspector said (para 3.20):

The descent was intentionally continued below the VMC limit specified by CAD and Air New Zealand Limited, of 6,000 feet to an indicated 1,500 feet.

(f) In further reference to the airborne radar, the Chief Inspector said (para 3.66):

The aircraft's radar would have depicted the mountainous terrain ahead.

(g) And the Chief Inspector then ended his list of conclusions by saying (para 3.37):

Probable cause: The probable cause of this accident was the decision of the captain to continue the flight at low level toward an area of poor surface and horizon definition when the crew was not certain of their position and the subsequent inability to detect the rising terrain which intercepted the aircraft's flight path.

A major section of the Chief Inspector's report consisted of a mass of technical detail derived from the readout by overseas experts of the 'black box' and the flight-deck voice recorder tapes. These together described — or in the case of the voice recorder tapes purported to describe — the last stage of the flight of TE901. In particular, the 'black box', with its continual recording of all the movements of the aircraft, established that the aircraft had been locked on to its Nav track — in other words, its pre-computed flight track — from Cape Hallett southwards; that is, the aircraft was navigating itself along the sequence of latitude and longitude co-ordinates which led to the destination waypoint of the flight track.

Then, when the aircraft was about thirty-seven miles from its destination, the captain had unlocked the Nav track and had begun to fly on 'heading select'; that is, although the aircraft was still being flown by the auto-pilot, it would follow the course and speed pre-selected by the pilot on his instrument controls. Then, once the aircraft had begun to operate on 'heading select', the pilot had turned the aircraft into a right-hand descending orbit. The turn travelled through a full 360° and when the aircraft levelled out at 10,000 feet, it was once again flying directly to the true south. Then Captain Collins had locked the aircraft back on to its Nav track.

The aircraft flew on for about ten miles. Captain Collins then unlocked once more from Nav track and commenced a left-hand descending orbit. The aircraft turned 180° and then flew to the true north slowly descending to 7,500 feet and then turned left again until it had once again completed a 360° orbit. Once again Captain Collins locked the aircraft on to its Nav track.

The DC10 was once more on the computer track which it had been following since flying over Cape Hallett, and it thereafter maintained a steady descent from 7,500 feet to 2,000 feet. Then, when it was about seven miles from impact, it had descended to 1,500 feet and maintained that altitude on its approach to the mountainside. The aircraft was still flying on Nav track over this last stage of seven miles and was maintaining a steady speed of 260 knots. Because it was locked on to its Nav track, its flight path did not vary left or right. Then, seconds before impact, there suddenly sounded the Ground Proximity Warning System (GPWS). This is a device which sounds a warning when the aircraft is flying at too low an altitude and in between audible warning signals a recorded voice keeps saying 'Pull up'.

The readout from the 'black box' indicated that immediate action had been taken by the crew in response to the GPWS in that Captain Collins had said, 'Go round power, please.' This meant that he was about to move the throttle levers forward to the pre-selected position marked 'Go round power' and either the co-pilot or engineer would have to place his hand on the throttle levers behind the hand of Captain Collins so as to ensure that the forward thrust of the throttles did not exceed the 'Go round power' position. The term 'Go round power' means an emergency burst of power from the engines and it is so described because it is normally applied when an aircraft, in the course of landing, is obliged suddenly to abort the landing and climb away so as to 'go round' the airport. At the same time as he made his request, Captain Collins pulled back on the control column so as to lift the aircraft upwards, but the 'black box' recorded that impact took place only a fraction of a second after the request for 'go round power'.

Such was the story the 'black box' told, and it will be seen immediately that it recorded a most significant event — the action of Captain Collins in locking the aircraft back on to Nav track at the conclusion of the first orbit, and again at the conclusion of the second orbit.

The purpose of these manoeuvres was to descend from 17,500 feet to 2,000 feet while still maintaining the same approximate distance from the destination waypoint. But why had Captain Collins been so meticulous in locking the aircraft back on to Nav track after the completion of each of the two orbits? I knew already that the navigation computer system of modern aircraft required the Nav track to be overprinted on the maps supplied to the aircrew for the journey. By this means the crew had only to look at the distance to run to the next waypoint (all the waypoints being marked on the map) in order to fix their exact position. If that were the case, then how was it that Captain Collins had been so intent, when levelling out after the second orbit, on the aircraft's resuming its computer track when, as we now knew, the computer track was aimed directly at Mount Erebus?

At this stage I can remember thinking back to the newspaper items published four months previously (in February 1980) which had referred to the belief of many pilots that the computer track for the flight had been altered without the crew being told. Back in February, the Chief Executive of the airline had announced that the correct co-ordinates had been typed into the aircraft's computer. There had been no admission that the flight path had been altered without the crew being told. But now it began to look as if the original newspaper reports might have been correct.

So much for the story of the last stages of the flight as revealed by the 'black box'. Evidence which might explain the orbiting sequence, and the maintaining of the Nav track, except during the orbit manoeuvres, would probably be available from the transcript of the voice recorder tapes, but before referring to this vital source of information it is essential first to draw attention to what was probably the major finding of the Chief Inspector as the result of his interviews with the management of Air New Zealand.

It appeared that ever since the Antarctic flights commenced in 1977, there had been an official minimum safe altitude (MSA) for aircraft approaching McMurdo. The MSA had at all times been 16,000 feet and this was the keynote of the finding of fault against the aircrew contained in the interim report. And now in the final report this finding was confirmed. The instructions from the company to flight crews had permitted in specified conditions a letdown from 16,000 feet to 6,000 feet once the aircraft had 'overflown' Mount Erebus and was over the general locality of the buildings and ice runway some twenty miles to the south of the mountain. But this exception did not apply in the present case, because the aircraft had not flown over Mount Erebus.

Very clearly the aircraft had commenced its descent below 16,000 feet on the approach to Ross Island, and after the two orbiting sequences, it descended to 2,000 feet and then 1,500 feet, maintaining that latter altitude until impact, and it was this breach of the MSA which dominated the Chief Inspector's report, and as far as I could see then, rightly so. But again, there seemed to be a lingering uncertainty about this apparent breach of the company's regulations. I have already referred to the opinion held of Captain Collins by his fellow pilots and by the company. He was painstaking and careful and had never been known to depart from any of the rules or restrictions controlling any flight of which he was in command. Why had he acted on this occasion so out of character? And his decision to let down to 2,000 feet must have had the approval of his co-pilot and his engineers.

Still, so far as I could see, there was no escape from the Chief Inspector's conclusion, not only that the MSA of 16,000 feet on the approach to McMurdo was a company instruction, but that it was also one of the conditions upon which Civil Aviation Division had approved the Antarctic flights.

So there now remained the task of reading the transcript of the voice tapes. The flight deck conversations would no doubt explain many things. Would they explain the decision to disregard the MSA?

When the report was published there was nothing which caught the imagination of the public so rapidly and which made so vivid an impression as the transcript of what had been said on the flight deck during the last stages of the flight.

Probably not many members of the public would have known that flight-deck conversations were recorded for the benefit of investigators in the case of disaster or some dangerous incident. The fact that such a device was installed in modern passenger aircraft had been revealed shortly after the crash in Antarctica, because the aviation reporters and various newspapers had made it clear that the 'black box' and the voice recorder tapes would be the most vital components of the aircraft as far as the investigators were concerned. But I do not believe that the public understood this fully until extracts from the Chief Inspector's transcript were published in the newspapers.

The story told by the transcript was this. The aircraft had received an initial forecast for McMurdo before it left Auckland and, as it flew from Cape Hallett towards McMurdo, an up-to-date report was received as to weather conditions at McMurdo. Unless the conditions were suitable for sightseeing the aircraft would turn away to the north and fly over the South Magnetic Pole which was the alternative sightseeing area. The last weather report received by the aircraft was that for the McMurdo and Ross Island areas — a cloud base at 2,000 feet and below that forty miles of clear visibility. Mac Centre at McMurdo suggested that the DC10, once within forty miles of McMurdo, could be picked up by radar and could then let down to 1,500 feet under radar control so as to emerge below the cloud cover. This invitation was accepted by Captain Collins when the aircraft was just over 100 miles north of McMurdo.

Captain Collins advised passengers on the PA system that the McMurdo radar would let the aircraft down through the cloud into an area with a visibility of forty kilometres and he said that, subject to any changes in the weather, he was hopeful that the crew would be able to give passengers a look at McMurdo. Then, as the aircraft flew on to the south at 16,000 feet, flying over a cloud layer at about 10,000 feet, the crew noticed large areas of cloudless sky below them. It was at this stage, when the aircraft was forty-three miles north of its destination waypoint, that Captain Collins decided to take advantage of these very large cloud-breaks to descend in visual meteorological conditions (VMC) which meant that a radar letdown was not then required.

The sea ice was clearly in view below the aircraft and once the aircraft had been flown downwards in clear air to 2,000 feet it could then proceed under the cloud base reported at McMurdo. The crew therefore notified McMurdo that a radar letdown would not be required as they were flying at 10,000 feet and that they were VMC. They asked permission to let down and proceed visually to McMurdo. This request was granted by Mac Centre and the aircraft, which had already carried out its first orbit in clear skies, then proceeded to carry out its second orbit. It was then apparent from the conversation between crew members that the second orbit was also completed in clear skies.

Once the aircraft had reported its altitude at 2,000 feet, the crew then decided to descend a little further to 1,500 feet which was the altitude recommended by Mac Centre, but in the course of these decisions, there were apparent expressions of discontent or doubt on the part of the two flight engineers and these were the extracts from the transcript which irresistibly attracted the public eye.

The Chief Inspector said in his report that from the voice tapes it appeared that Flight Engineer Moloney had been relieved at the flight engineer's panel by Flight Engineer Brooks but that Moloney had remained on the flight deck throughout the last stage of the flight.

The flight commentator had been Peter Mulgrew who was familiar with the Antarctic region and who was very well known throughout New Zealand as a mountaineer. He had had the misfortune when climbing in the Himalayas some years before to have lost both of his lower legs through frostbite and since that time had worn artificial limbs. Over the last stage of the fatal flight he would have been sitting in the commentator's seat just behind the pilot.

In the extracts which follow, the speaker on any given occasion is sometimes identified and sometimes not. The abbreviation CAM means Cockpit Area Microphone, and the different speakers are designated in the transcript as follows:

CAM 1	Captain Collins
CAM 2	Flying Officer Cassin
CAM 3	Flight Engineer Brooks
CAM 4	Flight Engineer Moloney
CAM 5	Peter Mulgrew
CAM ?	Unidentified voice speaking in flight deck area

Here are the extracts which attracted so much public attention. The figures appearing alongside the extracts represent minutes and seconds in Greenwich Mean Time:

0037:20
CAM 4	You're through ten thousand are you going to hold it here
CAM 1	Yep

0037:45
CAM 2	I'll go back to HF Jim
CAM 1	OK

0037:54
CAM 1	Well we're having trouble with communications right now so if you'll just wait there and see what we come up with
	(Comment to persons unknown.)

0038:23
CAM 1	I've got to stay VMC here so I'll be doing another orbit
	(Here follows remarks about difficulties in radio communication with McMurdo.)

0041:34
CAM 1	Well look go back to HF
CAM 2	Yes

0041:40
CAM 1	Tell him we can make a visual descent descending

0041:45
CAM ?	(Interjection) My God
CAM 1	on a grid of one eight zero
CAM 2	Yes
CAM 1	and make a visual approach to McMurdo
CAM 2	OK

0042:49
CAM 1	We're VMC around this way so I'm going to do another turn in

0042:59
CAM 1	Sorry haven't got time to talk but
CAM 5	Ah well you can't talk if you can't see anything

0043:02
CAM 1	Both the VHF channels that they use here we're not picking them up at fifty miles

0046:39

> CAM 3 Where's Erebus in relation to us at the moment
>
> CAM ? Left about (twenty) or (twenty) five miles

0046:43

> CAM ? Left do you reckon
>
> CAM ? Well I don't know . . . I think
>
> CAM ? I've been looking for it
>
> CAM 2 Yep Yep

0046:46

> CAM ? I think it'll be erh

0046:48

> CAM 3 I'm just thinking of any high ground in the area that's all
>
> CAM 5 I think it'll be left yes
>
> CAM 4 Yes I reckon about here
>
> CAM 5 Yes . . . no no I don't really know

0047:02

> CAM 5 That's the edge

0047:28

> CAM 1 Speed, nav track, alt . . .
>
> CAM ? Altitude (acquired)
>
> CAM ? What's wrong?
>
> CAM ? Make up your mind soon or . . .

0047:43

> CAM 1 We might have to pop down to fifteen hundred here I think
>
> CAM 2 Yes OK

0047:47

> CAM 2 Probably see further in anyway

0047:55

> CAM 2 I see vert speed for fifteen hundred feet
>
> CAM 4 * * it's not right
>
> CAM ? Bit thick here eh Bert?

0047:59

> CAM 4 Yeah my . . . oath

0048:05

> CAM 4 You're really a long while on . . . instruments at this time are you

0048:46
CAM 1	Actually those conditions don't look very good at all — do they?
CAM 5	No they don't

0048:55
CAM 1	Have we got them on the tower?

0048:59
CAM 2	No . . . I'll try again

0049:00
CAM 4	Only got 'em on HF that's all

0049:04
CAM 1	Try them again
CAM 2	OK

0049:08
CAM 5	That looks like the edge of Ross Island there

0049:24
CAM 3	I don't like this

0049:25
CAM 1	Have you got anything from him?
CAM ?	No
CAM 2	No

0049:30
CAM 1	We're twenty-six miles north we'll have to climb out of this
CAM ?	OK

(Here follows discussion between pilots as to whether they should turn left or right — then GPWS sounds at 0049:44 and impact occurs six seconds later at 0049:50.)

As will be seen, there was an apparent reference to the weather condition being 'thick'. There was another reference to the aircraft flying a long time 'on instruments at this time'. There are queries as to where Mount Erebus is. There is the remark attributed to Flight Engineer Brooks, 'I don't like this', and then a few seconds later Captain Collins decides to climb away to the north and, while he and First Officer Cassin are discussing whether to fly to the right or to the left, the GPWS suddenly sounds.

From this it could only be deduced that the aircraft was flying in cloud during the last stages of the flight. Also, there were indications of alarm from other persons on the flight deck.

So, it was not just a question of the crew's being in breach of the MSA of 16,000 feet. The pilot and co-pilot, after descent to 2,000 feet, had flown downwards from that point in spite of what the Chief Inspector called the 'mounting alarm' on the part of the flight engineers. And that was not all. The discussion about the location of Mount Erebus seemed to make it clear that the crew was uncertain of the aircraft's position. Admittedly, it did not look quite like this when you examined the remarks passed by the pilot and the co-pilot. They appeared to have no doubts at all. Indeed, the Chief Inspector accepted that their demeanour was calm and composed at all times. But the public could only go on the extracts published in the newspapers and when those extracts were looked at, there could surely be only one explanation: the aircraft had been flying in cloud, and the crew did not know where they were.

The allegation of 'low flying' was something the public particularly understood. Low flying? The very phrase was like a knell. It was a frequent cause of light aircraft accidents. Pilots flew into power lines, or into valleys shrouded in mist, and in this particular case, in addition to the low flying, the crew of the big jet had not even known where they were.

The newspaper summaries of the content of the Chief Inspector's report, and in particular the publishing of extracts from the transcript of the voice recorder tapes, were immediately understood by the general public who had never heard of the inertial navigation system or of the polar ocular illusions which occur when an aircraft is flying over snow. In the public mind, the story of the last stages of the flight was rather like a movie film involving war-time flying. The Air Force bomber has been hit by anti-aircraft fire and is struggling home through the night. The navigator is anxiously trying to work out on his plotting table where the aircraft is. The pilot and co-pilot are peering anxiously out the windows through the swirling cloud trying to get a sight of land. With their insulated flying jackets and their leather helmets and goggles, the crew are ceaselessly, but helplessly, trying to find out where they are, and in the end it is only the gallant devotion of the crew, coupled with the aid of divine providence, which finds them eventually over their home airfield. So, the impression conveyed to the public by the Chief Inspector's report was uncomplicated and clear. They had seen all this before on late night television.

VI

THE COMMISSION HEARINGS BEGIN

The public sittings of the Commission began on July 7, 1980. The parties represented by counsel were Air New Zealand, the Civil Aviation Division, the New Zealand Airline Pilots' Association, the estate of Captain Collins, the estate of First Officer Cassin, the consortium claimants representing the estates of deceased passengers, the estate of Peter Mulgrew, the New Zealand Engineers' Institute (representing the flight engineers), McDonnell Douglas Corporation and the Office of Air Accident Investigations, a division of the Ministry of Transport.

The hearings were conducted in a large room in a building in downtown Auckland. I sat behind a raised and very long table, which was very useful in view of the large number of documents and maps which required frequent consultation. The tables reserved for counsel and their technical advisers were dispersed widely around the room, with microphones on counsel's tables. The raised witness-box was over to my right and was also equipped with a microphone, and there were tables reserved for the press, radio and television reporters.

The evidence was recorded first by the witness producing a typed statement of what he had to say. He would then read this out and his statement would become part of the record. When cross-examined, the questions and answers would be typed into a word processor. This method of recording cross-examination was painfully slow, but had the inestimable advantage of producing for the benefit of every party a complete printout at the end of the day of all that had been said. All the same, in the whole course of my professional career, I have never been engaged in a case or an inquiry which proceeded at such a leisurely pace.

Counsel assisting the Commission were Messrs W.D. Baragwanath and G.M. Harrison. Mr Baragwanath made an opening speech, setting out the details of procedure which had been agreed between him and counsel for the other parties. All counsel were to be entitled to cross-examination. With the exception of the Chief Inspector of Air Accidents, who would be the first witness, the evidence of each witness would be prepared in advance in the form of a typed statement and the witness would give his evidence in chief by reading out his prepared statement. The evidence of the Chief Inspector would merely consist of amplifying his statutory report, and Mr Baragwanath would ask the Chief Inspector to discuss, and if necessary elaborate upon, various selected parts of his report.

Before the taking of evidence began, a statement was made to the Commission by counsel for the Airline Pilots' Association. It referred to the text of the CVR transcript which formed part of the Chief Inspector's report and it was claimed that the tape was transcribed in Washington in the presence of a New Zealand Inspector of Air Accidents and of three Air New Zealand personnel — two airline pilots and a flight engineer, all of whom were experts in DC10 aircraft and familiar with Air New Zealand's flight deck procedures. Although the length of the tape was only thirty minutes, the preparation of a transcript had occupied not less than five days. The two pilots and the flight engineer were familiar with the voices of Collins, Cassin, the two flight engineers and Mulgrew. The expert in Washington who controlled the production of the sound from the tapes was Colonel Paul Turner of the National Transportation Safety Board. He and the New Zealand personnel, so I was told, had the greatest difficulty in producing a transcript from the very bad quality tape. Finally, although many parts of the contents of the tape had not been decipherable, an agreed transcript had been prepared.

It had been the understanding of the pilots and the flight engineer that the agreed transcript would be typed out in New Zealand and would be the official transcript of the CVR tape. But, after publication of the Chief Inspector's report, the Airline Pilots' Association had discovered that amendments had been made to the Washington transcript without their knowledge. The Chief Inspector was said to have taken the tape to England in early 1980 and there, in conjunction with an expert at Farnborough, amendments had been made. Counsel for ALPA therefore gave notice that the association would not accept the accuracy of the CVR transcript except in respect of what had been agreed in Washington. At this stage, I merely noted the point and the hearing proceeded.

However, this might be an appropriate time to interpolate

THE COMMISSION HEARINGS BEGIN

some facts about CVR tapes in general, and this tape in particular, because it may assist in understanding the nature of the objection by ALPA. In the first place the existence of a flight deck microphone which recorded the conversations and the comments of the flight crew was not a system which had ever found favour with the International Branch of the Airline Pilots' Association. It meant that every flight crew member was under surveillance as to what he said at different stages of the flight. After a tape had run for thirty minutes, a fresh recording commenced with the original thirty minutes being progressively erased. Therefore, a person transcribing a CVR tape had access to only the last thirty minutes before it stopped when the aircraft crashed.

As will be obvious, the whole purpose of always having a tape of the last thirty minutes of flight was to be aware of what the crew had been saying over that vital period. In particular, the time sequence of the CVR tape could be synchronised with the information retrieved from the 'black box'. So an investigator would have on record a running verbal commentary to accompany the control of the aircraft by the crew over the last thirty minutes before the occurrence of the incident or accident under inquiry. Thus the practical advantage of the CVR was well known in aviation circles.

ALPA had always been concerned about the CVR tapes being used for purposes other than accident investigation and for motives other than the collection of information related only to flight safety. Suppose that remarks had been passed by a crew member about the management of the airline, stressing some unsatisfactory feature of its operations, or criticising some of its senior personnel. That information could well be used if it ever became available to an employer as a means of procuring the dismissal or resignation of the speaker.

Then again, there was the risk that persons seeking to sue an airline would press for production of the CVR tapes so as to use them against the airline in litigation. The latter point had already cropped up in court cases in England, Australia and the United States. Within the British, Australian and New Zealand context, the tapes were the property of the airline but would nevertheless have been transferred into the exclusive custody of air accident investigators as from the time when the two recording boxes were found among the wreckage, or safely located in an undamaged aircraft which had been involved in a 'near miss' or other incident which required investigation. The point had arisen in litigation because a plaintiff, claiming damages against an airline, would issue a subpoena against the air accident investigator requiring him to appear at court and bring with him the CVR tape.

The view of airlines and of pilots, and also of inspectors of air accidents was that the CVR tapes should be available only to accident investigators and used for the single purpose of preventing further similar occurrences, and thus promoting flight safety. This attitude was quite reasonable, it seemed to me, but it was based upon the presumed production of a clearly decipherable tape recording. However, in the present case, the recording had been so poor that parts were not decipherable at all. The only perfectly clear segments of conversation were the words spoken by the two pilots into their individual microphones. All this material derived from the cockpit area microphone (CAM) had been interpreted and analysed subject to various rules of caution prescribed by Colonel Turner. Some of these rules were:

1. Only transcribe word by word those words that were unanimously agreed to have been spoken.
2. Do not credit any words to a specific person unless there is unanimous agreement as to whom the speaker was.
3. Be careful of making editorial comments.
4. Be careful about interpreting what might have been said.

These rules were of general application, but in the case of the type of microphone installed in a DC10 there were further and very formidable difficulties. An all-purpose microphone is located in the roof of the flight deck just above and between the two pilots. It will pick up with reasonable clarity anything the pilots say to each other, and will pick up a considerable part of what might be said by the flight engineer who is sitting behind the co-pilot. But the microphone also records various voices including speech emanating from the rear part of the flight deck and from the galley.

The basis of the objection by ALPA to the whole of the contents of the published transcript arose from two factors. One was the addition by the Chief Inspector of remarks or comments which had not been agreed upon by the official group who prepared the Washington transcript; the other was the interpretation which the Chief Inspector appeared to have placed on some of the remarks or supposed remarks which had been made.

Under the first heading there were two very significant remarks which in the view of the Washington transcribers were not made at all. They included the two remarks of flying 'on instruments' and it being 'a bit thick here eh Bert'. Neither of these remarks appeared in the Washington transcript. On the second point,

ALPA was very critical of the interpretation placed by the Chief Inspector on various statements made or appearing to have been made by one or other of the flight engineers. The pilots present at the production of the Washington transcript did not agree that there were any remarks made by either engineer which expressed alarm or dissatisfaction with the descent of the aircraft. They pointed out that neither pilot made any reply to the remarks alleged to have been made and it was their view that no expression of opinion on the part of any engineer could safely be interpreted from the transcript except for the remark of Flight Engineer Brooks, 'I don't like this', recorded as being twenty-six seconds before impact and followed only six seconds later by the announced decision of Captain Collins to fly away.

The opinion of ALPA, therefore, was that the Chief Inspector had no grounds whatever for interpreting the transcript as if it disclosed expressions of alarm by the engineers. The association had a very hostile view about the suggestion that the pilots would have heard these questioning comments by an engineer and not replied immediately. They did not believe that the Chief Inspector properly understood the operational techniques of the three-man crew of a DC10 aircraft.

This detailed criticism by ALPA of part of the published transcript and of part of the Chief Inspector's interpretation was not known to me until a later stage of the inquiry. At the commencement of the inquiry I knew only that ALPA had strong criticisms about the reliability of some parts of the transcript and about the Chief Inspector's interpretation of them. But later, when I heard evidence about the production of the American transcript, I came to see that if you read the conversations between the pilots alone, and if you disregarded the pieces added to the transcript in England, and if you disregarded the Chief Inspector's interpretation of the alleged remarks of the engineers, then the transcript contained nothing which reflected upon the flying skills or judgment of either pilot, and indeed made it clear beyond doubt that the two pilots were certain at all times of their exact position, for the simple reason that with the DC10 in the Nav mode no uncertainty could arise.

The office of Air Accident Investigation in New Zealand is a division of the Ministry of Transport. However, the Chief Inspector and the small group of investigators which form his staff are, by statute, independent of the department to which they belong. The Chief Inspector addresses his statutory reports to the Minister of Civil Aviation (who is also the Minister of Transport), but his independence is illustrated by the fact that he can if necessary criticise or blame the Civil Aviation Division if, in his view, the circumstances of some aircraft accident justify that course.

Neither the Chief Inspector nor any of his staff were or had been jet pilots. Their duties in accident investigation almost always involved accidents or incidents involving light fixed-wing aircraft or helicopters. New Zealand is a notoriously bad place to fly in, with its mountainous terrain and strong winds, and great care is needed by pilots of small light aircraft and helicopters. Accidents involving these two classes of aircraft are very frequent — at the time of the Antarctic disaster, they were running at the rate of over 100 per year.

In the vast majority of such cases, the cause of the accident is not very difficult to determine. In the case of the light fixed-wing aircraft there were many accidents involving amateur pilots who had been careless in the way they manoeuvred their aircraft or handled the adverse weather conditions. Then there were the professional pilots of small aircraft and helicopters. In many cases, their work necessarily involved an acceptance of some degree of risk. Suitable examples are aerial top-dressing aircraft and helicopters engaged in commercial operations such as deer hunting and the like. Here again the main causes of accidents were predominantly decisions of pilots to take a risk. Again, a considerable proportion of these accidents occurred in sparsely populated hill or mountain country where, in the case of a fatal accident, there was usually no one who had seen exactly what had happened to the aircraft.

When the Chief Inspector, Mr Ron Chippindale, entered the witness box I took a careful look at him. He was a tall, lean figure with dark hair, going bald on top, and he wore a fairly full dark moustache with distinctly military overtones. He looked exactly what he was — an ex-Squadron Leader of the Royal New Zealand Air Force.

He was in the witness box for several days. In part he amplified, under the guidance of Mr Baragwanath, various aspects of his report. Then he was cross-examined in turn by the various counsel for the parties attending the inquiry. The main object of their questions was to seek clarification of a great many of the technical matters referred to in his report and to test the various opinions which he had formed as to the conduct of the flight crew on the latter stages of the flight. In so far as the technical questions were concerned, the Chief Inspector carefully avoided any positive response, being content to say that he believed or thought that the situation was this or that, but preferred that those inquiries be made from experts in the particular field. He admitted that, although 16,000 feet was the official minimum safe altitude for the approach to McMurdo and 6,000 feet was the official minimum safe altitude over the McMurdo area but within a defined sector, he was nevertheless aware, from discussions with the crews of previous flights, that there was doubt as to whether 6,000 feet was understood to be a minimum safe altitude, and that there were apparently pilots who believed that lower altitudes could be maintained in terms of the official briefing given by the airline.

However, the Chief Inspector could not be deflected from his opinion that no aircrew had any authority to descend below 16,000 feet on the approach to McMurdo. He could also not be enticed away from his view that the aircrew had flown, if not in cloud, then towards an area of deteriorating visibility and that this had been the real cause of the disaster. He agreed that if, in the light of evidence which would be given, he had reason to change these views then he would do so without hesitation. But as I studied his composed and imperturbable demeanour, I very much doubted whether he was likely to change his mind. He did not look to me like a man who changed his mind after reaching a conclusion. After all, his opinion as to the 'probable cause' had been published not only throughout New Zealand, but throughout the world.

The Chief Inspector had certainly been a model witness. As already indicated, he could not be trapped, in spite of all the practised skill of counsel, into any statement of fact which he could not support. And he had scrupulously avoided any opinion on the technicalities of the inertial navigation system or of the procedural aspects of flying big passenger jets. He had been courteous and co-operative throughout the whole of his long sojourn in the witness box.

But I was considerably concerned to find that he appeared not to have taken any written statement from any person except three brief statements from U.S. Navy personnel at McMurdo who had been due to depart for the United States at the end of the summer season. No statements had been obtained from anyone in Air New Zealand or Civil Aviation.

Annex 13 to the International Convention relating to civil aviation deals with accident investigation and it contemplates written and signed statements from all material witnesses. The New Zealand Civil Aviation Accident Regulations contain similar provisions. I must admit that I thought it incomprehensible that the Chief Inspector could have published his conclusions on the cause of the disaster without the firm evidence which only a series of written and signed statements could provide.

I felt obliged to make an informal inquiry as to the way in which air accident reports were prepared in New Zealand. I found the Chief Inspector was acting in accordance with established procedures, contrary though they may have been to the policy of Annex 13 of the International Convention and to the country's own air accident regulations. The general practice adopted by the Air Accident Branch in New Zealand was to undertake verbal interviews with anyone who might know something about the cause of the incident or accident and then to formulate a report based on these verbal inquiries. Whereas a police officer, directed to make a report as to a fatality, must reduce all interviews to the form of signed and written statements, for otherwise his report will not be accepted, the air accident investigation procedures in New Zealand were said to follow the contrary course. Although I do not say it occurred in the present case, there is a danger that conclusions reached, which are not supported by written statements, may have left on one side verbal statements which do not coincide with the view of the investigator. In a police inquiry, statements from every material witness are taken whether or not they accord with the police officer's view. In the case of the Commission of Inquiry, the future course of events was to illustrate in a vivid manner the very real necessity to take extensive written statements from all persons involved at the earliest possible stage of the air accident inquiry.

Following the evidence of the Chief Inspector, counsel for Civil Aviation called the evidence of two weather experts. They were both members of the New Zealand Meteorological Service, one a senior officer and the other a junior officer who had been in the McMurdo area, although many miles to the west of McMurdo Sound, on the day of the disaster. The former, Mr J.S. Hickman, gave evidence of the general functions of his service, in particular in relation to the Antarctic flights. He also expressed the opinion that from the passengers' photographs there was no 'whiteout' condition. His proposition was that passengers' photographs, taken shortly before impact, showed that the sea ice surface was dotted with patches of sunlight and that some landmarks were visible and identifiable. He also supported the Chief Inspector's statement that the flight, just prior to the accident, was 'toward an area of poor surface and horizon definition . . .'.

Mr M.R. Sinclair, the other weather expert, had constructed a very useful sequence of weather probabilities as deduced from passengers' photographs and from the location of the aircraft at the different points when these photographs were taken. He expressed the view that the overcast to the left and right of the aircraft had in all probability been lower ahead of the aircraft than it appeared to be from the photographic views taken to the left and the right.

Junior counsel for Civil Aviation, who had been conducting the examination-in-chief of these witnesses, caused some measure of suppressed amusement among other counsel as he valiantly attempted to get the witness to say that there might well have been, ahead of the aircraft, cloud which had descended virtually to sea level. Any such admission would, of course, have been very much in favour of those persons, possibly including the Chief Inspector, who were sure that the aircraft had in reality been flying into cloud before impact.

But the youthful employee of the Meteorological Service could not be induced to go so far, despite this diligent pressure (which would not have been tolerated in a court case) exerted upon him by one of his own department's counsel.

I had to remember, I thought at the time, that both these weather experts were part of a service which was itself a division of the Ministry of Transport. Their overall contribution to the weather information was certainly valuable and their work had been carefully done, but I had to bear in mind the fact that their own department might later be accused by counsel for other parties of having not paid enough attention to the planning of these Antarctic flights. This could be detected from the Chief Inspector's report. But, in particular, I was quite unable, by examining the passengers' photographs, to detect the supposed lowering of the cloud base forward of the aircraft.

It was at this stage that there occurred to me a fact which I later regarded as being of more and more significance. There were photographs taken from the aircraft showing views to the east, to the west and to the north. Where were the photographs showing views to the south? The aircraft had performed two orbits and many of the photographs produced had been taken during these orbiting sequences. On four separate occasions there had been ample opportunity for passengers to take photographs of the views to the south, i.e. towards Ross Island. It seemed to me that such photographs must surely have been taken. Where were they? Of course, the inquiry was only at an early stage. Further photographs might be produced.

At the close of the weather evidence it appeared that no one, apart from the persons on board the DC10, had ever actually seen the precise weather conditions obtaining at the northern aspect of Ross Island at or about the time of the disaster. But it was being suggested that the overcast was becoming solid as the aircraft flew into Lewis Bay, and the photographs appeared to confirm this. But was the base of the overcast also lowering as the aircraft flew on? That was the real question. And I was not certain at all that this had been established. I had to consider all the probabilities. Would the aircrew of the DC10 have flown onwards towards an area where a cloud base was sharply descending at a point only a few miles ahead? With the aircraft travelling at 300 miles per hour? And when neither pilot had made a single spoken reference to the base of the overcast descending in front of them? Surely not.

My overall impression was that the weather experts deeply desired to establish the theory that the aircraft was flying directly towards, and possibly into, an area of visible cloud, but their evidence had stopped short of that.

VII

THE AIRLINE STARTS ITS CASE

We had been quite some time waiting for the opening of the case for Air New Zealand. We had heard the evidence of the Chief Inspector and we had heard something of the considerable range of issues which the occurrence of the disaster appeared to involve. I had begun to realise that there was far more to the inquiry than the points made in understandably abbreviated fashion by the Chief Inspector in his report. I had also begun to identify an emerging confrontation between the management of the airline and the counsel and witnesses for the Airline Pilots' Association.

By the time the Chief Inspector's evidence had finished, I had recalled, on several occasions, the information received before the hearings started from my apparently well informed source in Wellington, the man who warned me that, despite the apparent simplicity of the Chief Inspector's report, I was going to find various areas of strongly disputed evidence and that the inquiry might primarily involve the evaluation of conflicting evidence. At the stage we had reached so far, this prediction certainly seemed well founded, and it already appeared that the major confrontation would not be between ALPA and the Chief Inspector, but between ALPA and the airline management.

Then I had heard the technical evidence as to the type of aircraft involved, together with a description of the maintenance procedures applicable to a DC10 Series 30, and I had been entirely satisfied that the aircraft was operationally perfect in all respects at the time when the disaster occurred. This technical evidence had been completed by the testimony of Mr L.S.H. Shaddick, the DC10-qualified air accident investigator from the United Kingdom. He had described the operational abilities of the aircraft and had expressed the opinion, not questioned by anyone, that it was in all respects an entirely suitable aircraft with which to carry out this type of long range sightseeing venture.

Then we had heard the evidence about the weather which had

prevailed at McMurdo at the time of the disaster. Those two witnesses had analysed the whole weather situation in great detail.

So now, after these opening days of evidence, we were to hear what the airline had to say. Like everyone else in the courtroom, with, of course, the exception of counsel for the airline and with the possible exception of counsel for Civil Aviation, I had confidently expected that counsel for the airline would make an opening statement as to the position of the airline in the matter, and as to the nature of the evidence which it intended to call. On the latter point I was not wholly uninformed, as counsel for the Commission had asked the airline counsel what airline witnesses would testify and had received at least a general answer sufficient to assist them in their own determination of what evidence might need to be called by counsel for the Commission. But the matter which was creating most interest was the nature of the expected opening address by counsel for the airline.

This is where I received yet another of the surprises which were to form such a significant feature of the inquiry. Counsel for the airline saw me in chambers, in the company of other counsel, and said that it was not proposed to make any opening statement 'at this stage'. They went on to say that they would reserve the right to make some opening submissions 'at a later stage'. I did not think it appropriate to offer any comment. The manner in which the airline intended to handle its case was, of course, its own affair. Nevertheless, I was taken aback at this unexpected announcement.

I thought I knew already what the management's attitude was going to be. I had been guided in this respect by a public statement by the Chief Executive which had appeared in the newspapers within a day or two of the publication of the Chief Inspector's report on June 12, 1980. In that statement the Chief Executive had referred to the salient features of the report as far as they affected Air New Zealand. He had said that the Chief Inspector had made five specific criticisms of the briefing procedures used by the company in relation to these Antarctic flights. He had then referred to the recommendations of the Chief Inspector with reference to future Antarctic flights. But Mr Davis had said that because there would be no future flights to Antarctica, the Chief Inspector's recommendations were not now relevant. He had then returned to the five criticisms of the briefing procedures, making it quite clear that these were now the only relevant features of the Chief Inspector's report as far as the airline's position was concerned, and he had stated that each one of these five criticisms would be totally and conclusively answered at the pending Royal Commission hearing.

I had checked these press cuttings and read them on several occasions. From the standpoint of the Chief Executive the company's position was clear. There was nothing in the Chief Inspector's report which, after the appropriate explanation, could possibly result in any blame for the disaster being attached to the management of Air New Zealand. There had been no other public statement by the Chief Executive. This had been his final word.

In these circumstances, how was it that the airline had elected to present no opening submissions to the Royal Commission? They were the operators of the aircraft. They were the employers of the aircrew. They were the party whose actions and procedures would be the object of the most sustained scrutiny during the course of the inquiry. I remembered how the cross-examination of the Chief Inspector by counsel for the airline had been centred upon the five supposed briefing defects to which the Chief Inspector had referred. I remembered how the Chief Inspector had readily agreed with the propositions put to him by counsel for the airline in relation to the five suggested briefing procedures, in that he had been prepared to accept that his views on those matters might have to be withdrawn once the briefing procedures had been fully explained by the airline witnesses.

The restricted nature of this cross-examination had been entirely unexpected. But, of course, when one looked back, it had been logically and tactically correct. The Chief Executive, in his public statement, had accurately isolated the only effective criticisms of the airline which had been published in the Chief Inspector's report. There had been one or two other criticisms, direct or implied, which were separate from the briefing procedures. One example was the continuing error, undetected for fourteen months, in the computer flight plan printout, but in the Chief Inspector's opinion this had not been identified as a causative factor. Other comments by the Chief Inspector on the airline's procedures had been in the same category.

So in the end, counsel for the airline had concentrated on the Chief Executive's analysis, and on his evident but unspoken belief that the only relevant criticisms of the airline could be with reference to its Antarctic briefing procedures. Such had been the suggestion, though not made directly, which had been the single basis of the very brief cross-examination of the Chief Inspector by the airline's counsel. And I could not deny the logic of that approach. If I had been the airline's counsel I would have done exactly the same. Demolish the validity of the five criticisms of the briefing procedures, then what was left? Only the inescapable and unfortunate conclusion that the sole blame for the disaster lay with the aircrew. And when the time came to begin the airline's case, an opening address along those lines would have been perfectly natural.

The theme of pilot error could have been advanced with becoming deference and expressed with suitable regret. It would have confirmed the Chief Inspector's ultimate opinion. It would have fortified existing public opinion as formulated by the newspaper headlines which followed the Chief Inspector's report. But for some reason, no opening address on the part of the airline was to be made.

I must admit that when I heard the news that the airline did not propose to make any opening submissions 'at this stage' I began to entertain a slight doubt as to their motives. They seemed to me to be regarding themselves in the same light as defendants in a court case. And there is very often a good reason why counsel for the defendant in a court case, whether in civil or criminal proceedings, will elect not to make any opening submission in the sense of describing what the evidence is going to be. When this occurs in the courtroom, as it does so frequently, the usual explanation is that counsel for the defendant, or counsel for the accused as the case may be, is not quite certain what his witnesses will say under cross-examination. So when a judge discovers in court proceedings that counsel for the defendant either is making no opening submissions or that his opening statement is in general terms, not complicated by any reference to the evidence to be called, he begins to suspect that counsel for the defendant is not quite sure about the reliability of his evidence and does not wish to be placed in the position of asserting that his evidence will prove certain facts and then, at its close, have to face the unpleasant situation that those facts, or some of them, have not been proved at all.

Still, this is only a working rule of general application. I thought that perhaps it might not apply here. The right to make an opening submission at a later stage in the evidence had been specifically reserved. It was possible that this early impression which I gained was not well founded.

The first witness for the airline was Captain Peter Grundy, one of the executive pilots for Air New Zealand. He was the Flight Operations Manager (DC10/DC8) and had been with the company for twenty-two years. He had been promoted to Flight Operations Manager (DC10/DC8) not long before the date of the disaster. He confirmed what we had learned from the Chief Inspector's evidence as to the original proposals for Antarctic flights. In November 1969 he was one of the group which had visited Scott Base in Antarctica to carry out a survey of the possibility of operating an air service from New Zealand to McMurdo Sound. He produced a report later prepared by the Ministry of Transport which set out the results of that investigation and confirmed that it had not been possible for a DC8 long-range aircraft to carry out the operation, having regard to the mandatory fuel requirements and the landing weight limitations.

Of more immediate, and I may say compelling, interest was the witness's evidence that he had manned the second flight to Antarctica in February 1977. His first officer had been a Captain Caudwell and his senior flight engineer had been Gordon Brooks, one of the aircrew on flight TE901 on November 28, 1979. He had been to a briefing at Christchurch with American flying personnel on February 4, 1977 and had gone there in the company of the Chief Pilot, Captain Ian Gemmell. The briefing had apparently only been verbal. The witness said that at his own briefing for the flight of February 22, 1977, the people in charge of the briefing had been Captain Gemmell and a member of the navigation section. He produced a copy of the written briefing material and said that it was made clear at the briefing that the flight track went directly from Cape Hallett over Mount Erebus and terminated over the NDB (Non-Directional Beacon) located at the McMurdo landing runway, known as Williams Field.

The witness's description of his flight on February 22, 1977 was very brief. He said he did not track directly to Williams Field but flew down the Victoria Land coast to the west of the computer track, and at no time flew below 16,000 feet. He said that the flight was conducted throughout at 16,000 feet in the McMurdo area and that, upon leaving McMurdo, he climbed to cruising altitude for the return to Christchurch.

Such was the nature of the evidence-in-chief of Captain Grundy. It was explained to me that he had been called at this stage for the purpose of establishing flight planning procedures and would be recalled at a later stage.

The witness was then cross-examined at considerable length. In fact, he was in the witness box for more than two days. The briefing for these Antarctic flights and the exact procedure adopted on his own flight was gone into in considerable detail and a number of significant pieces of evidence emerged.

Captain Grundy said that on his approach to McMurdo he had

flown the aircraft over the NDB. He had fixed a positional error of four nautical miles which was well within the tolerance of the AINS (Area Inertial Navigation System) after so long a flight.

He confirmed the fact that the AINS system provides a very accurate 'cross track' reading, that any deviation of the computer track can immediately be read on the instrument panel, and that a pilot would always know exactly where he was in relation to the computer track.

He was asked about the dispensation from the statutory requirement that a pilot in command must have flown in the area before. This, of course, did not apply to the witness himself as he had been to Antarctica in 1969, but he maintained the view that an adequate route qualification briefing was an appropriate substitute.

He was questioned about the contents of the airline records with regard to the planning of the commercial flights to Antarctica and agreed that there was internal correspondence within the airline relating to the proposed flights. He said that this correspondence would be on the airline files. He said that Captain Gemmell, the Chief Pilot, had handled most of the correspondence on this matter. Apart from Captain Gemmell, it would have involved the Commercial Planning Division, the Flight Navigation Section, and the Engineering Division.

The witness was closely cross-examined on the briefing procedures. He agreed that there were certain errors in the briefing but maintained that they would not be of any consequence.

(The position of the 'incorrect' destination waypoint had been ascertained by reading the Chief Inspector's report, and had been clarified by his evidence. The original flight track plotted for the Antarctic flights, and typed into the DC10 navigation computer before each flight, had been programmed so as to fly the plane from Cape Hallett to the NDB, which meant flying over the summit of Mt Erebus which is an active volcano. But in 1978, when the standard flight tracks for all the company's routes had been inserted into the company's newly acquired ground computer, it appeared that an error had been made when the longitude of the destination waypoint had been typed. A wrong digit had been typed, and the result had been to shift the destination waypoint twenty-seven miles to the west, thus placing it at the head of McMurdo Sound, and thus plotting the last leg of the flight track down the centre of the sound. It was said that this mistake went undetected until shortly before the fatal flight some fourteen months later, but had been corrected a few hours before Captain Collins left for McMurdo, and it appeared that he had not been told of the correction. As will be recalled, the Chief Executive had been asked about this some months before the inquiry began its hearings, and he had responded by telling the Press that the correct co-ordinates had been fed into the DC10 computer. In other words, as it had appeared from the Chief Inspector's evidence, the 'false' waypoint had been corrected.)

Captain Grundy was asked whether the computerised flight track of 1978, terminating at the 'false' waypoint, had been deliberately plotted. He said he preferred that the Chief Navigator be asked such questions.

He was asked about the airborne radar and said that the use of weather radar for navigation purposes was not encouraged because of misleading returns which might convey erroneous ground returns. He emphasised that the aircraft was navigated not by its radar but by the AINS.

Then a rather delicate question arose. The flight report in respect of the witness's own flight was produced for his inspection. An altitude of 10,000 feet was very clearly recorded on that section of the report which dealt with the over-flight of the McMurdo area. This appeared to contradict the witness's evidence that he had at no time descended below 16,000 feet, but an explanation for this insertion of '10,000 feet' was advanced. It was not lacking in detailed elaboration. It was said to refer not to the operating altitude over McMurdo, but to the fuel planning for the flight. The entry was said to be the result of inflight confirmatory calculations designed to establish what fuel would be consumed if an aircraft had to return to New Zealand at 10,000 feet.

But it seemed to me, as I listened to all this, that a slight shadow of doubt was starting to drift across this altitude question. I remembered the witness's demeanour when he had said he had maintained a flight level of 16,000 feet. He had seemed to me to be not entirely adamant about this part of his evidence. If, of course, there was a standard minimum safe altitude of 16,000 feet then any descent below that level would have involved the witness in difficulties with Civil Aviation, a fact of which I was already well aware. Anyhow, here was this distinctly inconvenient entry in the flight report. All I could do was to consider the explanation which went to show that the entry did not mean what it said, and to keep an open mind on the matter.

Then another point arose. It had been established that on November 22, 1979, six days before the fatal flight, the Civil Aviation authorities had passed on to Air New Zealand a complaint from the U.S. Navy at McMurdo that a civil airliner had been seen to fly at about 1,000 feet over a glacier. Leaving

71

CENTRE LANDING GEAR IS EXTENDED FOR TAKE OFF

```
OPS FLASH
NZN NZAA-NZCH RT NO    /    CAPT DALZIELL    RADIO LOG
06/11/79-1900Z  TRK.T  W/V  G/S  DIST ZEET FUELRM STN
M82 TE 901/07  TRK.H DDUUU FL   ZATA ZETA RQFUEL GMT


NZAA   AUCKLAND                              .  FREQ P
3700.6S17446.9E                   S/H ....  101.4     S

NP   NEWPLMTH  193.6      400  123   21
3900.2S17410.9E 174.3     CLB  .... ....   XX.X

NS   NELSON    199.3 23037 448  146   22    .
4117.8S17308.0E 179.3     FL31 .... ....   91.3

RY   MT MARY   216.2 24037 444  208   28    .
4408.2S17016.8E 195.2     FL31 .... ....   86.5

NV   INVRCRGL  211.8 27037 457  163   21    .
4624.8S16819.1E 189.2     FL31 .... ....   83.1

AUKIS AKLND IS 198.4 29078 478  271   34    .
5042.0S16610.0E 173.4     FL29 .... ....   77.5

55S   55S      185.7 29098 497  259   32    .
5500.0S16527.2E 156.2     FL29 .... ....   72.5

60S   60S      185.7 31060 504  302   36    .
6000.0S16431.1E 150.2     FL33 .... ....   66.8

BLYIS BALENYIS 185.7 31053 504  407   48    .
6645.0S16300.0E 349.5     FL31 .... ....   59.6

CPHLT C HALLET 155.8 31063 532  367   41    .
7220.0S17013.0E 322.4     FL31 .... ....   53.6

MCMDO MCMURDO  188.9 34054 517  337   40    .
7753.0S16448.0E 357.4     FL35 .... ....   47.9

CPHLT C HALLET 008.9 34054 425  337   47    .
7220.0S17013.0E 177.4     FL33 .... ....   41.5

70S   70S      358.8 33060 420  139   20    .
7000.0S17003.6E 168.9     FL33 .... ....   38.8

65S   65S      358.8 31068 425  300   42    .
6500.0S16946.6E 168.7     FL33 .... ....   33.2
```

On the left, the standard flight plan; on the right, the plan for the fatal flight.
Note the variation in the McMurdo positions (fourth from bottom)

```
ZKNZP ON GATE 2. CLG DOWN FOR DEPARTURE.
OPS FLASH
NZP NZAA-NZCH RT NO    /    CAPT COLLINS    RADIO LOG
27/11/79-1900Z  TRK.T  W/V  G/S  DIST ZEET FUELRM STN
M82  TE 901/28  TRK.M DDVVV FL   ZATA ZETA RQFUEL GMT


NZAA  AUCKLAND                                      FREQ P
3700.6S17446.9E                    S/H .... 100.9      S


NP    NEWPLMTH  193.6       425   123   20
3900.2S17410.9E 174.3       CLB  .... ....  XX.X


NS    NELSON   199.3 30027 486   146   21      .
4117.8S17308.0E 179.3       FL31 .... ....  91.0


RY    MT MARY  216.2 31027 481   208   26      .
4408.2S17016.8E 195.2       FL31 .... ....  86.5


NV    INVRCRGL 211.8 31029 485   163   20      .
4624.8S16819.1E 189.2       FL31 .... ....  83.3


AUKIS AKLND IS 198.4 32029 495   271   33      .
5042.0S16610.0E 173.4       FL29 .... ....  77.9


55S   55S      185.7 31033 498   259   31      .
5500.0S16527.2E 156.2       FL29 .... ....  72.9


60S   60S      185.7 30034 487   302   37      .
6000.0S16431.1E 150.2       FL33 .... ....  66.9


BLYIS BALENYIS 185.7 29026 481   407   51      .
6645.0S16300.0E 349.5       FL31 .... ....  59.3


CPHLT C HALLET 155.8 29021 490   367   45      .
7220.0S17013.0E 322.4       FL31 .... ....  52.8


MCMDO MCMURDO  188.5 24015 463   336   43      .
7752.7S16658.0E 357.0       FL35 .... ....  46.5


CPHLT C HALLET 008.5 24015 483   336   42      .
7220.0S17013.0E 177.0       FL33 .... ....  40.8


70S   70S      358.8 29024 465   139   18      .
7000.0S17003.6E 168.9       FL33 .... ....  38.4


65S   65S      358.8 29024 465   300   39      .
6500.0S16946.6E 168.7       FL33 .... ....  33.3
```

aside any company rules about altitude in Antarctica, the standard operational rules required all aircraft to maintain clearance of 2,000 feet above any mountain terrain and a glacier qualifies as such. It had already been established that the Chief Inspector had mentioned this matter verbally to this witness in the course of his inquiries after the disaster but, very surprisingly, the Chief Inspector appeared to have taken his inquiries no further. Here was the man to whom the information had been passed in the first place by Civil Aviation. What had he done? Apparently, he had done nothing. He said he might have mentioned it to one or two pilots who had flown to Antarctica prior to the day of the fatal flight. He also thought he had passed it on verbally to the officer in charge of the simulator briefing procedures.

All this seemed to me to be very strange, having regard to the insistence which was said to have been placed by the management of the airline, including this witness, upon compliance with a minimum safe altitude of 16,000 feet at the time of his flight, and the subsequent variation to 6,000 feet in a defined area south of Ross Island to which I have already referred. I had been at a loss to understand how the Chief Inspector, with his official pre-occupation with minimum safe altitudes, had not been at pains to follow up this American complaint. All he had done was to mention it casually to this witness on a chance meeting in a corridor of the head office of Air New Zealand. And now we had the apparent failure of this witness, in his capacity as Flight Operations Manager, to enter upon a diligent pursuit of the complaint.

I was therefore taken aback on the morning of July 29, 1980, being the second day of his evidence, to see the witness produce a typed supplementary brief which covered the point which I have just been discussing. The witness explained, in terms of the brief, that he had indeed taken official action. He had checked that there was to be only one further flight in 1979. He had been shown a company memorandum of November 8, 1979, confirming the 6,000 feet height limitation. He had confirmed that this limitation had been mentioned at the briefing of Captain Collins in the simulator by Captain Johnson, the author of the memorandum. He had then notified Civil Aviation. He then produced a letter, signed by himself, dated January 11, 1980 (six weeks after the disaster), which he had sent to Civil Aviation replying to their letter of December 24, 1979, (nearly a month after the disaster), inquiring whether he had taken any corrective action. In his letter the witness had set out all the steps which he had taken to remedy this complaint from McMurdo.

Now this 'supplementary' brief of evidence was produced by the witness and read, as I have indicated, at the start of his second day in the witness box. But on the preceding day he had been cross-examined by counsel for ALPA on this very point. Why had he not then produced this correspondence with Civil Aviation which described so clearly the positive and entirely correct action which he had taken, in his official capacity, in response to the Civil Aviation message received by him six days before the disaster? As I have said, the 16,000 feet requirement on the approach to McMurdo had formed the very basis of the Chief Inspector's report. Once past Ross Island, descent to 6,000 feet was permitted under stipulated conditions. I was by now quite sure that the minimum safe altitude factor had dominated the whole approach of the Chief Inspector, of Civil Aviation, and of the Air New Zealand management, in respect of the pending Commission of Inquiry.

Surely this inquiry by Civil Aviation, conveyed to this witness only six days before the disaster, and recorded in correspondence shortly after the disaster, must have been the subject of anxious consideration by the airline management as they prepared the evidence to be given before the Commission? I thought it scarcely conceivable that this witness would not have recalled, when first questioned about the incident, that he had taken immediate and decisive action as soon as the Civil Aviation message was received. Why had he not disclosed to me on July 28, when first questioned on the point, the detailed and wholly responsible action he took as set out in his 'supplementary' written brief produced on July 29? I was very tempted to take him to task about it, but I decided to let the point go. After all, he had been briefed to explain the 1977 planning procedures. He had been told he would be called again as a witness and he may have decided, when the point was raised with him on July 28, to defer any reference to his post-accident correspondence until he had refreshed his memory, or had it refreshed for him. Nevertheless, the Chief Inspector had been asked about the 1,000 feet complaint. There had been ample warning that this witness, who had received the complaint, was likely to be asked about it.

Again, the thought crossed my mind that Air New Zealand might be running the inquiry as if it were a court case in which they were defendants. Admit nothing, unless compelled to do so. Do not volunteer evidence. If a witness is in doubt how to answer a dangerous question, then spar for time until the evening adjournment. These are all commonplace courtroom situations. Sometimes they are 'counsels of perfection', especially the 'sparring for time' tactics, for such measures are usually identifiable, but they often succeed. Once more, I thought I must leave the matter open. It was possible that on July 28 the witness had forgotten the details of the action he took, and the related correspondence, until reminded of it by someone that night. Such things happen.

But this incident relating to Captain Grundy was the first of a good many of the same type. It became a standard feature of the inquiry for someone in the management to monitor the daily record of evidence and to correct or patch up any defect or supposed defect in the company's case which cross-examination appeared to reveal. The stage was reached where, during our normal conference at the end of the day, Messrs Baragwanath and Harrison and I would identify some evidential setback which the airline seemed to have suffered and we would then wait for that evidential fact to be modified or explained and, in some cases, contradicted by the same witness the next day or by some other witness on some future day. We were able to predict with considerable accuracy these future shifts and changes in the evidence. The procedures just described were certainly not popular with the two senior counsel for the airline. They evidently complained to other counsel, and they certainly informally complained to me on at least four occasions, that the airline 'was changing its evidence without telling us'. All this demonstrated the vigilant attention with which every word of a day's transcript was being checked by someone or by some group in the airline management.

A considerable part of the cross-examination relating to the altitude question was concentrated upon whether Captain Grundy had read, or heard of, various published accounts of Antarctic flights in the latter part of 1977 and in 1978. Various documentary exhibits, produced by counsel for the consortium, were put to him.

On October 22, 1977 an article had appeared in the *Auckland Star* containing a description of the flight of October 18, 1977. It described a flight over Scott Base at less than 2,000 m. Later in the text was a reference to flight at 200 m., namely about 600 feet. The writer of the article had been on the aircraft and when he described the overflight of 200 m. he had said that the aircraft was 'well below the towering volcano Erebus belching smoke only 50 kms away'.

Had the witness, who lived in Auckland, seen this article in the *Auckland Star*? No, he had not. Nor had he ever heard of it. Had the pilot in command of the flight of October 18, 1977 been at that time the senior DC10 training captain? Yes, he had.

Then the witness was shown a copy of a magazine called *Travelling Times* published in September 1978. It contained an account by Mr John Brizindine, President of the McDonnell Douglas Corporation, of being a guest of Air New Zealand on the last Antarctic flight of 1977. Mr Brizindine had written in enthusiastic terms and described how the pilot in command, Captain Gordon Vette, had approached Ross Island at an altitude of 3,000 feet and had flown over the Scott Base area at a height of 'perhaps half a mile'.

Had the witness ever seen this article? No, he had not. Had he ever heard of this descent by Captain Vette described in a trade magazine by the President of McDonnell Douglas as being to 3,000 feet? No, he had not.

The witness was further questioned on the same topic. He was shown a news clipping from another Auckland paper, the *Central Leader*, published on November 28, 1978. This contained an article by a Mr McGregor, who had been on the Antarctic flight of November 7, 1978. He referred to flying at 2,000 feet, which was low enough to see the huts and vehicles at McMurdo. Had the witness seen that article? No, he had not. Had he ever had it drawn to his attention? No, he had not. The same article had been published in another Auckland suburban paper, the *Western Leader*. But the witness had neither seen nor heard of that either.

Since these flights had been the subject of such wide newspaper comment, with favourable attention being drawn to the relatively low altitude of those sightseeing flights, why had the witness not acquired some knowledge of their occurrence? He replied by saying that he thought he had heard 'a rumour' in 1977 that one or two flights had been carried out at less than 6,000 feet. But it had only been a rumour. This is why he had not mentioned the matter to Civil Aviation when he received their message about six days before the fatal flight.

But the troubles of this witness on the altitude question were not yet over. Counsel for ALPA, who had cross-examined the witness on the previous day, was permitted to ask some further questions. He raised with the witness the flight of November 7, 1978, which had been the subject of the McGregor newspaper articles. Counsel told the witness that it would be established that a passenger on this flight had been the company's former Director of Flight Operations, Captain Douglas Keesing, and that this man, who was head of all the airline's flying operations, had described with apparent approval, the flight being conducted over McMurdo at 2,000 feet.

Had the Director of Flight Operations ever mentioned this fact to the witness? No, he had not. He knew nothing of it at all. If the descent to 2,000 feet had been unauthorised, yes, he would have expected the Director of Flight Operations to have taken official action. But as far as the witness knew, the Director had not taken the matter up with anyone.

I was starting to be mystified over this altitude question. If as at November 7, 1978 the then Director of Flight Operations, apparently the predecessor of the present Director, had known of the two minimum safe altitudes of 16,000 feet on the approach to McMurdo and 6,000 feet over McMurdo, how could he have condoned the action of the pilot on his flight in flying over McMurdo at 2,000 feet? Yet this had been the tenor of the question asked by counsel.

I had to bear in mind that the question had been hypothetical. 'If it were established that Captain Keesing...' But, knowing counsel for ALPA, I thought it unlikely that he would have put the questions unless he had, or expected to have, solid evidence to support the hypothesis. Captain Keesing must have described the 2,000 feet flight to someone, or he might have prepared a written memorandum.

There was another factor which also seemed to support the probability that Captain Keesing had told someone about the 2,000 feet flight, and this was the way in which the witness had answered the questions of counsel. First, counsel had asked whether the witness knew that Captain Keesing had been on the flight of November 7, 1978. Not at the time, the witness said, but he knew of it later. Then had come the following question and answer:

> **Q.** Would it be a difficult matter for a captain with the experience of Captain Keesing to determine at any stage whether the aircraft in which he was travelling was flying at 2,000 as opposed to 6,000 feet? Is that a difficult judgment?
>
> **A.** If he was on the flight deck it would be very easy. Looking outside a passenger window not as easy. Height estimation viewed from the cabin in the vastness of Antarctica would be considered to be difficult.

I remembered how readily the witness had given this reply. And I also remembered being disconcerted at the suggestion that any pilot with thousands of flying hours' experience, which I assumed Captain Keesing to have had, could possibly mistake

6,000 feet for 2,000 feet in broad daylight, no matter what window he was looking out of. But the point was that it looked as if the witness had known in advance what the ultimate question was going to be. If this were so, then this alert and intelligent witness had made a mistake which is frequently made by courtroom witnesses. He had given a premature explanation for the proposition which he knew was going to be put to him by counsel. And if this were so, how had he known that Captain Keesing had described to someone his flight at 2,000 feet?

I could only hope that this confused altitude evidence would all be cleared up as time went on. After all, the altitude levels of 16,000 feet and 6,000 feet had been considered inviolate by the Chief Inspector. The basic fault of the aircrew, according to him, had been the decision to descend below the authorised minimum level of 16,000 feet on the approach to Ross Island, and there had been no doubt that this opinion was also shared by the present witness. But what had been the instructions to pilots as to the minimum safe altitude? This was going to be the real question, and as the evidence now stood, some doubt as to the answer was emerging.

The witness may or may not have made two slight tactical errors in his testimony. But even if he had, he did not make any others, and he was under sustained cross-examination for two days. One piece of his evidence had been a minor masterpiece, and this was when he spoke of the aircraft flying onwards at low altitude towards Ross Island.

Basing his opinion on the detailed evidence already given by the weather experts, with which he seemed closely familiar, he had apparently postulated a situation in which the DC10 had flown onwards at 1,500 feet either in or towards impenetrable cloud in strange and mountainous territory. But this had to be reconciled with his previously expressed admiration for the well known flying skills of each member of the three-man crew, and his evidence in this respect had combined in a most effective manner a reverential eulogy of the dead aircrew with a deeply reluctant indictment of their conduct on this specific occasion. Of all the evidence given by this witness, this had been his most masterly presentation. And if one accepted the thesis upon which he had proceeded, he was clearly correct. It was not only what he said, it was his demeanour, and his manner of testifying. With his courteous attitude, and his dark hair and good looks, and his persuasive fluency, I began to think of him as an ideal public relations man. The airline was fortunate, I thought, to have available, as its first witness, such an impressive individual.

At this stage I began to wonder to what extent I should allow management personnel, no matter how well qualified, to give their individual opinions as to the quality of the conduct of Captain Collins. Would the other airline witnesses offer the same opinions? I rather thought they would. But were such opinions permissible? They did not involve any technical feature upon which their opinions might be of value. If the opinion of this witness was based on the simple non-technical ground that given a certain set of circumstances a pilot should have climbed away rather than continued on, then I did not need any advice on this topic. This was the old and familiar question as to whether in a given situation a specific person had been negligent or not. I was not very interested in what one particular witness might have done or not done. I decided for the moment to leave the point open, but I thought that my reservations on this type of opinion might have to be disclosed as the inquiry went on.

The evidence of Captain Grundy came to an end on the morning of July 30. He was to be followed by Captain Ian Gemmell, the Chief Pilot of Air New Zealand.

VIII

THE CHIEF PILOT'S EVIDENCE

I had heard something of Captain Gemmell before he gave evidence. He was one of the most senior members of Flight Operations Division and one of the dominant figures in the airline. He was said to be a close friend of Mr Davis. I knew that he had been the airline's accident investigator and had accompanied the first party of officials to the scene of the disaster. He was said to have been the principal adviser — perhaps the only adviser — to the Chief Inspector in relation to the technicalities of jet flight and of the inertial navigation system. He had accompanied the Chief Inspector when he visited the McDonnell Douglas Corporation in California in the course of his inquiries.

I knew that Captain Gemmell, in his capacity as Chief Pilot, had been one of the architects of the original planning of the Antarctic flights. It had been agreed that his evidence at this stage would cover only the planning procedures of the Antarctic flights, as subsequently approved by Civil Aviation, and it was understood that he would be recalled at a later date in order to give further evidence.

Captain Gemmell began by reading his prepared brief of evidence. He said that his present position was that of Flight Manager (Technical) for Air New Zealand Limited, but, in this narrative, I shall continue to refer to him as the Chief Pilot. He had started with the company in April 1946 and had then become a licensed pilot and had been transferred to Flight Operations Division in January 1953. He subsequently became a flight captain on all varieties of aircraft used by Air New Zealand. In 1966 he had attended an accident investigation course at the University of Southern California, in 1971 he had become a DC10 Flight Captain and in August 1975 he had become Chief Pilot. In that position, he had been responsible to the Manager of Flight Operations for overall supervision of Air New Zealand's flight operations, and these included the Antarctic flights which had

81

begun in February 1977.

In the course of reading his brief of evidence, Captain Gemmell described the process by which the Antarctic flights had been inaugurated. There had been considerable interest, he said, in the publicised proposed operations by Qantas Airways of a service from Sydney scheduled to fly over Antarctica in early 1977. It was apparent that, as a result of this information, Air New Zealand decided that it would begin comparable scenic flights itself.

Captain Gemmell said that, being aware of the original proposal to operate a DC8 service to McMurdo, he had made himself familiar with the reports on that file dated November 25, 1969. He had also discussed the possibilities of the operation with Captain Grundy who had been to McMurdo when the earlier DC8 proposals had been under consideration.

Captain Gemmell explained how it was decided that, in preference to an original proposal of flying to the South Magnetic Pole, the airline would operate flights over McMurdo itself. He said that a study of the route was undertaken and it was shown to be feasible, having regard to various considerations, such as weather and fuel. He described the decision to make the McMurdo flight the primary scenic flight, and to provide an alternative flight to the South Magnetic Pole, followed by a flight over the Mertz and Ninnis Glaciers, returning to Christchurch via Cape Hallett and the Campbell Islands. The secondary flight was to be used in the event of weather conditions preventing the operation of the primary scenic flight to McMurdo and back.

The proposal to operate two of these Antarctic flights in January 1977 or shortly thereafter, was submitted to the Director of Civil Aviation by letter dated January 18, 1977. The approval was requested in respect of two flights to be operated in February. These flights were approved by Civil Aviation by letter dated January 19, 1977, subject to compliance with certain operational conditions. The airline then wrote to Civil Aviation on February 2, 1977, setting out the proposed conditions, and the appropriate air service licence to operate the flights was then granted.

On February 4, 1977, Captain Gemmell had accompanied Captain Grundy and one of the Civil Aviation airline inspectors to an Antarctic briefing given by the U.S. Navy at the Christchurch headquarters of the Navy.

The first Air New Zealand flight to Antarctica took place on February 15, 1977. Captain Gemmell was the pilot in command and his co-pilot was Captain A.A.E. Lawson who was at the time the company's RCU Briefing Officer. This meant that Captain Lawson was in charge of the Route Clearance Unit which was responsible for briefing pilots in respect of various flights. Also present on this flight was an airline inspector from Civil Aviation.

Captain Gemmell said that the last stage of the flight was on the computer track between Cape Hallett and the McMurdo NDB. He said that the aircraft followed this track throughout and that the minimum safe altitude of 16,000 feet was maintained at all times. The aircraft flew over Mount Erebus and just to the east of its peak in conformity with the computer track. After flying at 16,000 feet around the mountain and over the McMurdo area, the aircraft then tracked northward from McMurdo and up the coast of Victoria Land, before returning to Christchurch.

There was one more flight in February 1977, and it was then decided, later in the year, to ask Civil Aviation for approval to conduct four more flights towards the end of 1977. But it appeared that in the meantime, there had been some query about a scenic flight operating at an altitude as high as 16,000 feet. Evidently, a request had been made from the Commercial Division of the airline to the Flight Operations Division to see whether future flights could descend to a lower altitude. Captain Gemmell went on to say that he discussed this possibility with one of the airline inspectors of Civil Aviation, and that at the conclusion of this meeting the company put a proposal in writing to Civil Aviation for consideration. This was done by letter dated August 10, 1977.

This letter requested approval to fly over Mount Erebus in accordance with the original planning, and then to descend in appropriate conditions to 6,000 feet within a specified area. The altitude of 6,000 feet was calculated to ensure a sufficient safety margin over the highest ground within that area south of Ross Island.

Captain Gemmell did not, at this stage, indicate whether any written approval was obtained from Civil Aviation in response to this letter. However, approval was evidently obtained, because he said that the four flights which operated in the latter part of 1977 were controlled by this extension of the minimum safe altitude. In other words, the aircraft could let down to 6,000 feet once it had flown over Mount Erebus, and provided that this level of 6,000 feet was maintained only within the specified sector south of Ross Island.

Captain Gemmell was then cross-examined, at considerable length, by counsel for other parties. Many criticisms of the flight planning were advanced and it was interesting to see how the witness responded to the detailed and challenging questions which were addressed to him.

The answers which he gave were unhesitating and positive. When possible, his answers were monosyllabic and he seemed to treat the various counsel with thinly veiled contempt. His lean figure, standing upright with an almost military stance, reminded me of someone; but I could not for the moment remember who it was. I looked at his bronzed, immobile aquiline features, and his close-cut grey hair, and I surveyed his uncompromising demeanour. Then I remembered who it was that the Captain reminded me of. In his general appearance, he was very similar to photographs I had seen of the celebrated Field Marshal von Manstein, probably the most brilliant army commander of the present century. And as the hearing went on, I came to see that his similarity to the Field Marshal was not exclusively visual.

As I have indicated, his answers were given with almost military precision. Everything he said was clear and brief. If he considered a question repetitive, he did not hesitate to say so. After he was asked a question, he would immediately lean forward towards the microphone, pronounce his answer, then lean backwards and regain his former posture.

Under cross-examination, the Chief Pilot maintained his iron composure. He was completely unperturbed and his answers continued to be concise and clear. No matter how valid some criticism seemed to be, his attitude never varied. He plainly maintained the view that the planning of the flights by the airline had been impeccable in all respects.

The questions put to Captain Gemmell by cross-examining counsel were very much the same as had been put to Captain Grundy. He was asked about the programming of the flight so as to fly the aircraft over the top of an active volcano. The witness replied by saying that there would be no danger unless the volcano were in eruption, and he would expect the airline to be given adequate notice of such an event.

It happened that I had been reading whatever material I could find about Antarctica. I had seen many photographs of Mount Erebus and I was aware that there was a permanent high plume of steam floating away from the crater, almost always in an easterly direction. The computer track lay a little to the east of the mountain, and 2,500 feet above its summit. I could see no escape from the conclusion that the aircraft, while flying on its computer track, must inevitably fly through this thick plume of steam and gas. I naturally would not have expected the aircraft to stay on that course when the pilot saw, in front of him, this high and dense wall of steam. Nevertheless, it seemed a strange thing that the computer programme had been so designed as to expose the aircraft to this obvious danger.

The witness was asked why the flight had not been programmed to follow the military track in the centre of McMurdo Sound. It was suggested that such a flight path would be better for scenic purposes. It was also suggested that it had the obvious advantage that the air traffic control operators at McMurdo would be able to pick up the aircraft at forty miles range and follow its progress on the radar screen.

The witness replied that the scenic advantages of programming the flight down the centre of the sound were only marginally better than the flight path actually selected. As to the other advantages of the military flight path, the witness maintained that it was desirable for the aircraft to fly over the NDB by a direct route so that the crew could check the accuracy of the AINS system. It was put to him, however, that an aircraft flying down the centre of the sound could turn to its left at the Byrd reporting point and then fly over the NDB. The witness said that this would take more fuel. I remember measuring off the comparative distances on one of the maps and coming to the conclusion that the fuel explanation could certainly not be supported.

The Chief Pilot was questioned as to whether it was necessary to check the accuracy of the AINS by 'overheading' the NDB. It was pointed out to him, and he agreed, that the system was extremely accurate and had always been known to be so. He agreed that it would be accurate to within two to three miles after the long flight from New Zealand but he steadfastly maintained that it was the correct operational procedure to fly over a beacon of this type so as to verify the accuracy of the AINS.

Then there arose the whiteout question. Captain Gemmell was asked why the aircrews had not been adequately briefed on this visual factor. The counsel asking these questions had in mind, of course, the description of this type of whiteout given briefly by the Chief Inspector in his report. They were referring to the existence of a solid, pale, low overcast, coupled with white forward terrain, and the consequent inability to perceive that the apparently flat terrain is in fact rising. But the witness continually associated the term 'whiteout' with cloud. There was no doubt from his answers that he was using the term 'whiteout' in its other sense, meaning an area in which the air is filled with drifting flakes of snow. This appeared to be the only sense in which he understood that term. And, of course, the maintenance of 16,000 feet until entering the 6,000 feet sector was adequate, in his view, to overcome any type of visibility problem.

Another topic pressed in cross-examination was the act of the airline in procuring from Civil Aviation a dispensation from the ordinary requirement that a pilot in command must have flown over the area previously as a pilot under supervision. Why had this dispensation been sought? Was it not essential in flying over this strange and unfamiliar territory for a pilot to have been there before? To these questions the Chief Pilot maintained a constant attitude. He said that a previous flight over the area was of no significance because of the accuracy of the very careful briefing given to the pilots at Auckland.

At this stage, I thought there was some validity in the criticism being advanced by counsel. Going by the photographs which I had seen of the Antarctic terrain, with its unvarying, white assembly of ice and snow and of various snow-covered mountain peaks, I could not see how any pilot in command would have been able to identify through the cockpit window which peak was which. But on further reflection, I decided that the Chief Pilot was probably correct. The aircraft was programmed to navigate itself along a determined track, and it was not possible for it to deviate from that track unless the Nav mode was disengaged. But much later on, when I eventually went down to Antarctica myself, I saw that I had been wrong. There was simply no substitute for having flown in the area before. But all that was in the future.

The witness was asked whether the U.S. Navy at McMurdo had been advised that the flight path of the Antarctic flights would be over the top of Mount Erebus and that, following the first two flights, they were permitted to descend to 6,000 feet in the special sector south of Ross Island. He replied that at the initial Christchurch discussion with Navy officials, the proposed flight track had been mentioned, but he agreed that no further notice was given to the U.S. Navy. This being the case, he was asked, would not the radar and radio operators at Air Traffic Control first see the aircraft on the radar screen only when it appeared over the summit of the mountain? Did this not give ground control insufficient notice of the arrival of this big jet? Captain Gemmell maintained his steadfast refusal to accept that there was anything valid in this criticism.

The barrage of questions continued. Why did the computer flight plan not refer to the destination waypoint being at the NDB? Why was there no written briefing material describing the NDB as the destination waypoint? Why were the crew not given a topographical map with the computer track printed on it? These questions had no effect upon the Chief Pilot. He dismissed them all as being of no consequence. He thought that possession of a topographical map on the flight deck would be of only marginal assistance.

I had been giving some thought to this point about the aircrews not being supplied with a topographical map. I knew that the computer track could be printed over the map so that the crew would know at any given moment exactly where the aircraft was when flying in the Nav mode. I could not help but think that the absence of such a map was a defect in the flight plan, although it appeared that there was going to be evidence that Captain Collins, along with other pilots, had taken the precaution of plotting the computer track on a map which he had obtained for himself. However, the attitude of the Chief Pilot was as stated. He thought there was nothing in the point.

At one stage in cross-examination, a rather curious point emerged. It appeared that on December 24, 1976 the airline had advised Civil Aviation that the first of the proposed two flights to Antarctica would be to the South Magnetic Pole, and that this would be the destination of both flights. Then it seemed that the New Zealand Ministry of Foreign Affairs, having been notified by Civil Aviation of the airline's intention, had told Civil Aviation that the present location of the South Magnetic Pole was in the ocean. It appeared as if the airline had notified Civil Aviation of this destination without knowing where the South Magnetic Pole was. I had a mental vision of an aircraft flying far away to the south and then circling around an unknown part of the dark, cold sea before returning to New Zealand.

It was in consequence of this notification from the Foreign Affairs Department that the South Magnetic Pole route was altered so as to include the two glaciers previously mentioned. But it was clear enough that the airline had made a formal request to Civil Aviation without taking the opinion of their own Flight Operations Division, the members of which would immediately have pointed out that the South Magnetic Pole varied its position from year to year and was at the present time out at sea. There seemed to be some hint here of hasty planning on the part of the airline.

Mr Baragwanath, senior counsel assisting the Commission, asked the Chief Pilot about the published accounts of flights to Antarctica which had maintained low flight levels in the McMurdo area. The three published accounts which had been put to Captain Grundy were also put to the Chief Pilot. He said that he had never seen any such account before. He said that he had never heard, prior to the disaster, of any Air New Zealand DC10 descending below 6,000 feet in the McMurdo area.

I noticed that the Chief Pilot was not asked about the flight of which Captain Keesing had apparently written. I assumed from this that counsel was awaiting some verification of the Keesing flight before this particular inquiry was pressed further, and I assumed that the Keesing incident, if correctly described, would be put to the Chief Pilot when he gave evidence at a later date.

The Keesing incident was, of course, of major importance. I had not heard any direct evidence about it, but if the allegations about that flight as put to Captain Grundy were correct, then there really seemed no answer to the suggestion that senior members of Flight Operations would have known of Captain Keesing's experience. However, all I could do was wait and see.

And now the evidence of Captain Gemmell had come to an end. He stepped down from the witness stand and departed as he had arrived — intelligent, taciturn and impregnable. Throughout the process of skilled cross-examination, he had not deviated one hair's breadth from his basic position that the airline's planning procedures had been impeccable. He walked to the back of the courtroom and sat down amongst the management contingent.

Right throughout the long hearing, throughout all the weeks which lay ahead, Captain Gemmell sat day by day behind the airline counsel. Now and then he was away through being engaged on conversion courses relating to the Boeing 747 aircraft then being bought by Air New Zealand, and on such occasions his place would be taken by another senior official from Flight Operations Division. Whereas at one time Captain Gemmell had been technical adviser to the Chief Inspector, he was now technical adviser to the airline counsel.

There was another airline employee who was present daily at the hearings, right through to the end of the inquiry. This was a retired pilot named Captain J.P.Wilson, and we shall meet him again in this narrative. He used to sit in the public seats right at the back of the courtroom, just on the left of the main doorway. He was armed with a notebook in which he would make frequent entries and I noticed, as the hearing went on, that he always made a written note whenever some counsel got a reluctant admission out of an airline witness, or whenever an airline witness was induced to depart from his prepared brief. And, with other witnesses, he always noted any point which seemed to be against the airline. I wondered to whom he was reporting next day. It would not be to the Flight Operations Division, because Captain Gemmell was there himself. And it would not be to the airline management generally, because both Captain Gemmell and the airline counsel would be reporting to the management. I presumed that Captain Wilson was reporting directly to the Chief Executive. I would have given a great deal, in the stormy days which lay ahead, to have had a look at Captain Wilson's notebook.

The evidence of Captains Grundy and Gemmell had been restricted at this stage to their participation in the planning procedures for the Antarctic flights. However, Captain Grundy had been asked, by various counsel and by me, various questions which went beyond the specific planning evidence and these questions had been objected to by counsel for the airline. I permitted these questions to continue to a limited extent, but accepted the assurance of counsel for the airline that both these witnesses would be testifying again.

However, there were one or two features of Captain Grundy's evidence which I could see had caused some measure of discontent among the management personnel sitting behind their counsel. One had been Captain Grundy's apparent agreement that Captain Collins might have plotted his computer flight path on a map before the commencement of his flight. This had led to questioning of a specific kind, and I had asked the relevant questions myself.

I had asked Captain Grundy to consider the following hypothesis: If Captain Collins had plotted his computer track on a topographical map, then he would have seen that the destination waypoint terminated some thirty miles to the west of the TACAN (Tactical Air Navigation System). That being so, he would therefore have been at all times confident that as long as he maintained the aircraft in the Nav mode, his flight path must take him down the centre of McMurdo Sound. This meant that he would be satisfied that as he passed Ross Island, the peak of Mount Erebus would be about twenty-five miles to his left. Captain Grundy had agreed with this hypothesis.

Then I had gone on to suggest that if that hypothesis were correct, and if the computer track had been changed a matter of hours before the departure of the aircraft, then would not the computer mistake be the major originating cause of the disaster? To that proposition Captain Grundy had replied: 'On that hypothesis, I would have to agree.'

But, despite that admission, Captain Grundy had not moved away from the position that there was a minimum safe altitude of 16,000 feet on the approach to Ross Island, and that it was not permissible to descend below that altitude under any circumstances.

In summary, it was clear that both these airline witnesses were

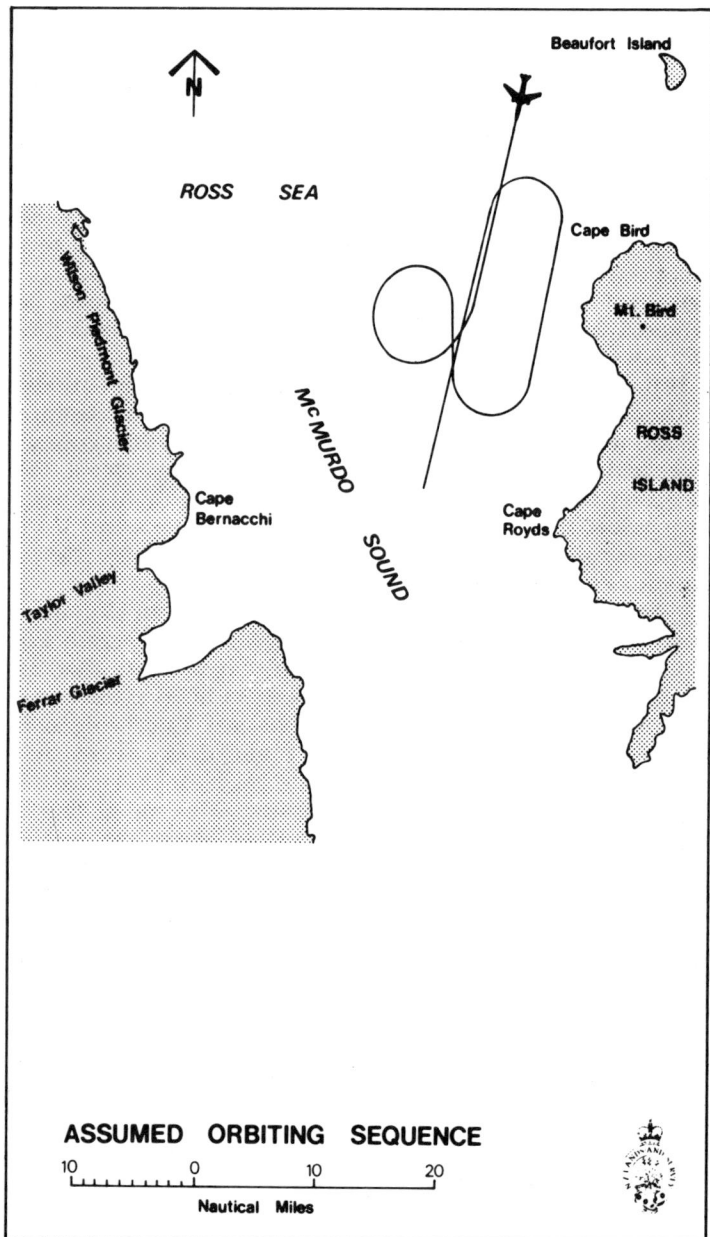

These two diagrams show the orbiting sequence in McMurdo Sound where Captain Collins thought it was being performed and the orbiting sequence just north of Lewis Bay where, in fact, it was being performed

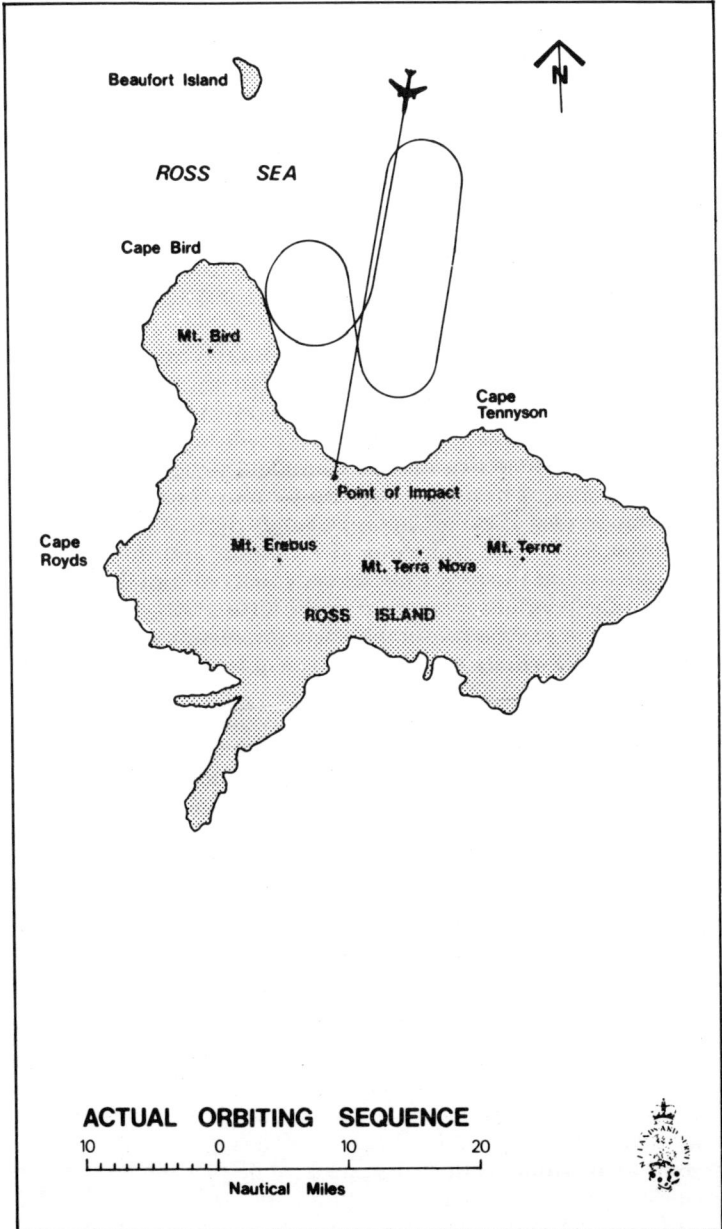

Beaufort Island

ROSS   SEA

Cape Bird

Mt. Bird

Cape
Tennyson

Point of Impact

Cape
Royds

Mt. Erebus

Mt. Terra Nova

Mt. Terror

ROSS   ISLAND

ACTUAL   ORBITING   SEQUENCE

10   0   10   20

Nautical   Miles

reflecting the positive stand taken by the Chief Executive when he issued his press release of June 24, 1980. It was an inevitable conclusion from the terms of that release that he denied that the operational planning and procedures of the airline itself were in any way at fault and this had clearly been the view of the first two witnesses for the airline. It seemed to me that the case for the airline was now fairly clearly foreshadowed. There may have been a computer mistake, there may have been some unusual weather conditions which produced an ocular illusion, but no factor of this type could possibly have resulted in disaster had the aircraft been maintained at a level of not less than 16,000 feet until over the top of Mount Erebus.

I had wondered why the airline did not call Captain Gemmell as its first witness. Instead he had sat in the courtroom and listened to the evidence of Captain Grundy. Captain Gemmell had been responsible for the ultimate planning details of these first flights to Antarctica and had commanded the first flight. But when I compared him with Captain Grundy, I could see why it had been decided to make Captain Grundy the first witness. With his persuasive and courteous demeanour and his obvious intelligence and fluency, I had already marked him down as an ideal public relations man so far as the airline was concerned. If one desired to make a favourable early impression on a tribunal, then Captain Grundy was just the type of witness to be used for that purpose.

Here I should explain that the decision as to the order of witnesses is always of considerable importance in a jury case. It may be that the best witness for one party is not as persuasive in his demeanour as one or two of the others. It would not do, for example, to call as the first witness a man who might be rude or self-assertive or otherwise liable to set the tribunal against him and therefore against the party calling him. So there is a standard procedure in jury cases whereby you select as your first witness, if you can, a person who is not only a reliable witness, but also with a demeanour which will favourably impress itself upon the tribunal.

I strongly suspected that this manoeuvre had been attempted here. If so, I could only regret its occurrence. This inquiry was in no sense a court case. In addition, it was being heard by a man who had spent all his working life in courtrooms. It was idle to expect that I could be taken in by this type of device.

But, apart from all that, it seemed to me that the airline had made a tactical mistake in not calling Captain Gemmell first. He and Captain Grundy were obviously men of high intelligence, and it goes without saying that they were accepted, without question, as being pilots of long experience and great skill. But I could not imagine Captain Gemmell ever making the evidentiary concession to which I have referred.

Captain Grundy was perfectly correct to answer my hypothetical question in the way he had, and indeed such an answer was logically inevitable once the opening hypothesis was stated. But I was satisfied that Captain Gemmell would not have been enticed into that type of concession, and that he would have raised the point that he was being called at this juncture only on the question of flight planning procedures.

Baragwanath and Harrison, as counsel assisting the Commission, ran into difficulties with the airline fairly early with regard to the production of its written statements of evidence. The idea had been that the statements of witnesses would be supplied to me and to counsel a day or two before each witness testified, but it soon transpired that the airline had no intention of carrying out this procedure. Not until the airline counsel called a witness would his statement of evidence be distributed to counsel and to me, so that no one had any warning of what any witness was about to say. I was well aware that these statements had been prepared well in advance of the appearance of each witness, but Baragwanath and Harrison had no success whatever in obtaining early production of the statements.

The reason given by the airline was that the statements might require deletions or additions in the light of evidence previously given and that they had to be retained until the last moment for this purpose. There was, of course, no reason why any additions could not have been made verbally in the witness box and it soon became clear that the object of the airline was simply to prevent other parties knowing what their witnesses were about to say. However these manoeuvres· had no effect at all. The parties opposing Air New Zealand all had access to expert advice in the courtroom, the process of cross-examination was almost painfully slow because of the methods used to transcribe the evidence, and the full content and effect of a witness's statement of evidence was known and fully understood by all of us before he had even finished reading it out. Counsel for the airline would have known all this.

The preliminary evidence for the airline was now completed. The two witnesses who had been the pilots in command of the first two flights, had described the parts they played in the planning procedures involved. The next section of evidence to be produced before me was that of the appropriate officials from the

Civil Aviation Division. They were now going to describe the part they played in the planning operations and the conditions which were imposed by Civil Aviation upon the proposed flights to Antarctica.

IX

THE CIVIL AVIATION WITNESSES

Three officials were called to give evidence on behalf of Civil Aviation — Captain E.T. Kippenberger the Director of Civil Aviation; Captain E.J. Omundsen, the Controller of Airline Operations and Captain J. Spence, an airline inspector.

The Director first of all gave his personal history in aviation. He had joined the Royal New Zealand Air Force in 1940 and was commissioned as a pilot in 1941. He had then been an instructor for some years and had flown on transport operations in the Pacific area in May 1945. After the war he became a civil airlines pilot and flew in various parts of the world from 1947 until 1953, when he resigned from BOAC and returned to New Zealand and farmed a property for the next five years. In 1959 he had joined the New Zealand Civil Aviation Department as an airline inspector. When the department merged with the Transport Department in 1968 he had become part of the Civil Aviation Division of that department. The Director related his various promotions within Civil Aviation over the years, up to his present position of Director of Civil Aviation to which he had been appointed in 1978. It is, of course, the senior position in that particular division of the Ministry of Transport.

The Director had in the course of his career become qualified to pilot DC8 aircraft and his general background of experience made it clear that he was suitably qualified to be the Director of Civil Aviation.

The next part of the Director's evidence was devoted to a description of the organisation of Civil Aviation and the functions of its various branches. He then went on to describe the relevant provisions of the Civil Aviation Act 1964 and the Civil Aviation Regulations made pursuant to that act. It was pointed out that in his capacity of Director, the witness had powers under the regulations to issue various documents and requirements that were in the nature of tertiary legislation and which have the force of regulations.

Then the Director went on to describe some matters of more immediate interest. He explained that every airline operator must carry out his operations under the authority of and in accordance with an Air Service Certificate issued by the Director. At all times Air New Zealand was in possession of two Air Service Certificates — one covering DC8 and DC10 operations, and the other covering B737 and F27 operations. The Director is empowered by law to attach conditions to the Air Service Certificates covering matters which he considers to be necessary in the interests of safety, and the standard practice had always been to include such conditions in a document called the Operations Specifications.

Pursuant to Regulation 141, Air New Zealand was required to provide for the use of its operations personnel an approved Operations Manual containing the matters set out in Regulation 141. It is also a requirement of the law that the Operations Manual used by an airline operator must be approved by the Director of Civil Aviation. The manual is required by law to be carried upon an aircraft and it contains many provisions, but, in particular, it contains the text of the special conditions imposed by Civil Aviation in its Operations Specifications. Therefore, in the case of any given flight, the aircrew can always refer to the manual to see what special conditions have been applied to the route upon which they are flying.

The Director went on to describe the part which he had played in the setting up of the Antarctic flights. The Division had approved the proposed conditions of the flights as submitted by Air New Zealand in the early part of 1977, but as the Director had not been appointed to his present post in the following year, he had not been involved personally with any further aspects of Antarctic flight planning. However, as he pointed out, his subordinates had been involved.

It would be tedious for me to attempt to describe the course of the Director's evidence, and the evidence of his co-employees, as covered in detail during the very prolonged cross-examination by various counsel. The primary point was that, in the view of the three Civil Aviation witnesses, the minimum safe altitude on the approach to McMurdo was 16,000 feet. They held the unalterable opinion that the disaster was due to the failure of Captain Collins to maintain this minimum safe altitude. This was the essential basis upon which depended the whole case for Civil Aviation.

The three Civil Aviation witnesses also held the combined view that Captain Collins had been solely responsible for the disaster in that not only had he departed from the 16,000 feet minimum safe altitude, but he had flown on towards an area of deteriorating visibility. It was also perfectly clear that, in the opinion of these three witnesses, the aircrew had in fact been flying in an area of impaired visibility. In this respect they had very carefully, as it seemed to me, aligned themselves with the opinions of the Chief Inspector, who, despite his autonomous powers as an air accident investigator, was nevertheless their co-employee in Civil Aviation Division.

During the course of lengthy cross-examination of these three Government officials they were pressed with some very testing questions and there were occasions on which they gave some very unfortunate answers. But their opening position was that the 16,000 feet limit was inviolate, that they had never heard of Air New Zealand aircraft descending below that limit, and that the failure to comply with the MSA of 16,000 feet was the sole cause of the disaster.

Broadly speaking, the attitude taken by these three witnesses was based upon the report of the Chief Inspector, coupled with the evidence which had been given by the weather experts, who were employed by their own department.

In this latter regard, I recalled how junior counsel for Civil Aviation had done his level best in questioning the weather experts to get them to agree to a proposition that, having regard to the passengers' photographs, the view to the south during the final approach to Ross Island would have shown that a cloud base was descending down to ground level. But the experts, despite pressing invitations from their own counsel, had not felt themselves able to agree with that view. They were prepared to go as far as to say that the proposition being put to them was possible, but they were hindered by the fact that none of the passengers' photographs displayed a view to the south. Nevertheless, they had expressed an opinion that the aircraft may well have been flying in and out of cloud on the final approach and they were of the opinion that some miles ahead of the aircraft there was an area of deteriorating visibility.

To put the matter succinctly, I thought the weather people would very much have liked to have said that the aircraft flew on at 1,500 feet towards an area of clearly discernible cloud which descended down to ground level, but there was no positive evidence which could have supported such an opinion.

This opinion of cloud immediately in front of the aircraft would obviously solve the difficulty created by the known fact that no one on the flight deck had ever seen the mountainside. But of course, that same opinion was open to an insuperable objection of the kind which I have mentioned before: On what basis could this experienced aircrew have possibly flown towards a low-lying cloud bank without ever deviating direction or height? On what basis could this same experienced flight crew have continually spoken to each other up to the very last seconds reconfirming that they were flying throughout in VMC?

Of course, these were not questions for the weathermen to answer. Nor was it their function to see the logical inconsistency inherent in the opinion which they were being asked to endorse. The Chief Inspector, denied of any evidence to suggest that the aircraft was flying in cloud at the time of impact, had then modified his original view by stating that the aircraft was flying 'towards' an area of impaired visibility. That area was only a few miles forward of the aircraft which was flying at 300 miles per hour. So the logical anomaly was, how could there be any difference between flying in cloud and flying towards cloud at such close range?

But I must come back to the main points of the evidence given by the three Civil Aviation witnesses. They were each cross-examined for long periods of time and were asked to explain many matters which, upon analysis, seemed to defy explanation.

Why did the Division accept the airline's proposal to programme the computer flight path over Mount Erebus? How could they possibly have agreed to have the aircraft flying over an active volcano? Some vague answers were given to the effect that several other airline routes in the world flew over active volcanoes, but no example was given of an airliner being programmed to fly so close to a volcanic crater that it must encounter a plume of steam and gas which drifted permanently across the flight path and gradually ascended to some thousands of feet.

In view of the fact that actual knowledge of the topography was vital in a flight to this unknown and hostile terrain, why was it not stipulated by the Division that the flight track be overprinted upon a topographical map and the crews provided with such a map? I could detect no satisfactory answer to that obvious criticism.

Why had the Division not cleared with the U.S. Navy the approved flight track, and in particular, the amended altitude provisions, about which the Division had been informed, authorising a descent to 6,000 feet in the immediate location of the U.S. Navy field? Again, I could not see that any satisfactory answer had been given to this query.

Was it not clear that the aircrew had been deceived by the last-minute alteration in the flight track? Was it not clear that Captain Collins must have plotted the original flight track himself on a map and then relied upon that track in order to determine his position? Was not this theory completely vindicated by the care which the flight crew had taken to lock the aircraft back on to its computer track immediately after the conclusion of each orbit? To these questions, and disregarding variations of opinion among the three witnesses, the general answers seemed to be that there was no satisfactory evidence that Captain Collins had in front of him a topographical map upon which the last leg of the computer path had been plotted.

What about the whiteout phenomenon? Had not the briefing of all Antarctic crews been totally inadequate with regard to the variety of whiteout alluded to by the Chief Inspector in his report? Why had the aircrews not been warned that when flying over snow-covered terrain under the type of overcast prevailing at McMurdo at the time of the disaster, all the white terrain in front of them would appear to be uniformly flat? Again, no satisfactory answer could be obtained to the various questions on this topic. The witnesses could only say that there had been some reference in the briefing to difficulties in defining the horizon in those latitudes, and it was thought that professional pilots would have understood the difficulties of horizon perception. So far as I could see, none of the witnesses seemed able to answer the proposition that in those particular conditions, an aircrew is not even aware that any visibility problem exists forward of the aircraft's track.

The Director had made a most unexpected assertion with regard to this whiteout question. He had said that, in his opinion, there was no whiteout problem on the day of the disaster. When asked the basis upon which he advanced this surprising opinion, he seemed to have been uncertain. He was obviously faced with the simple difficulty to which I had previously referred: If there had been no whiteout problem, then how was it that this experienced aircrew, with Peter Mulgrew sitting with them in the flight deck, had flown straight into the mountainside without one of them being aware that the icy slopes of Mount Erebus lay directly in their path?

The Director then explained that, having given careful consideration to these matters, he had formed the view that Captain Collins must have been suddenly afflicted by some medical or psychological malady which made him oblivious to the mortal danger looming in front of him. This was a most incautious remark. Everyone in the courtroom immediately saw that if this theory were sound, then the same insidious malady must simultaneously have affected not only the two pilots, but also Peter Mulgrew. The Director's theory was so nonsensical that I was surprised that a person of his long experience and authority could have put it forward. And, unfortunately, in consequence of this unhappy piece of evidence, the Director's evidence as a whole then began to suffer from general doubt as to its reliability.

But, of course, this was only one expression of opinion. I could not discount the long experience of the Director in aviation and his subsequent long experience as an official within the Civil Aviation Division. Overall, he was not a good witness, but many very well informed people are frequently not seen at their best in the witness box. I felt that I should perhaps place the Director in that category.

The overall effect of the Civil Aviation evidence was that their witnesses agreed with every observation in the Chief Inspector's report which tended to place blame either on the airline management or on the dead aircrew. On the other hand, they strongly disputed every opinion of the Chief Inspector which appeared to place any blame, or to attach any undesirable responsibility, to Civil Aviation itself.

The stance of Civil Aviation was a simple one. The aircrew was prohibited from descending below 16,000 feet, upon the approach to Ross Island. This was the simple single cause of the disaster. When told that there would be evidence that on all the flights from October 1977 onwards — that is to say, for two years before the disaster — the crews had flown their aircraft in the McMurdo area at altitudes well under 6,000 feet, the Civil Aviation witnesses immediately indicated that they had never heard anything about that and that no aircrew had ever had any authority to transgress the minimum safe altitudes of 16,000 feet and 6,000 feet respectively.

It was obvious indeed that the operational conditions submitted to Civil Aviation by Air New Zealand had contained a number of deficiencies. But it was equally obvious that Civil Aviation took a contrary view, and their main justification, so it appeared, was that they always relied very strongly upon the high professional skills of the Flight Operations Division of the airline.

I was satisfied by this time that Civil Aviation, in all matters relevant to the occurrence of this disaster, had simply accepted without question whatever proposals were submitted by the airline. Despite their various file notes and memoranda, they did not seem to me to have ever paid real attention to their statutory obligation to monitor effectively the Antarctic operations of the airline.

It might be apposite to give just one example of the casual attitude adopted by Air New Zealand towards Civil Aviation which was its supposed governmental controlling agency. It had become obvious to Air New Zealand at an early stage that an overflight of the McMurdo area at 16,000 feet was unsatisfactory for scenic purposes. Almost all the passengers would have cameras and they would no doubt take many photographs of the spectacular white expanse of the Ross Sea ice shelf covered with snow and of the high snow-covered jagged peaks of Victoria Land. Some passengers might conceivably get photographs of the crater of Mount Erebus. But at an altitude of 16,000 feet (over three miles in the air) what chance would there be of passengers obtaining successful photographs of the Scott Base buildings, of Hut Point, of the team of huskies tethered in a long line in the snow?

Then there was the place at which the famous Polar explorer Captain R.F. Scott and his companions perished when only a short distance from the safety of Scott Base. It was the practice of some Antarctic aircrews to fly some distance to the south of Scott Base and the commentator would point to the approximate location of the place where Captain Scott and his companions met their deaths. How could a picture taken through a cabin window from three miles in the air possibly have any credence, when shown to friends and relatives after the flight, as indicating this historic spot?

Indeed, as I well knew, there had been complaints from passengers after the very first flight in 1977 of the high altitudes which were being maintained. Thus it was that on August 10, 1977 Air New Zealand had directed the inclusion in its briefing material of its permission to descend to 6,000 feet over the Scott Base area within a defined sector.

In view of my terms of reference, I had no interest in the position of the insurers of Air New Zealand with regard to future civil litigation. It was quite obvious that any claim for damages on behalf of a deceased passenger must succeed against Air New Zealand. On the other hand, the airline was party to the international Warsaw Convention by which it could not be liable for a greater sum than $42,000 in respect of any individual claim, unless the claimants could show that there had been 'reckless misconduct' on the part of the airline. If this latter proposition could be maintained, then the airline's liability would be unlimited.

As it happened, claims for damages for personal injury or death had been abolished in New Zealand by the Accidents Compensation Act 1972. Whereas previously damages could be obtained on proof of negligence, this had all been swept away. Under the act, a widow who has lost her husband by negligence on the part of any other person could receive payment to the order of only $6,000 or so, coupled with an annual pension of some moderate amount. But the Accidents Compensation Act did not apply to this Antarctic disaster. The act does not apply to any claims by or on behalf of airline passengers in respect of an accident occurring outside New Zealand, and for this purpose the words 'New Zealand' are defined in the act to mean only a specified geographical area in which no part of the Antarctic continent is included. The words are clear. Therefore, the original claim for damages for negligence still subsisted in the New Zealand courts in respect of claims by relatives of the passengers who were killed.

The setting up of this Royal Commission was therefore of great value to the lawyers representing the passengers' consortium. One of my responsibilities as Royal Commissioner was to determine the cause or causes of the disaster. This was a matter, therefore, upon which counsel for the consortium were entitled to cross-examine. They took full advantage of this opportunity, and they concentrated particularly, as I could see, upon the witnesses called for Civil Aviation Division. The Division, as a department of the Ministry of Transport, was not an airline operator and consequently was not covered by the Warsaw Convention. If negligence could be proved against any official of Civil Aviation, in the sense of an act or omission which either caused or contributed to the disaster, then the Ministry of Transport stood exposed to claims for unlimited damages.

The whole tenor of the Chief Inspector's report had been that the sole cause of the disaster was pilot error. If this were shown, then the $42,000 limit would apply to claims against the airline and such a finding, if established in court proceedings, would entirely exonerate the Ministry of Transport from any successful claim for damages.

I could not doubt that these considerations weighed very heavily with Civil Aviation Division, and with the three witnesses whom it had called. It was not merely the understandable attitude that the Civil Aviation personnel did not wish individually to be thought to be responsible for what had happened. The central point was that the Ministry itself did not want to be held liable for millions of dollars in damages.

There was one particular point upon which Civil Aviation seemed particularly vulnerable. This was its decision to excuse Air New Zealand from compliance with the requirement that the pilot in command of an Antarctic flight must have flown in that area on a previous occasion so as to make himself familiar with the topography, the weather and the general environment of this far-distant region.

The requirement of a previous flight to Antarctica was established by law. It was contained in Regulation 141 of the Civil Aviation Regulations 1953. The statutory requirement was in fact contained within the Operations Specifications which were part of the Air Service Certificate No. 22 issued to Air New Zealand and which covered Antarctic flights. A condition was attached to the certificate, in conformity with Regulation 141, requiring that pilots in command of any Antarctic flight must previously have completed a flight in the Antarctic area under the supervision of a person authorised by the Flight Operations Director.

The first two flights operated by Air New Zealand in February 1977 had complied with this mandatory provision in the sense that both Captains Gemmell and Grundy had been to Antarctica before. But, in the case of all subsequent Antarctic flights, including the fatal flight, this requirement had not been carried out. No pilot or co-pilot had ever flown to Antarctica before.

Evidence had been given by all three Civil Aviation witnesses that the Division had decided in October 1979, only a month before the fatal flight, to give Air New Zealand an official dispensation from this requirement, but it had also been proved that the Division had not provided Air New Zealand with written approval for the dispensation until December 5, 1979 — a week after the disaster.

Like all other persons in the courtroom — with the exception of the Air New Zealand and Civil Aviation officials, and presumably their counsel — I had regarded this last-minute dispensation as being so providential as to require close examination. I myself had a particular reason for adopting that attitude. By reason of inquiries made by counsel assisting the Commission, I had become aware of the fact that when the first investigation team had arrived at McMurdo within days of the disaster, they had been greeted with expressions of astonishment on the part of McMurdo personnel, both Americans and New Zealanders, that the aircrew of the fatal flight had never been to Antarctica before.

The Royal New Zealand Air Force, the Royal Australian Air Force and the U.S. Navy flying personnel all had a standard procedure in this respect. No pilot was allowed to command a military flight into Antarctica without past experience of flying in that region. This was such an obvious precaution that the personnel at McMurdo could scarcely believe the verified fact that neither pilot on TE901 on November 28, 1979 had previously flown in the region.

The universal opinion at McMurdo was that if the pilot in command had flown to Antarctica before, he would have observed one significant but vital fact on his approach on Nav track to Ross Island. He would have seen that Beaufort Island was about fifteen miles to his right, when in terms of the computer flight track which he was following, it should have been fifteen miles to his left. He would have realised immediately, after checking on his HSI (Horizontal Situation Indicator) panel, that the aircraft was exactly on its computer track, and that the destination waypoint fed into the aircraft's computer was approximately thirty miles to the east of the destination waypoint previously existing, and which had appeared on the sample flight plan displayed to him and his co-pilot at the briefing. The computer error had become well known at McMurdo shortly after the disaster, and during the months which had followed, the McMurdo personnel had taken the simple and accurate view that the failure to identify Beaufort Island had prevented the aircrew from finding out that the long-standing flight path to McMurdo had been altered without their knowledge.

As the reader will see, this last-minute dispensation from the requirement of a previous familiarisation flight was now of critical importance as far as Civil Aviation was concerned. Their witnesses had been at great pains to explain it and they had taken the same line as the Air New Zealand witnesses — a previous flight under supervision could safely be dispensed with having regard to the careful briefing of Antarctic crews. But the fact remained that the only persons fully informed on the matter, namely the operational officers of the various military services flying to Antarctica, took an absolutely contrary view. There was no substitute, they said, and there could never be any substitute, for a previous flight into that distant and unique environment.

As I say, I had all this information in my possession as I listened to the cross-examination of the Civil Aviation witnesses. And there was no doubt that Mr J.S. Henry Q.C., leading counsel for the consortium, was also similarly informed. Like myself, he evidently felt it not appropriate to reveal the extent of his knowledge. But his cross-examination of the Controller of Flight Operations for Civil Aviation left no doubt as to the primary method of attack which was going to be used against the Division in civil litigation.

I should here explain that in his prepared brief of evidence, the Controller of Airline Operations for Civil Aviation had referred to a discussion which he had with Captain Spence (the airline inspector), who had evidently discussed the proposed dispensation with Captain Gemmell. The Controller had said that he had accepted Captain Spence's recommendation that the requirement be deleted. He said that he had sent a signal to Air New Zealand on October 24, 1979 'confirming their understanding that the requirement for flight under supervision would be deleted'.

Having made these preliminary observations, I now quote from the cross-examination by Mr Henry of the Controller of Airline Operations as to who had been responsible for the Civil Aviation decision and why that decision had been reached.

Captain Omundsen questioned by Mr Henry:

Q. Referring to the earlier requirement that a pilot in command should first have a flight under supervision down the Antarctic, what was the reason for that requirement?

A. The reason was that the pilot would become familiar with the operation.

Q. Did you regard it as a prudent requirement?

A. I regarded it as a valuable experience.

Q. And a prudent requirement?

A. Yes it would be a prudent requirement.

Q. Did you first learn of the suggestion that it be deleted through Captain Spence?

A. That's correct.

Q. To what extent did you discuss that proposal with Captain Spence, how long, how many times?

A. It would have been a discussion of — it's hard to recall — I would say it would be an initial discussion of thirty minutes and it would have been the result of more than one discussion.

Q. In relation to your message to Air New Zealand dated October 24, when would that discussion have taken place?

A. I can't really tell you. The communication with Air New Zealand was sent by myself as I recall it because Captain Spence was not in the office at the time, so the discussion would have taken place when Captain Spence was in the office.

Q. Days, weeks or months before that message?

A. I can't recall, but I would be quite sure they would be days.

Q. Being a variation from a prior prudent requirement, you would have given it a lot of consideration?

A. Correct.

Q. Whom did you consult other than Captain Spence?

A. I don't recall I discussed it with anyone else.

Q. If you had you would recall it no doubt?

A. I would believe so.

Q. What was your reason for approving that change?

A. Previously, and I'm speaking of 10-15 years prior to this, a pilot could only be cleared to operate a scheduled air transport route by having gained experience and demonstrated that he was familiar with and proficient at operating that route. International practice with established carriers and respected aviation authorities had studied the situation and considered that the items which were necessary to be understood and applied, could be handled from a properly established training organisation using modern training aids. This was accepted by the international Civil Aviation organisation, and was the subject of an amendment to Annex 6 of Operation of Aircraft by that organisation. The CAD regulations were amended subsequent to Annex 6 changes, and this then enabled these procedures to be followed within New Zealand. Air New Zealand, after discussions with the CAD, proposed to us that credit be given for the use of the Route Clearance Unit and their aircraft flight simulator for this purpose.

Q. I might have missed it, but I don't recall you telling me the reason for the change. Were not all those things you spoke about in force in 1978?

A. Yes they were. The reason for the change was that it was considered that adequate information and experience could be gained in the Route Clearance Unit which had been established by Air New Zealand for this purpose.

Q. When had that Route Clearance Unit been established?

A. I can't recall offhand, but I think we have letters which will indicate it was about 1977, but I don't wish to give that as a date.

Q. What I would like to find out from you if I can is what was different in late 1979 from what had been the position in 1978?

A. The difference was that the company asked for the Route Clearance Unit to be used for compliance with Regulation 77.

Q. So far as you are aware that same Route Clearance Unit had been used for the purposes of the 1978 flights had it not?

A. I believe it had.

Q. So what you are telling me is really no more than Air New Zealand requested this alteration and you approved it for no particular reason.

A. I couldn't agree to that statement.

Q. Do you consider that it was an unnecessary requirement for 1978?

A. No I wouldn't agree with that statement.

Q. Meaning it was necessary for 1978?

A. Desirable.

Q. Was it not desirable for 1979?

A. Yes I would say it would be desirable.

Q. Prudent?

A. Yes I must agree it would be prudent, but I wouldn't agree that because it was not required in 1979 that it was imprudent.

Q. If it was prudent for 1979 why delete it?

A. Because the company said they could not comply with it in 1979, and the Route Clearance Unit had been established to replace this kind of activity. We were satisfied with the Route Clearance Unit, and it was properly utilising the investment that Air New Zealand had made to achieve safe and economic use of their facilities and personnel.

Q. What was the reason Air New Zealand had given you to establish that they could not comply with this requirement in 1979?

A. I don't recall they gave a reason.

Q. If that were a factor surely you would have inquired about it?

A. If I considered it important I would have.

Q. Did you not just a minute ago tell me it was one of the reasons the requirement was deleted?

A. I can't follow the question.

Q. I thought you told us Air New Zealand informed you that it could not comply with the requirement?

A. Yes I made that statement.

Q. Was that one of the factors which led you to give your

107

approval to the deletion of the requirement?

A. Yes it was.

Q. But you didn't bother to inquire as to why Air New Zealand could not comply with it?

A. No, I don't think that's correct. By you using the word 'bother', I did not bother to inquire, you infer I was doing something less than was necessary. I don't accept that.

Q. If it was a factor for deleting a requirement, surely you would want to check its importance and genuineness. Wouldn't you?

A. I have had no reason prior to that with Air New Zealand to doubt their integrity as an operator. I have found that the company themselves are reliable, responsible. I have also found their flight crews to be professional people who are persons of integrity who were dedicated to the operation of Air New Zealand, and this was over the years a situation which gave me every confidence in the airline and their flight crew.

Q. With that degree of confidence, is the situation that their proposal in an area such as this, would be treated by you as being satisfactory merely because it's put forward anyway?

A. I have lost the question.

Q. Well I'll phrase it another way. I'm suggesting to you that what happened in this instance was, because of your trust in Air New Zealand and knowledge of their operations, you rubber-stamped this proposal?

A. You made that statement, I wouldn't agree with that.

Q. I made a statement. I was wanting you to agree or disagree. Can you however, give me any other reason why that requirement should have been deleted for 1979 flights?

A. There is to my mind no other necessary reason.

When the witness had explained that Air New Zealand 'could not comply' with the requirement of a previous flight under supervision, we all knew what he meant. The airline had no shortage of pilots. Indeed, as was generally known right throughout New Zealand, the airline was heavily overstaffed. What Air New Zealand meant was, as previously established in evidence, that the most senior of their international pilots had the right to apply to command one of these flights and the company ran a system of rostering the crews in accordance with the priority which the pilots were claiming. That was why the airline could not 'comply' with the requirement. The system which they were operating was based upon the indication that any pilot in command with suitable seniority was entitled, as a change from ordinary duties, to fly to Antarctica and by reason of the large number of applications it was simply not feasible to have senior pilots go to Antarctica merely as observers.

As I listened to the cross-examination just quoted, I had a mental image of the scene in the courtroom in future civil litigation with Civil Aviation Division under attack by counsel representing some particular estate. I had no doubt that it would be suggested to the Civil Aviation witnesses that there had never been any verbal discussion between airline personnel and Civil Aviation on or about October 23, 1979 or at any other time, and that the alleged teletype messages had been fabricated. It would be suggested that, following the disaster, both the airline and Civil Aviation became equally anxious about the fact that the statutory requirement of a previous flight under supervision had not been complied with for over two years before the disaster, and had not been complied with in the case of the fatal flight itself. It would be suggested that both Air New Zealand and Civil Aviation were well aware of the long-held opinion at McMurdo that if Captain Collins had been on a previous flight, the disaster would not have occurred.

But that accusation was never made before me during the Royal Commission hearings. If it had been, I would have required much more evidence on the point. I would have recalled, naturally, that Captain Gemmell had not himself referred in his evidence to any conversation with Civil Aviation about a month before the fatal flight, but I would certainly not have been prepared to accept such accusations as proved on the basis of the evidence which I had heard. But what would a jury think? I had the uneasy impression that a jury might think that such serious allegations were true. And if it did, then it would presumably follow the practice of all juries, and reflect its indignation in a very high award of damages against Civil Aviation.

As I say, from my own point of view, the written post-accident dispensation seemed to me to be very providential and I was certainly anxious about it, particularly when Mr Henry appeared successfully to have established that there was no really solid basis for the approval. But so far as I was concerned, the view that a jury might take was beside the point. I was prepared to accept the Civil Aviation's evidence on the question, despite all its weaknesses, and I not only put the matter on one side, but made no reference to this destructive cross-examination in my ultimate report.

The transcript of the cross-examination would be available in any civil litigation. And it was now established as a matter of record that the dispensation by Civil Aviation had been based upon considerations which a jury was certain to reject. Any jury, in my experience, would on the basis of Mr Henry's cross-examination, hold that Civil Aviation had been guilty of negligence which caused or contributed to the disaster.

The Civil Aviation witnesses had had their opportunity to avoid the trap which Mr Henry had set for them. They could have denied that the dispensation was granted as a matter of convenience to Air New Zealand. But now it was too late, and their answers had made the Ministry of Transport liable for damages unlimited in amount.

The trap was closed.

X

THE OTHER EXECUTIVE PILOTS GIVE EVIDENCE

I have referred already to the evidence of Captains Gemmell and Grundy. They both came of course within the definition of 'executive pilot', but the evidence now to be described is that of the other executive pilots who testified on behalf of the airline.

In Air New Zealand, as in the case of other airlines in the world, some administration positions within the Flight Operations Division of an airline are often held by pilots who are also carrying out ordinary flying duties. This is certainly not a wholly satisfactory procedure because, for some part of every working month, the executive pilot will be away from his desk carrying out his flying duties, and will have to inquire upon his return as to what has taken place within his particular sphere of responsibility, and what decisions or duties have been made or carried out on his behalf in his absence.

However, it is of prime importance that these administrative positions involving operational decisions and training duties be carried out by pilots who are experienced in the most recent type of passenger jets being operated by the airline. Hence the necessity, which certainly existed within Air New Zealand, for executive pilots to combine their flying duties with administrative work. They were paid higher salaries in consequence of being executive pilots, and within Air New Zealand they were clearly part of the airline operational management. It was in that capacity that they testified before the Royal Commission. Without exception, their evidence was in favour of the company. Without exception, their evidence supported the proposition that neither the company management nor the company organisation had committed any error or omission which had been a cause, or even a contributing cause, of the disaster.

111

There seemed at first sight to be a fairly formidable list of administrative operational positions in respect of a very small airline with a total of thirty-five aircraft flying both domestic and international routes (only ten aircraft were flying internationally — seven DC10s and three DC8s). All the executive pilots were employed administratively within Flight Operations Division and were subject to the overall control of the Director of Flight Operations.

As I have given details of the evidence of Captain Grundy, it is perhaps only necessary to say that the other executive pilots testified to the same facts — they all denied knowledge of any flights in the Antarctic region which had been below 16,000 feet on the approach to McMurdo, or below 6,000 feet to the south of Ross Island.

The executive pilots were adamant that no authority to descend to less than 16,000 feet or 6,000 feet had ever existed. In other words, they all took the position that the minimum safe altitude of 16,000 feet settled in correspondence between Air New Zealand and Civil Aviation was conclusive and was in no case allowed to be departed from.

Two of the executive pilots who testified in this manner, as well as being referred to various published accounts of flights below 6,000 feet of the kind which had been drawn to the attention of Captain Grundy, were also confronted with a particular published report concerning a flight which they themselves had been on. These two executive pilots had been respectively pilot in command and co-pilot on the third Antarctic flight which had taken place on October 18, 1977, that being the first occasion upon which the 6,000 feet limitation was operative. The co-pilot on that flight said in evidence that although Mac Centre had invited the pilot in command to descend below 6,000 feet, the invitation had been declined. Mr Henry, on behalf of the passengers' consortium, then confronted this witness with an extract from the *Auckland Star* of October 22, 1977. This was an article written by a Mr Graeme Kennedy and it referred clearly to a flight over Scott Base Station 'at less than 2,000 metres'. There was also a reference in the same article to the pilot in command having brought the DC10 down to 200 metres over Scott and McMurdo Bases, 'well below the towering volcano Erebus belching smoke only forty kilometres away'.

Mr Henry said that Mr Kennedy had been interviewed and indicated that the reference to 200 metres ought to have read '400 metres' — in other words, approximately 1,300 feet. The witness maintained that Mr Kennedy's report was incorrect and said that 'to the best of my recollection the flight did not descend below 6,000 feet'. The witness admitted that Mr Kennedy was known to him personally.

Whatever the correct version of this altitude report in the *Auckland Star*, it was nevertheless clearly established that the report had in fact appeared in that paper on October 22, 1977 and, of course, the head office of Air New Zealand is located in Auckland.

Then this same executive pilot was cross-examined about a newsletter published by the airline and entitled *Air New Zealand News*. The article was dated November 30, 1978 and consisted of a brief description of a flight to Antarctica on November 7, 1978. The article described a report from Captain Keesing, at that time Director of Flight Operations, of his experience on that flight as a passenger. The opening two paragraphs of this article read as follows:

> The flight deck crew of TE901 took the boss flying with them on November 7 ... And as the DC10 cruised at 2,000 feet past the Antarctica's Mount Erebus and over the great ice plateau, Captain Doug Keesing, Flight Operations Director International, was as interested in sightseeing as the other 230 passengers aboard.

It was admitted that the airline's newsletter was distributed as a matter of course to every member of the staff of the airline which at that time numbered 8,700.

The witness said that he had read this item in the airline newsletter. He also agreed in cross-examination that this issue of the newsletter would have provided ample evidence to people in authority who could have acted on it if they so desired.

But this witness was the only pilot called by the airline who admitted any knowledge of the contents of this airline newsletter. No other executive pilot admitted ever seeing that article. Additionally, when the present Director of Flight Operations (who had succeeded Captain Keesing), was called as a witness at a later stage, he also denied ever having seen the article. And when the Chief Executive gave evidence, he also denied having ever read the article.

Coming back now to the evidence of the executive pilots, it was apparent that their professed combined ignorance, with the exception of the one witness just referred to, of any knowledge of this article was being treated with palpable and contemptuous disbelief by those counsel opposing Air New Zealand. It had referred, after all, to the aircrew of TE901 on November 7, 1978 having taken 'the boss flying with them'.

And then there was one other executive pilot who gave the very unexpected evidence that when he himself had been pilot in command of the Antarctic flight of November 8, 1977, he had descended to 3,000 feet in the McMurdo area because, as he said, of the fine and clear weather at that time prevailing. The commentator on this flight had been Bob Thomson, who had given evidence of being commentator on four separate flights and who had said that apart from some doubt about the first flight, captained by Captain Gemmell, the other three flights had all descended below 6,000 feet.

This witness, in his prepared brief of evidence, admitted that he had descended to 3,000 feet following authority from American Air Traffic Control. I confess to having been mystified at the time as to why this admission had been made. Perhaps the witness had decided that he was going to testify honestly as to the altitude to which he had descended on his own flight, and had done so in the sure knowledge that this apparent breach of the minimum safe altitude rule would place him in jeopardy with the airline management. But I doubted whether he would have done so voluntarily. The evidence of Mr Thomson in respect of the three flights other than the first flight had been given without any qualification. Perhaps the witness felt he could not contradict Mr Thomson. Perhaps he was only being honest. No one could say for sure what the reason was for an executive pilot, called by the airline, unequivocally admitting a breach of what he himself maintained was an inflexible minimum safe altitude regulation. The thought even crossed my mind, though perhaps I was wrong, that there might have been some other convincing evidence available to the passengers' consortium or to the Airline Pilots' Association confirming the descent allowed on this particular flight, this evidence being known to the airline management.

This witness was cross-examined in the most hostile manner by leading counsel for Civil Aviation. The witness agreed, again and again, that he had committed a deliberate breach of one of the most sacred rules imposed upon commercial pilots. The continual pressing of this accusation upon the witness became almost embarrassing, having regard to his penitential attitude in the witness box. It seemed all too clear that the witness was well aware of the disciplinary powers possessed by the Director of Civil Aviation in respect of any pilot who committed so grave an infringement of the department's minimum safe altitude requirements.

But the witness was adamant that he knew of no other Antarctic flight which had descended below 16,000 feet on the approach to McMurdo and below 6,000 feet in the McMurdo area itself. He was evidently disposed to condemn himself as being the only known culprit, but I noticed that there was no evidence of any disciplinary action having been taken against him by the airline, and that he still retained his responsible executive position within the airline.

The evidence of Captain J.P. Wilson deserves special mention. He had been called just before the executive pilot whose evidence I have just been discussing.

Captain Wilson had had operational experience as a Royal New Zealand Air Force pilot in the Pacific theatre during the war, and had been awarded the Air Force Cross. Like many other military pilots he had declined an aviation career in the Air Force, and had elected to transfer to Civil Aviation. He had flown with different overseas airlines in the Caribbean area and had also held various aircrew training positions. He had joined Air New Zealand in 1965, becoming a command pilot in 1968. From that time onwards, he had flown as a pilot for Air New Zealand on DC8 and DC10 aircraft, and had operated on all routes through the company's network, except to Antarctica. He had also held a First Class Navigator's Licence. On reaching Air New Zealand's compulsory retiring age for aircrew, he had accepted, in December 1977, the position of Route Clearance Unit Supervisor, and he still held that position.

The witness then gave a long and detailed description of the manner in which the Route Clearance Unit was operated, and he described the various steps which he had taken to add to or improve the material used at the briefings for Antarctica, including the simulator briefings. He referred to the cyclostyled briefing sheets which were handed over to the flight crews when they were briefed for an Antarctic flight. He then referred to the briefing of the two aircrews on November 9, 1979. It happened that he had been on an Antarctic flight himself only two days before, but that flight had been diverted to the alternate route of the South Magnetic Pole because the weather had been unsuitable at McMurdo. It appeared that Captain Wilson had previously made requests to go to Antarctica on one of the sightseeing flights, but they had been declined. However, on November 7, 1979 his persistence had been rewarded, but unfortunately he had been on the only flight to Antarctica which had been required to divert to the South Magnetic Pole. Consequently, he was in charge of a briefing procedure for flights to McMurdo when he had never been there himself. Captain Wilson obviously considered this situation unsatisfactory. So did I.

The witness gave detailed evidence as to the exact nature of the briefing which he had delivered on November 9, 1979. Two proposed Antarctic flight crews had been present — the pilot in command of one crew had been Captain L. Simpson; of the other, Captain Collins. Needless to say, the very considerable group of counsel, representatives of interested parties, and the press and radio reporters all concentrated upon this evidence, and naturally, I was myself giving it my closest attention.

Captain Wilson went in detail through the briefing material. It comprised the audio-visual presentation and the taped commentary of which a copy had been produced in evidence, followed by verbal amplification of the written briefing material. He had noticed that Captain Collins had brought his own atlas to the briefing and he found this consistent with the pilot's conscientious nature.

The witness went on to say that he had thought it helpful to utilise the latest flight plan in the course of his briefing. He said that before departing himself on the November 7 flight (two days previously), he had obtained a copy of the flight plan from the Flight Despatch Office, and he had taken it with him on the flight. On his return he had requested Flight Despatch to give him a copy of the aircrew's flight plan which had been returned to Flight Despatch by the crew on that flight, and he had apparently secured copies of that flight plan, which was, of course, the standard Antarctic flight plan.

It appeared that during the briefing of November 9, Captain Wilson had not only referred to the flight plans but put them on the desk in front of the people attending the briefing, and that the flight crews had had access to them for a considerable period of time.

Then Captain Wilson went on to say that at the conclusion of the briefing he had recovered the flight plans from the two aircrews, and he had retained them in his possession. This was a significant point. It suggested that Captain Collins had not taken away with him a copy of the flight plan which showed the destination waypoint to have been near the Dailey Islands at the head of McMurdo Sound, twenty-seven miles to the west of Williams Field.

It appeared from the evidence of the witness that the two aircrews had been specifically told that their flight path was not the military route as depicted on the RNC-4 chart which he

116

demonstrated to them. He said that he had pointed out the Air New Zealand route with his pen on the RNC-4 chart. He said that before leaving for Antarctica the crews would receive from Flight Despatch an envelope containing charts and topographical maps, and he said that someone had said (and he believed that it was Captain Collins), that they would have 'about five hours to study them on the way down'.

So it emerged from all this detailed evidence of the operation of the Route Clearance Unit and of the vital description of the briefing of the crew on the fatal flight (which occupied thirty-five pages of Captain Wilson's prepared brief) that there had never been any doubt that the flight crews believed that the computer track which would be stored in their respective aircraft would take them on the last leg to the south from Cape Hallett directly over Mount Erebus to the destination waypoint now established at the TACAN. And, in addition, he had said that there had been no doubt that the crews both understood that the minimum safe altitude was 16,000 feet until south of Mount Erebus, and 6,000 feet in specially defined conditions once over the McMurdo area.

Then there came a piece of evidence, contained in the last page and a half of his prepared brief, which fell like a bombshell in the courtroom. (I could not help but observe that this final portion of the brief, which comprised four paragraphs, had been prepared with a different typewriter from that used in the previous thirty-eight pages.)

Captain Wilson disclosed that in 1978 he had become aware, by overhearing various comments, that certain flights had descended below 6,000 feet. He also believed that he had heard these remarks at a time when his office was located on the seventeenth floor of Air New Zealand House within Flight Operations Division. He also said that he might have read the *Air New Zealand News* article concerning the flight described by Captain Keesing which had been cruising in Antarctica at 2,000 feet.

He went on to say that he believed that the condition about descent to 6,000 feet had been laid down by the McMurdo authorities. It was therefore his belief that, because of the way this particular specification had been worded in the Air New Zealand documents, the McMurdo authorities had retained what he called 'the ability' to give consent to descending lower than 6,000 feet.

Captain Wilson said that at some of his Antarctic briefings he had remarked to aircrews that some flights had been below 6,000 feet, but he could not recall whether he had made such a comment during the briefing of November 9, 1979. And he said that when making various comments of this kind to aircrews he had assumed that the descents below 6,000 feet had been effected with the prior authority of Air Traffic Control at McMurdo.

As may be expected, Captain Wilson was extensively cross-examined on this surprising disclosure. It became quite clear that, at various Antarctica briefings, his remarks had been interpreted by aircrews as indicating authority by the airline to descend to any altitude in the McMurdo area which might be authorised by American Air Traffic Control.

All this was grossly at variance with the management evidence already given. I had been led to believe up to this time that any descent below 16,000 feet on the approach to McMurdo and any descent below 6,000 feet at McMurdo would have been in flagrant breach of the airline's operating instructions.

The airline's implacable and persistent 'altitude defence' had now disintegrated. And what is more, the Chief Inspector's report, which was essentially based upon breach by Captain Collins and his crew of the official minimum safe altitude provisions, was now a matter of little moment. It seemed as if the Chief Inspector had not been told of the authority given to aircrews by Air New Zealand to operate into McMurdo at whatever altitude was suggested by American Air Traffic Control.

Naturally, the more I thought about this belated disclosure, the more I could see how reasonable the real operating instructions had been. I had never been able to understand how passengers could be expected to take worthwhile photographs of the detail of ground installations and other low level features of interest from heights of 16,000 feet and 6,000 feet respectively. I had, by that time, travelled on many occasions on the flight decks of DC10 and other jet passenger aircraft and had on every occasion taken careful note of the visual appearance of objects on the ground at heights of 16,000, 6,000, 2,000 and 1,000 feet. I had taken photographs at these different altitudes myself. I had no doubt that any worthwhile photograph, taken without any special equipment and designed to illustrate the interesting features on the ground at McMurdo and at the area where Captain Scott had died, could only be effective at heights not exceeding about 2,000 feet.

And, in addition, I had become aware of the great interest taken by all personnel at Scott Base and at McMurdo Base at the occasional appearance of one of these big jet airliners flying at about 2,000 feet across the McMurdo area. I knew that with helicopters operating daily at low levels in and around this part of Antarctica, the McMurdo Air Traffic Control system, when it suggested an approach altitude, would have been keeping in mind the known altitudes of other aircraft operating in the area.

So, as I said, the real truth about the operating instructions given to pilots had been at last revealed, and Captain Wilson had been the twenty-fourth witness called at the inquiry, which by that time had been in session for no less than ten weeks. No better illustration could be given of the implacable opposition of the airline management to any suggestion of organisational fault on its part. I could only wonder how it was that Captain Wilson had dared to brave the storm which now had arisen in consequence of this last-minute addition to his evidence.

(It may be worth interpolating here that the recollection of Captain Wilson that he collected and retained all copies of the flight plan produced at the briefing is apparently at variance with a fact later discovered. After the disaster, a senior pilot who had been a close friend of Captain Collins had been assisting Mrs Collins and her family in the sorting out of various documents at the Collins' home. This pilot was asked by the Director of Flight Operations, this being about two days after the disaster, whether he had found a copy of a flight plan in the documents because Captain Collins had taken a copy of the flight plan away with him when he left the briefing of November 9, 1979. The pilot reported to the Director of Flight Operations that no flight plan had been found.)

The principal part of Captain Wilson's evidence was his description of the manner in which he conducted his briefing of crews who were to fly on the Antarctic scenic flights.

First of all there was the audio-visual display, and then he went through the written briefing notes with the crews. He would from time to time verbally amplify or correct some aspect of the briefing notes. After this process was completed the crews would then go over to the simulator which was operated by Captain Johnson and there they would sit at the controls and be briefed further with the aid of this appliance.

It was noticeable that, as Captain Wilson read his brief of evidence, he was describing many remarks which he had interpolated by way of addition to the written briefing notes as he went through them for the benefit of crews. It was also noticeable that almost every such verbal addition conveyed either a direct or indirect reference to the computer flight track taking the aircraft over the top of Mount Erebus.

In particular, there had been a statement by Captain Wilson that at one point he ran his pen down a navigation chart and said that he pointed out that the computer track would take the aircraft from Cape Hallett 'over Erebus to McMurdo'. Other remarks of similar kind were said to have been made.

Then there came the evidence of Captain Ross Johnson in which he described in considerable detail the briefing which took place in the simulator. Once again, there were remarks which he said he had made which made it quite clear that the flight track took the aircraft over the top of the mountain.

As an example, Captain Johnson said that his practice was to indicate on the RNC-4 chart the computer track by making a circle around the Balleny Islands, Hallett Station and McMurdo Station. This, of course, would mean a visual briefing to the various crews that the flight track lay over the top of the mountain.

Captain Johnson also said that his practice was to position the simulator at a point fifty miles true north of the TACAN. The crew then looked at a dark night sky scene which admittedly conveyed no particular information. However Captain Johnson was conveying the impression to flight crews, so he said, that the aircraft on the approach to McMurdo would be to the true north of Williams Field and, therefore, the computer track would take the aircraft over the top of Mount Erebus. In addition, Captain Johnson had stated, so he said, that he told crews that if weather conditions were not good, they should maintain their cruise altitude on the computer track until over the runways at McMurdo. Once again, this intimation would certainly have warned each aircrew that the computer track lay over the mountain.

Captain Johnson made other references to similar remarks, and it was clear from his evidence that he had in fact gone out of his way to demonstrate at different times during the simulator briefing that the flight track went directly from Cape Hallett to the runways at McMurdo Station.

The response of ALPA to this testimony was to call a succession of pilots who had, at different times, been briefed in relation to Antarctic flights. Included among those pilots were those who had attended the briefing on November 9, 1979 along with Captain Collins and First Officer Cassin. These pilots were Captain Simpson, Captain Gabriel and First Officer Irvine.

First of all, I should describe in summary form what was said by the pilots who had attended Antarctic briefings other than the briefing on November 9, 1979. Without going into unnecessary detail, it is sufficient to say that not one of them agreed with those parts of the evidence given by Captains Wilson and Johnson as to the verbal interpolations by the briefing officers which were said to have made it clear that the flight track lay across the top of

Mount Erebus. The understanding of all these pilots was that the computer track would take the aircraft down the centre of McMurdo Sound, and that the aircraft would pass Mount Erebus with the mountain many miles away to the left of the aircraft.

Indeed, the audio-visual display demonstrated at the briefing showed the approach to McMurdo with Mount Erebus located far to the left of the flight track. It was ascertained that this particular slide represented a photograph taken from an aircraft pointing north, not pointing south, but it would certainly fix in the mind of any crew member watching the audio-visual presentation that the approach to McMurdo was down the centre of the sound.

But the most positive evidence given in opposition to that of the airline about the briefing procedures was that given by Captains Simpson and Gabriel and First Officer Irvine, in respect of the briefing of November 9, 1979.

Captain Simpson had been a particularly impressive witness. He was forthright, clear, and quite unshakable. He reviewed in detail the various verbal comments said to have been made by Captains Wilson and Johnson in the course of the briefing.

Captain Simpson went through the evidence of these verbal comments with meticulous care. He simply said that he 'did not recall' any of those comments which were said to have pointed to the computer track lying over the peak of Mount Erebus. He was positive that no such remarks were made at the audio-visual briefing or at the simulator briefing. He made it clear that if he had suspected that the computer track would take his aircraft over the top of the volcano, he would have objected immediately. And he did not conceal his astonishment that these verbal comments were now alleged to have been made by the briefing officers.

Captain Simpson was under no misapprehension about the flight path. He had noted the destination co-ordinates on the sample flight plan produced at the briefing and, without using a map, he had been able to see that the destination waypoint lay approximately at the head of McMurdo Sound and was located many miles to the west of the airfield at McMurdo. In other words, the computer track for the DC10 flights to Antarctica was just where he would have expected the computer track to be.

Captain Simpson's robust and forthright evidence was confirmed in every respect by Captain Gabriel and First Officer Irvine. These two pilots were also clear that no suggestion was ever put to them that the computer track lay over the mountain. They all believed that the track lay down the centre of McMurdo Sound.

And, as a matter not without significance, Captain Simpson

had not agreed at all with a remark said to have been made by Captain Collins to Captain Johnson in the course of the briefing. Captain Johnson had said that someone — he believed it was Captain Collins — had made a query as to what should happen if weather conditions were not suitable for the approach to McMurdo. Captain Simpson was adamant that Captain Collins had made no such remark, and Captain Gabriel and First Officer Irvine were also satisfied that they had heard no such remark passed by Captain Collins.

By the time the ALPA witnesses had testified as to these briefing procedures, and in particular as to the briefing procedures adopted on November 9, 1979, the atmosphere at the hearing had become one of sustained hostility between the airline management on the one hand, and the Airline Pilots' Association on the other.

As may be imagined, I had listened with some anxiety to the direct confrontation between the two briefing officers and the succession of airline pilots whose evidence I have just described. I could not help but be struck by the direct conflict of evidence which had emerged.

I was now faced with the familiar courtroom dilemma which confronts judges when they have to consider conflicting accounts of an event which had taken place. Sometimes the accounts vary in minor aspects of detail, and sometimes they vary in point of emphasis. But here a very different situation had developed. The pilots who had attended these various briefings, and in particular those who had attended the briefing of the crew of the fatal flight, had directly opposed every piece of evidence given by the briefing officers which had tended to suggest that all crews were reminded, although it was not on record, that the flight track to McMurdo passed over the peak of this dangerous mountain.

In such a situation, a judicial officer will normally examine with some care the motives which might have inspired the two sides in their respective versions. I had to apply the same test here. I read through the notes of evidence, and I brought back to mind the demeanour of each witness and the general tone and manner of his presentation. I looked first of all at the evidence given by the briefing officers.

How was it that the evidence which the briefing officers gave was contradicted at every material point by the succession of pilots who had attended their briefings? The general nature of the audio-visual briefing and of the reading through of the briefing notes had been in no way contested. Nor had it been disputed that the evidence of the briefing officers in relation to the simulator had been correct in so far as it had purported to show that magnetic navigation had to be converted to grid navigation at a certain point. Nor had it been contested that the simulator briefing had also been directed to the approved 6,000 feet sector and other conditions necessary for a letdown in the area. Before the briefing of November 9, 1979, the letdown procedure had been associated with the navigation aid provided by the NDB, whereas at the briefing of November 9 it had been revealed that the NDB was no longer operating, and consequently, any letdown had to be in visual conditions.

Thus the purpose of the simulator briefing had in effect been twofold (and this was not contested by the pilots) in that it first related to the changing of the aircraft compasses to the grid system of navigation, and secondly, that it related to the conditions under which a letdown in the McMurdo area could be accomplished.

Now, let me come back to the motivation of the two sets of witnesses. Why was it that Captains Wilson and Johnson both believed that the flight track lay over the mountain? Why had the Route Clearance Unit not provided them with an ordinary topographical map of the area over which the computer track had been overprinted? This would have shown without any doubt that the track lay across the top of the mountain peak. Would Captains Johnson and Wilson have agreed with the propriety of plotting the track in that location? I very much doubted whether they, as experienced pilots, could have agreed. On the other hand, it is standard practice on ordinary scheduled flight routes to terminate a destination waypoint at a navigational aid installed at an airport. But even so, no landing was contemplated at McMurdo and from any point of view, it seemed a very dangerous procedure to plot a computer track over the top of an active volcano. Perhaps it was not the place of these two briefing officers to disagree with what had been planned by higher authority.

But I could not get out of my mind that the two briefing officers, with all their experience, would surely have expected protests from the very experienced pilots whom they were briefing when it was disclosed that the computer track of each flight flew over the active volcano. Surely they would have expected questions from the pilots as to why the computer track was not plotted down the centre of McMurdo Sound? So why was it that each had insisted in the course of his evidence, on emphasising that he had taken the occasion — not once, but several times — of reminding flight crews that the flight path led over the mountain?

I wondered whether the two briefing officers were being held responsible by the airline for any failure to explain to pilots the actual track as settled between the airline and Civil Aviation Division before the first flight to Antarctica ever took place. Was their evidence dictated by this consideration? Was it possible that they really believed that their oral briefing had warned all aircrews as to where the computer track lay?

Again I was struck by the palpable absurdity of the position the briefing officers were seeking to maintain. Let us leave on one side for a moment the obvious and serious objection that all pilots would make to flying an aircraft with its computer track lying directly over the belching gas and steam from the volcano. They knew, I had no doubt, that it would be established by counsel for ALPA that the meticulous Captain Collins had in fact plotted his own track on a topographical map. The questions asked of the Chief Inspector had plainly foreshadowed that such evidence would be given. And the briefing officers were well aware, as everyone at the inquiry was well aware, that Captain Collins had been most assiduous in holding the aircraft on its computer track from Cape Hallett to the point where he had commenced his two descending orbits in clear air. And the briefing officers were aware, as all of us at the inquiry were aware, that at the conclusion of each orbit Captain Collins had instantly re-armed the navigation mode of the aircraft so as to lock the aircraft on to its Nav track.

In view of these careful flight procedures, confirmed as they were by the 'black box', how could it be said that Captain Collins and First Officer Cassin really believed that the flight path of their Nav track led them towards Mount Erebus? This could only mean that Captain Collins had deliberately flown the aircraft at 1,500 feet straight into the high icy slopes of a mountain which he knew lay straight in front of the aircraft.

And then I considered carefully the position of the ALPA witnesses who had been present at the various briefings. In particular, I may say, I considered the evidence of Captains Simpson and Gabriel and First Officer Irvine. Suppose that the briefing had indeed followed the lines indicated by the two briefing officers who had given evidence on behalf of the airline. What could be the motivation of the pilots who had all disputed so strongly the tenor of the evidence of the briefing officers?

One of the senior pilots had gone so far as to say that in reflecting upon the evidence given by the two briefing officers he could hardly believe that the briefing as described was the same he had attended.

I could see that it might be suggested that the pilots were

members of a union which would instinctively be opposed to any attitude on the part of the management which tended to suggest a gross breach of duty by the deceased aircrew. But could this really be so? The pilots who had testified in opposition to the two briefing officers were all actively engaged in operational flying duties on behalf of Air New Zealand. They all had their careers to consider. They were part of a company organisation which was highly dictatorial in its approach to all employees. It was publicly known that there were more pilots employed by Air New Zealand than were required for the flight routes operated by the company and it was clear that the management was very unlikely to tolerate any intransigent attitudes by pilots in respect of this inquiry and of any litigation which might follow. But, apart from this, why should this array of pilots be so intent on disputing the evidence of the briefing officers? It surely could not be that they were simply acting in defence of the deceased aircrew and were therefore combining together to give false evidence.

There is only one thing to do in such circumstances. One must wait and see. I had already noticed the absence of documentation on the part of Air New Zealand. Even Captain Johnson had admitted that his file for Antarctic briefings had been handed over to the management shortly after the disaster and that he had not seen it since. For all I knew, that file might appear, and other documents might appear, which might show that the evidence of the briefing officers was not as improbable as I, at that moment, believed. So I followed my customary procedure, and kept an open mind. Who could tell what future evidence would reveal?

But, just the same, if the pilots who testified against the management on this issue were correct, then it was clear that I was being presented in the courtroom with an attitude, on behalf of the company management, which was implacable and obdurate.

XI

CAPTAIN KEESING'S STORY

During the inquiry we had heard something of Captain Keesing because, until the early part of 1979, he had been the Flight Operations Director (International) of Air New Zealand. It appeared from the correspondence regarding the proposed Antarctic flights, which began late in 1976, that he had been the author of some of the letters from Air New Zealand, although the final arrangements with Civil Aviation with regard to altitudes and flight tracks had been settled by Captain Gemmell and a little later confirmed in respect of future flights by Captain Johnson.

I was aware of the fact that Captain Keesing had reached retiring age and had left the service of Air New Zealand some time before the disaster. It will be remembered that he had been referred to in the evidence as being on an Antarctic flight which had descended to 2,000 feet, and one day he unexpectedly appeared in the witness box, called as a witness by counsel assisting the Commission.

Captain Keesing said he had started off his civilian flying career, after wartime service in the RNZAF, in 1943. At that time he was a flying instructor and he spent some years in that capacity with Air New Zealand (or TEAL as it was then known), and then later flew different aircraft for Air New Zealand including DC6s, Lockheed Electras and DC8 aircraft.

It was the responsibility of Captain Keesing to accept the DC8 aircraft at the factory on behalf of Air New Zealand and deliver them all to New Zealand, and he operated DC8s as a pilot until 1969.

In 1969 Captain Keesing became the Flight Operations Manager of Air New Zealand. It was company policy that the pilot holding this position should not fly, as his administrative duties would not permit him to be away for any length of time. It was during Captain Keesing's term of office as Flight Operations Manager that the company decided to purchase the DC10 aircraft.

A year or two later, Captain Keesing became Director of Flight Operations, which meant that his previous job had a new name. From that time onwards he was directly responsible to the General Manager for all matters relating to Flight Operations Division.

Then, on April 1, 1978, came the merger between the National Airways Corporation and Air New Zealand. At this point someone else was given control of all operations and engineering functions and Captain Keesing became Flight Operations Director (International). This meant, in effect, that he was doing the same job but he was no longer reporting direct to the Chief Executive.

After something like thirty-five years of service as a civil airline pilot, Captain Keesing retired from Air New Zealand on April 2, 1979. He was replaced by Captain D.R. Eden. Throughout the rest of 1979 Captain Keesing was retained as a consultant by Air New Zealand. At the time of the Mount Erebus disaster, he was in fact in Auckland, but he went on to say that 'not one person from Air New Zealand' sought his views on what might have happened, nor did anyone in the airline management ever discuss the disaster with him.

Captain Keesing went on to explain that from December 1979 he had been working most of his time for Polynesian Airlines in Western Samoa and he was not aware of what was happening at the Royal Commission in 1980 until he was told that he had been referred to in evidence given to it. He then obtained and read a copy of the Chief Inspector's report and realised that there were certain facts which he thought the Royal Commission should know about. For that reason, he came down to New Zealand and approached counsel assisting the Commission and gave them details of the evidence which he thought would be of interest to them. This evidence was in respect of the original altitude and flight path negotiations which had developed between Air New Zealand and Civil Aviation. And, in respect of these matters, Captain Keesing had a curious tale to tell.

He first of all described the original proposals to fly Air New Zealand aircraft to Antarctica with the intention that the aircraft land on the ice shelf. He described the close inquiries which he and his colleagues made into this proposal, and how the proposal was rejected on his advice. Then he went on to describe the negotiations with Civil Aviation which began in late 1976. This proposal, as we know, envisaged a DC10 flying to Antarctica and back without landing on the ice.

Captain Keesing then went through the relevant

correspondence of which copies had already been produced to the Commission. His first letter was dated December 24, 1976 and in that he set out the fuel studies and other research which had been done into the feasibility of the flights. Then on January 18, 1977 he wrote to the Director of Civil Aviation and requested a flight route a little different from that originally envisaged, namely from Auckland to the Balleny Islands, to Cape Hallett, to McMurdo, and then back via the Campbell Islands and Christchurch. This letter indicated that some of the flight would be made at low level in the McMurdo Sound area, but no altitude was specified. Civil Aviation replied on January 19, 1977 asking for further details in respect of routes, altitudes and flight plan information, and a number of other items.

On February 2, 1977 Captain Keesing wrote once more to the Director of Civil Aviation and he there set out the required details for the flights. Reference was made to the possibility of sightseeing at lower levels and it was specifically stated in this letter that it was the company's proposal to descend for sightseeing purposes, so as to maintain at least 2,000 feet terrain clearance at the captain's discretion. This would be in compliance with the regulatory altitude requirement in respect of mountainous territory. The letter also indicated that on the first flight an area inertial navigation specialist would be carried to observe the operation of this sophisticated system and to ensure that it was satisfactory in those regions. It was also arranged that the pilots in command of the first two flights would attend a briefing with Christchurch Air Traffic Control and with the Christchurch Base of the U.S. Navy Antarctica Support Force.

Captain Keesing said that no formal reply was received to his letter, but that one of the Civil Aviation inspectors had gone on the first flight and that his report dated February 15, 1977 had indicated approval of the various matters specified in Captain Keesing's letter of February 2, 1977.

Captain Keesing stated that Captains Gemmell and Grundy had flown the first two flights. He said they did not raise with him any specific point after their return and his understanding was that both flights were successful and had been operated according to the plan settled between Captain Keesing and Civil Aviation.

Then Captain Keesing went on to say that it was not until the Royal Commission started, and he read the Chief Inspector's report, that he became aware that some further correspondence had taken place between Air New Zealand and Civil Aviation without his knowledge. The first document to which he referred was dated August 10, 1977 which was signed by Captain Gemmell in his capacity as Chief Pilot. This was the one which said that it was now proposed that there would be a further group of five flights and that permission was requested for descent to 6,000 feet in VMC conditions, or by the approved NDB procedure in IMC conditions, provided the cloud base was 7,000 feet or better. He also noticed that there had been previously introduced a company requirement that descent below 16,000 feet was not permitted.

Captain Keesing said that this was the first time he became aware that the Chief Pilot had altered the conditions previously settled between Captain Keesing and Civil Aviation. Captain Keesing could not understand why these alterations had been made without his approval. He was of course the officer in charge of the entire Flight Operations Division.

However, on August 24, 1977 a letter had been written to the Director of Civil Aviation and signed by Mr C.B. Hewitt, the Senior Navigation Officer, on Captain Keesing's behalf. This letter sought approval to operate eight DC10 charter flights to Antarctica. It went on to say, 'We propose to operate over the same routes as the previous charters and in accordance with the requirements of your letter of January 19.' At this stage, so Captain Keesing said, it was quite apparent that the arrangements which he had made to permit descent to 2,000 feet were still current in his mind, because he had dictated the letter, and presumably they were also present in the mind of the Chief Navigator.

Captain Keesing then referred to other letters which he had been shown by counsel assisting the Commission. One was dated August 30, 1977, written by one of the departmental inspectors to Captain Gemmell, in which the inspector had apparently accepted certain conditions put forward by Captain Gemmell. In that letter there was no reference to the letter of August 24 (six days beforehand), sent to the Department on Captain Keesing's behalf by Mr Hewitt. Then again, in respect of the 1978 season, a letter was written to Civil Aviation on September 19, 1978 by the new Flight Manager Line Operations International (Captain Johnson), in which he sought approval to operate four charters flying over Antarctica and said that the previous crew training and operational procedures would be adhered to.

Captain Keesing was still unaware that the Chief Pilot, and then Captain Johnson, had made different arrangements with the Department of Civil Aviation. The next correspondence referred to the forthcoming 1979 season but by that time Captain Keesing was no longer responsible for the Operations Division of the airline.

The impact of this evidence was, of course, very considerable. Here was the man occupying the position later known as Director of Flight Operations, who had himself concluded the altitude arrangements with Civil Aviation, and then there had been some other arrangement involving a minimum safe altitude of 16,000 feet, and in certain conditions 6,000 feet, with such new arrangements never having been referred to Captain Keesing by his subordinates.

In addition to all this, the evidence had been clear, as given before me, that the result of the 16,000 feet agreement was entirely anomalous. Whereas the DC10 aircraft were not permitted to descend below 16,000 feet over the immense wide and flat expanse of sea and sea ice which lay in the path of the approach to McMurdo, yet the minimum safe altitude over the mountain ranges of Victoria Land still only required a terrain clearance of 2,000 feet.

The same aircraft, on its approach to McMurdo, would therefore fly for some fifty miles towards Ross Island over flat sea or flat ice at not less than 16,000 feet, and then on the return journey, or, if it took the alternative route, it would fly over the menacing jagged ice-covered peaks of mountains at a terrain clearance of only 2,000 feet.

The evidence of Captain Keesing only served to reinforce the view of everyone in the courtroom that there had been the most consummate confusion in the planning by Air New Zealand and Civil Aviation over the altitude factors which should control the Antarctic flights. And the matter went a little further than that. It seemed to me that there was an unexplained gap in the airline's evidence. Why had the Chief Pilot reached an agreement with Civil Aviation which was so deeply in conflict with the altitude agreement reached only a week or two previously between his own superior and Civil Aviation? The answer to this enigma was never given.

Finally, Captain Keesing referred to the flight he made in 1978 as a passenger on the Antarctic journey. He was shown the edition of the *Air New Zealand News* of November 30, 1978 in which there appeared the article which described 'the boss' travelling on the flight and stated the altitude of the aircraft as being 2,000 feet above sea level as it flew past Mount Erebus. Captain Keesing emphasised that this article had been brought to him for approval before publication, and that he had approved it as being accurate.

Therefore, said Captain Keesing, his own experience on that flight had merely confirmed that the aircraft was being operated in accordance with requirements imposed by himself and by Civil

Aviation.

Captain Keesing referred to his knowledge of the flying abilities of Captain Collins and he praised the meticulous care with which Captain Collins had always carried out his duties. He said that there must have been something badly wrong somewhere for Captain Collins to have flown into the mountainside in broad daylight. He believed it probable that Captain Collins was of the opinion that the track he was to follow and which the crew had inserted in the inertial navigation system of the aircraft took them down the centre line of McMurdo Sound and that at the point of impact Captain Collins thought they were in fact over pack ice with flat areas on each side running for many miles.

Captain Keesing paid tribute to the Navigation Section of Air New Zealand. He said that when he was told that errors existed in the flight plan data, his reaction was that the staff of the Navigation Section were all top-line navigators on a world-wide basis and that their technical knowledge in the navigation sphere was unsurpassed. He said that these experts produced volumes of work on route structures and he said that their cross-checking of work was so meticulous that he, Captain Keesing, would have believed that it was not possible for any mistake to have slipped through.

This latter observation certainly seemed to have some merit. Mistakes can occur anywhere, but I was aware that Captain Keesing's view as to the meticulous and highly skilled accuracy of the Navigation Section of Air New Zealand was shared by every operational pilot within the company. So, in other words, Captain Keesing was indicating that in his opinion, based on his knowledge of the inertial navigation system and of personnel in the Navigation Section, it was difficult to accept that any mistake had been made by navigation personnel.

As a witness, Captain Keesing was a very impressive individual. He was evidently a man of strong personality, his evidence was clear and concise and he spoke from a platform of vast experience as an operational pilot and as a training pilot. In addition to that, when he was one of the team investigating the desirability of the type of new jet to be bought by Air New Zealand, he had been largely responsible for the technical specifications of the aircraft. It was decided, so he said, to purchase an aircraft with a technical specification identical to that of an airline group known as the KSSU Group (KLM, SAS, Swissair and UTA). It was this consortium which had fostered and encouraged the development of the area inertial navigation system in the DC10. This was the most sophisticated navigation equipment known at that time.

131

When Captain Keesing was cross-examined by counsel for Air New Zealand, I noticed that the questions put to him were very carefully selected and that the approach to this formidable witness was cautious in the extreme. No doubt the company was deeply concerned at the statement of Captain Keesing concerning the improbability of any error having been made by the Navigation Section. What he was saying to me in effect was: 'Do not listen to any evidence which has been given, or might be given, to the effect that these highly skilled navigation experts made a series of mistakes. I know the system, and I know the men, and I can tell you that it is impossible that between them they could have made just one mistake, let alone a series of mistakes.'

This admonition came from a highly-qualified and impartial source. I thought I should keep it carefully in mind.

XII

THE NAVIGATION EVIDENCE

I am here about to describe the second branch of the case advanced for Air New Zealand, the first being the alleged belief on the part of members of the company management, including the Flight Operations Division, that no flights to Antarctica ever descended below 16,000 feet on the approach to McMurdo. The second branch of the company's case comprised the navigation evidence.

The purpose and intent of the whole of the navigation evidence, as given by a number of witnesses, was to establish two propositions:

1. that the Dailey Islands waypoint had been fixed, not intentionally but by mistake; and
2. that no one in Flight Operations (including the Navigation Section) was ever aware that the Dailey Islands waypoint existed. They all believed that the destination waypoint for Antarctica flights was the NDB located at Williams Field, and that the computer track, if maintained by an aircraft, would take it over the top of Mount Erebus on its approach to the NDB.

The basis of these two propositions was stated in the navigation evidence to be the combination of a series of mistakes made by different people within Flight Operations Division. The nature of the evidence describing these mistakes was necessarily very complex and technical, and it cannot be described at any length in a book of this kind. However, here is a summary of the mistakes which the airline witnesses asserted had been made:

Mistake No. 1

In 1978 arrangements were made to computerise all the airline's flight plans for its different flight routes. Thus the ground computer unit of the airline would thereafter hold a flight plan for every route, containing the fixed waypoints and track and distance details associated with them, and shortly before the pre-despatch briefing for a flight the latest weather forecasts would provide the data necessary to determine the winds to be expected at different altitudes and the fuel calculations which would then need to be made in respect of each leg of a particular journey. These latter details would be typed into the ground computer shortly before the aircraft departed and they would appear as part of the standard flight plan which the computer held for that route. Then a printout of the complete flight plan would be obtained from the computer and this printout with the necessary copies would be delivered to Flight Despatch and the crew would be given two or three copies. In the case of the Antarctic flights, as has been explained, the crew would then type into the aircraft computer the series of co-ordinates contained in the flight plan.

The Chief Navigator typed into the ground computer the waypoints which would comprise the standard Antarctica flight plan. But he made a mistake. The current destination waypoint for the Antarctica flights was the NDB of which the position was 77° 51 minutes south and 166° 41 minutes east. However, the Chief Navigator mistakenly used the co-ordinates for Williams Field which had been the destination waypoint for the first two flights in 1977. Those co-ordinates were 77° 53 minutes south and 166° 48 minutes east. The Chief Navigator failed to observe that the Williams Field co-ordinates had been changed to the NDB co-ordinates in mid-1977.

Mistake No. 2

When the Chief Navigator typed the destination co-ordinates which were intended to read 166° 48 minutes east, he inadvertently typed the figures 164° 48 minutes east. This had the effect, unknown to him, of now moving the destination waypoint from the Williams Field area over to the Dailey Islands area which involved a shift of twenty-seven miles to the west.

Mistake No. 3

Having completed the typing of all co-ordinates, the Chief Navigator checked the display on the computer screen with his list of co-ordinates, but failed to ascertain that he had made this error. By pressing the appropriate key he could have obtained a printout of what he had entered and then he could have checked the entries one by one with his own list, but he did not do this.

Mistake No. 4

There was produced in evidence a track and distance diagram which was known as Exhibit 164. This was not a map, but a chart. It depicted what appeared to be a flight track travelling down the centre of McMurdo Sound and then circling the McMurdo Base area from west to east and then travelling back to join the original track at a point far north of Ross Island. The line representing the flight track was adorned with arrows. When the line had completed its semi-circle to the south of Ross Island it turned again to the north and an arrow was again inserted pointing north. The witness who drew this diagram denied that the last-named arrow was meant to indicate a flight path. He said that he had only marked the arrow so as to remind himself of the direction of true north. But it had been pointed out to him that the northward track at this stage followed exactly the line of the 170th meridian of longitude and since all meridians of longitude point north it would not have been necessary for this witness, who could safely be classed as a world expert in navigation, to remind himself of the direction of north. But he insisted that although the other arrows on the flight track indicated the path of the aircraft, this arrow did not, and it was in that respect mistakenly inserted on the diagram.

Mistake No. 5

After Mistake No. 1 had been made, the Flight Manager Line Operations called for a track and distance diagram to replace a previous one which had shown the track of the Antarctic flights to be over the top of Mount Erebus. He was supplied with a copy of Exhibit 164 which showed the flight track down McMurdo Sound. It was evidently not noticed that this new diagram showed an entirely different flight track and Exhibit 164 was supplied as part of the flight documents to the crews who flew all the 1978 flights. It was claimed by the airline witnesses that Exhibit 164 was never intended to be a true track and distance guide, and that its inclusion in the flight documents for 1978 was a mistake. I should here mention that Exhibit 164 was produced by counsel for ALPA and it was obvious that this came as a surprise to the airline counsel, and indeed I was told that at the next adjournment of the hearing there was an angry confrontation involving one of the junior counsel for the airline and counsel for ALPA, it being asserted that counsel for ALPA should have given notice that he possessed this document. It was observed, however, that the exhibit had not been mentioned in the airline's previous navigation evidence. In 1979 Exhibit 164 was withdrawn from the flight documents and was replaced by a Radio Navigation Chart which depicted a military flight track down McMurdo Sound, but this track also did not coincide with the airline flight track.

Mistake No. 6

Captain Simpson, who had commanded the flight of November 14, 1979, had been at the same briefing as Captain Collins and First Officer Cassin. He had noted that the co-ordinates on the Antarctica flight plan produced at that briefing were located at the Dailey Islands waypoint. Upon arrival at McMurdo he overflew the TACAN and then looked at his HSI panel which demonstrated to him that he was about twenty-seven miles 'cross track' from the destination waypoint on his flight plan, namely the Dailey Islands waypoint. Upon his return to Auckland he spoke to the Flight Manager Line Operations and pointed out to him that the destination waypoint was approximately twenty-seven miles west of the TACAN and he thought that aircrews should be notified of this wide cross-track difference.

When Captain Simpson referred to the TACAN position he was referring to a memorandum issued on November 8, 1979 to the effect that the NDB facility at McMurdo was now not operating and that descent to 6,000 feet south of Mount Erebus was now to be regulated by the position of the TACAN which is only two miles away from the NDB. Since it is conventional for all aircraft upon arriving at a destination to establish their position in relation to the airport beacon, Captain Simpson was merely pointing out that the beacon represented by the TACAN was nowhere near the destination waypoint and that pilots should be notified that if over the destination waypoint the TACAN would be 27 miles to the east and not close to the destination waypoint as might normally be expected. In his later explanation to the Chief Inspector, the Flight Manager stated that Captain Simpson had said to him that the McMurdo position was in error and should be 166° 58 minutes east which is the TACAN position. But there was no doubt in my mind at the hearing that Captain Simpson's version of the conversation was entirely correct.

Mistake No. 7

In giving evidence before the Commission, the Flight Manager altered the explanation which he had given to the Chief Inspector. He said his recollection now was that Captain Simpson had said that the McMurdo waypoint would be better positioned if it were

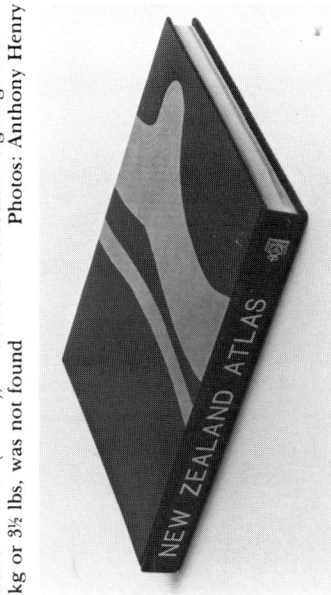

Top: Captain Collins's notebook. Centre: His ring binder (with the pages missing). Bottom: Diane Keenan's diary which has been charred by fire and has the name torn out

Photo: Anthony Henry

Many copies of Eliot Porter's book 'Antarctica' (above) were retrieved from the crash site but Captain Collins's copy of the 'New Zealand Atlas' (below), about the same size and weighing about 1.6 kg or 3½ lbs, was not found

Photos: Anthony Henry

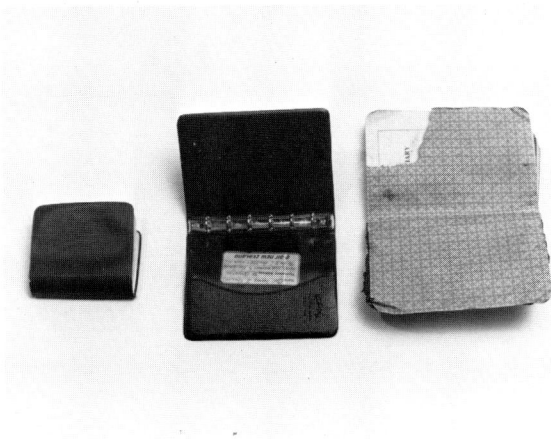

The crash site. Top: Sergeant S. J. Gilpin, Inspector R S. Mitchell and Constable S.B. Leighton

The hazards of Antarctic flying are demonstrated by these artist's impressions based on a photograph taken by the author. The top picture shows the clear air situation (with Mount Erebus quite visible); the lower picture shows the same scene with a 3000 ft overcast painted in   Artist: Sam Mahon

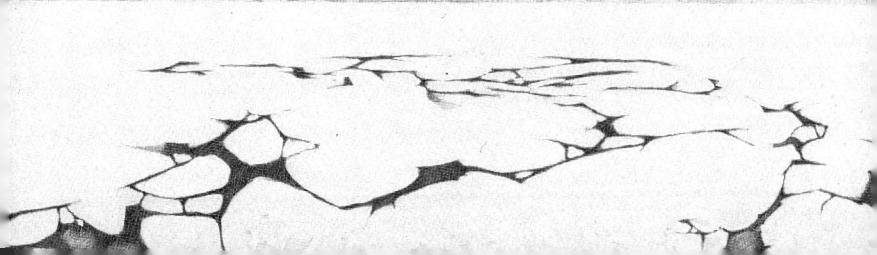

One of the passengers' photographs showing Beaufort Island surrounded by pack ice. 'Had Captain Collins seen Beaufort Island previously, and identified it on the fatal flight, he would certainly have realised that his nav track had been changed.' (Mahon report, Page 153)

The author on the flight deck of the Hercules, following the flight track of the fated DC10   Photo: Carmel Friedlander

at the TACAN. He was therefore saying that his explanation to the Chief Inspector had been a mistake.

Mistake No. 8

It appeared from the evidence that the Flight Manager had given yet another explanation prior to the Commission hearings which contained a further mistake on his part, but this had been contained in a document which evidently had been lost and was never produced at the hearings.

Mistake No. 9

Early in November advice had been received by the airline that the NDB at McMurdo was no longer operating and it was therefore decided to relocate the destination waypoint at the TACAN (as described already) which meant a cross-track difference of only 2.1 miles. When the appropriate instruction was then given to the Chief Navigator he therefore proceeded to alter the computer programme so as to make the longitude read 166° 58 minutes east (being the TACAN position), and did not notice that the standard flight path held by the computer was 164° 48 minutes east. Thus it was believed by everyone that the change in distance was only 2.1 miles and no one realised that it was 27 miles. I felt obliged to enquire whether there might not have been some blunder in recording the suggested 2.10° cross-track difference and the 2.1 nautical miles difference between the NDB and the TACAN. Had someone recorded 2.10° in such a way that someone else read it as 2.1 nautical miles? But I was assured that this was a purely coincidental similarity in the two sets of figures.

Mistake No. 10

Any change in a standard computer flight track is invariably notified to the flight crew to which the amended flight plan will be supplied. This is vital because no matter what route is being flown by an aircraft, it will ordinarily have various ground stations which will have the same co-ordinates as the various waypoints, and as the aircraft 'overflies' the ground station, the crew automatically checks their flight track against the known position of the ground station, and even a difference of 2.1 miles will be sufficient for the crew to believe that there is some malfunction in the computer system on the aircraft. But in this case, the alteration in the destination waypoint was never notified to the flight crew. The alteration could have been revealed to the flight crew by causing the computer to print out a warning to that effect on top of the flight plan.

Mistake No. 11

As part of the ordinary routine, the airline transmits to the destination airport what is called an Air Traffic Control (ATC) flight plan. This merely consists of a teletype message identifying the aircraft and listing in succession the waypoints to the destination and back. The air traffic controllers at the destination airport receive this ATC flight plan shortly after the aircraft has started on its flight and they are therefore able to determine the exact route which it will take on its journey. The same procedure was followed with regard to the Antarctic flights. The ATC flight plan for these flights comprised a list of the co-ordinates up to and including the destination co-ordinates and then a list of the co-ordinates which would be followed by the aircraft on its return to New Zealand. On previous Antarctic flights in 1978 and 1979 the destination co-ordinates had been shown as 77° 53 minutes south and 164° 48 minutes east, which of course represented the Dailey Islands waypoint. But, on the occasion of the fatal flight, the ATC flight plan had not referred to the destination co-ordinates. It used the word 'McMurdo'. In order to demonstrate the difference, here is the outward leg from Cape Hallett to McMurdo and the leg from McMurdo back to Cape Hallett as transmitted to Air Traffic Control at McMurdo on November 21, and November 28, 1979:

21 November 1979		28 November 1979	
72.20.0 S	170.13.0 E	72.20.0 S	170.13.0 E
77.53.0 S	164.48.0 E	McMurdo	
72.20.0 S	170.13.0 E	72.20.0 S	170.13.0 E

The effect of using the word 'McMurdo' on the day of the fatal flight therefore concealed from the air traffic controllers that the flight path had been changed. They believed (as was later ascertained from the U.S. Navy witnesses), that the word 'McMurdo' meant the same waypoint as the one to which they were accustomed and it lay twenty-seven miles to the west of their own position. If the actual co-ordinates for the new destination waypoint had been contained in the ATC flight plan, then the air traffic controllers would immediately have recognised those co-ordinates as representing the TACAN position and they would have radioed their Christchurch base and asked them to seek an explanation from Air New Zealand, for the simple reason that they would not have approved any proposed flight path over the top of Mount Erebus. This use of the word 'McMurdo' was therefore an event of great significance. Why had it been used? The explanation of the airline was that it was the result of yet another mistake.

A Navigation Section witness said that when he wrote in the new co-ordinates changing the destination waypoint (as was mistakenly thought) from the NDB to the TACAN, he inserted the new waypoints in the correct columns of the worksheet which would be used to programme the computer and he then wrote in the figure '5' which would tell the computer that a change in co-ordinates was being made. In order to bring about this result, the figure '5' had to be written in column 55 of the worksheet. But by mistake, the witness wrote the figure '5' into column 65. This had the accidental result of causing the computer, once the figure '5' was inserted in this manner, to obliterate the TACAN co-ordinates which had also been inserted, and to replace them with the word 'McMurdo'. A photocopy of this erroneous worksheet was produced in evidence. The occurrence of the error was almost impossible to understand, having regard to the close familiarity of this witness and others with every detail on this printed worksheet. In addition, counsel who cross-examined this witness pointed to a scarcely decipherable note on it which appeared to suggest that the worksheet did not in fact relate to this particular flight track alteration. In other words, the validity of this exhibit came under suspicion. But leaving all that on one side, this was yet a further mistake which was said to have occurred.

Mistake No. 12

It will be recalled that Captain Simpson had operated the Antarctic flight of November 14, 1979 and, immediately after the flight, had expressed the view that pilots should be told that the nearest airfield beacon (the TACAN) from the destination waypoint was 27 miles to the east. It will be recalled that this was mistakenly believed to have been a statement by Captain Simpson that the waypoint should be moved to the TACAN. It therefore followed that if this interpretation of Captain Simpson's statement was correct, then the flight plan should have been immediately altered so as to be corrected in time for the next flight which was November 21, 1979.

One of the Flight Despatch employees had taken a note in his log regarding an instruction from the Chief Navigator that the flight plan for the next flight should be hand-amended accordingly. But in the relevant page from the log book for

November 21, 1979, the entry seemed to be out of the time sequence in the log.

Three weeks after the disaster, the Chief Pilot asked this witness in writing why the message from the Chief Navigator had been sent on November 20, requiring a hand-amendment to be made for the flight on November 21, whereas no amendment to the flight plan for that flight had been made. Four days later the witness had written saying that he was unable to offer any explanation and could only express his regret. Some months later the witness discovered that during the Royal Commission hearing this mistake had been the subject of some inquiry — evidently not only the Chief Pilot, but the Chief Inspector had not been satisfied with the explanation.

The witness was then called at the Commission of Inquiry and explained that, although the log entry appeared to have been inserted out of sequence in the log (it was timed at 1301 hours but was followed by entries timed at 1058 and 1258 hours), it in fact had been correctly inserted on November 21. The witness said that he had used a large clip on this personal log and the clip had slipped and he inadvertently recorded entries for November 27 on a blank space which in fact had been left for November 21.

Then it appeared that the Chief Navigator now recalled that his instruction to the witness was on November 21, and not on November 20, which meant that the instruction had been given too late for the November 21 flight. The witness who kept the log explained this error in great detail and no good purpose would be served in further describing it. But again, it was a mistake of some consequence. If uncorrected, then it did not support the explanation that Captain Simpson's notification was immediately recorded as requiring an amendment to the Antarctica flight plan forthwith, and until the time sequence in the log entries was explained it could be alleged that the entry for November 21 was not inserted until after the disaster.

Such was the catalogue of errors which were alleged to have been made.

Mr S.J. Macfarlane, a senior lecturer in Law at Auckland University, constructed an appendix to Captain A.G. Vette's book *Impact Erebus* and in it he analysed, in the closest detail, the occurrence of multiple errors alleged to have been made by airline witnesses in the course of their evidence. In respect of the sequence of errors just described, Mr Macfarlane, verifying each conclusion by specific reference to the evidence and to specific exhibits, estimated that these basic errors gave rise to a connected series of consequential errors with the result that in all, there was a formidable total of fifty-four errors made by Flight Operations personnel in connection with this navigation question.

The suggestion that there could have been even the twelve basic errors which I have described was greeted with open disbelief by counsel who cross-examined the navigation witnesses. The navigation section of Air New Zealand was noted for its system of meticulous cross-checking, and the nature and extent of these mistakes on the part of a group of highly expert personnel was a source of considerable worry as far as I was concerned. I could understand that one or two of the errors I have mentioned may have been made, but I found it incredible, in the light of the totality of the navigation evidence, that there could have been this alarming number of mistakes.

Suppose that one accepted the Chief Navigator's account of his series of errors in 1978. This meant that the new destination waypoint had been fixed in error, and not by design. But it was alleged that no one in Navigation Section or in Flight Operations noticed the error, and that it continued to be part of the standard Antarctic flight plan for fourteen months — until some hours before the fatal flight. If this were so, and the new destination waypoint was never noticed, how was it that the publicity material issued by the airline and all the passenger information maps showed the flight path as proceeding down the centre of McMurdo Sound? And when Captain Simpson had his conversation with Captain Johnson, the briefing officer, was it not an inference from Captain Johnson's lack of reaction that he and everyone else had adopted and approved the Dailey Islands waypoint?

The nature of the general case for the airline, and in particular the nature of the navigation evidence, had now reached the stage where the representatives of ALPA believed that considerable harm was being done to the airline's public image. The counsel opposing Air New Zealand and their technical advisers were incredulous at the nature of the explanations being given by the navigation witnesses, quite apart from the purported lack of knowledge on the part of the management of the actual operating altitudes into McMurdo. In the view of ALPA, the altitude and navigation evidence being produced by the airline was not worthy of credence. They decided to do something about it.

On September 11, 1980, Captain Arthur Cooper and First Officer Rhodes both obtained an interview with Mr Davis, the Chief Executive. They entered his office to find him flanked by some of his senior management officials. They made their apprehensions known to him, but they did not get the chance to do very much talking. Captain Cooper later estimated that out of about forty minutes in the office of Mr Davis, he and First Officer Rhodes spoke for about five minutes and Mr Davis held the floor for thirty-five minutes. Mr Davis refused to listen to any suggestion that the management of the airline had been in any way at fault in relation to the disaster. He kept repeating that the two pilots were 'wholly culpable'. He described, in angry terms, the manner in which the Chief Navigator had been cross-examined. It was clear that he was in full touch with what had been going on at the inquiry. He was aware, so it appeared, of the destructive cross-examination of the Chief Navigator and he denounced Mr P. J. Davison, junior counsel for ALPA, who had taken a leading part in the exposition of the wellnigh incredible series of navigation mistakes which were said to have been committed. He described this very able counsel as 'that young whippersnapper'. Mr Davis promised full retaliation when the ALPA witnesses gave evidence. Captain Cooper and First Officer Rhodes, when they were able to get a word in, kept emphasising that the atmosphere of total disbelief in the courtroom was doing untold damage to the airline. They said it was obvious that I did not believe the altitude and navigation evidence. The readers of this chronicle will be pained to hear, I am sure, that the Royal Commissioner himself then came under hostile attack from Mr Davis. He described me as an 'amateur' who did not know what he was talking about. He further went on to say that I was 'incompetent' to decide these major issues and he hinted darkly that there was far more involved in this inquiry than the deputation from ALPA could ever realise. He did not elucidate this latter point.

When this confrontation was reported to me shortly afterwards, these uncomplimentary references to myself were tactfully deleted, as was only right and proper, but they were revealed later after my report had been published. But the point of the confrontation of September 11, 1980 was that the Chief Executive had point-blank refused to accept the urgent warnings being conveyed by these two experienced pilots who only had the welfare of the airline at heart.

Nor was this the only outburst delivered by Mr Davis. There were later occasions, also reported to me, when there would be a chance encounter between him and one of the pilots who did not approve the position taken by the management at the inquiry and on such occasions he loudly repeated the substance of his previous observations, adorned with offensive language, and he would now and then add the following remark, '... and I would like you fellows to know that I have the Government right behind me on this'. It was evidently thought by Mr Davis that this was a decisive factor. But I did not see it in that light. I replied in the sense that Mr Davis obviously had a fixed view and that these incidents were only his manner of expressing that view.

When I had listened to this narrative of consecutive mistakes on the part of the Navigation Section and the Flight Manager it occurred to me that someone, without the benefit of this explanation, might well have assumed that there had been only one mistake, and that it had occurred when the weather and fuel data were inserted into the flight plan for the fatal flight. Most company computers carry in their memories various experimental programmes, and the Air New Zealand ground computer would have been no exception. Suppose that the operator, or the person preparing the worksheet, had called up by mistake an experimental flight plan which showed the TACAN as the destination waypoint, and that the weather and fuel data had been typed into that flight plan, and printouts then supplied to the Flight Despatch office. This would be an error which certainly had the merit of simplicity, and it would explain why Captain Collins had not been told that the destination waypoint had been shifted to the TACAN. No one told him because no one realised that the waypoint had been moved. However, this possibility was never discussed, and no doubt would have been rebutted by the airline.

By this time I had become very concerned about the atmosphere of disbelief which seemed to have settled over the courtroom in respect of the evidence presented by Air New Zealand on the altitude and navigation questions.

As to the case put by the airline that no pilot was authorised to approach McMurdo at less than 16,000 feet and could only descend to 6,000 feet in the area to the true south of Ross Island in a defined sector and under specified conditions, all this seemed to have been negated by the evidence of Captain Wilson. It was now very clear that there had been a verbal briefing of aircrews which was inconsistent with the written material to which I had been referred.

As to the evidence from the navigation section, this had been aimed at demonstrating that the computer flight path to McMurdo had been altered by mistake about fourteen months before the occurrence of the disaster. I have referred to the general tenor of this evidence. But counsel for the consortium, counsel for

ALPA and counsel assisting the Commission had all made it very clear that this navigation evidence was impossible to accept in its entirety. It was not conceivable, in their view, that this extraordinary sequence of mistakes which had been related by the navigation witnesses could have occurred. The expertise of the navigation people had been well established. How could it be that this sequence of errors had been made, not by one man but by a variety of men in the manner which had been described?

Such was the reception accorded by all the counsel opposing Air New Zealand to the saga of the navigation errors. Even the press and radio reporters, sitting at their tables on the righthand side of the courtroom, were obviously contemptuous of this evidence. As for me, I had found it necessary to ask a few questions myself. I had endeavoured to make it clear that I had no preconceived view. I had asked my very limited number of questions in what I hoped was a tone indicative of pure inquiry, and not indicating any open disbelief of what I was being told. But, nevertheless, the witnesses in question could have been under no illusion that I was finding this part of the evidence difficult to believe.

The witness who was causing me particular anxiety in this respect was the Chief Navigator. He had first failed to ascertain the actual position of the standard destination waypoint, and this was an alarming error because he only had to look at a copy of the standard flight plan to see what these co-ordinates were, and, having regard to this long return journey to the frozen wasteland of Antarctica, it was essential that the destination waypoint be accurately fixed because of the vital need to calculate the fuel requirements. Then, having selected the wrong co-ordinates, he had made his second mistake by typing them incorrectly into the computer.

Seeing that the occurrence of these two errors was in their opinion almost impossible to believe, the stance of opposing counsel was that the witness was concealing the fact that he had intentionally moved the destination waypoint twenty-seven miles to the west. But as against this, the witness had produced a copy of his worksheet showing the incorrect co-ordinates. If his evidence was true, then this worksheet corroborated his story. But if his evidence was false, then the worksheet was a concocted document, a fact that I was not prepared to accept.

As a further point in the Chief Navigator's favour, it was clear that he had not altered the heading of the existing flight track, and this again suggested that the changing of the flight track had been accidental. On the other hand, changes to the headings of a flight track are made by a different computer, namely the NV90 computer. He could have altered the flight track intentionally on the main computer, and then instructed someone else to make the routine change of heading on the NV90 computer. He would have done that by putting a note on the file. But no file was ever produced. However, it was perfectly conceivable, in my mind, that the Chief Navigator's evidence was entirely correct.

It was certainly not impossible that the track may have been intentionally shifted without any alteration to the original heading printed on the flight plan. This was because a difference in the heading on the flight plan and the heading displayed on the instrument panel would be disregarded by the aircrew. The reason for this is that when an aircraft is being navigated from point A to point B across the surface of the globe then the shortest distance between A and B will be the great circle track between those two points. But the heading marked on a map in the form of a rhumb line (we will call it a 'straight' line) between A and B will not be the same as the great circle heading actually followed by the aircraft proceeding from A to B. In other words, the map is flat, but the Earth is round. But it is the 'straight line' heading which is printed on the computer flight plan supplied to the crew. Any pilot proceeding from Cape Hallett to McMurdo would expect to see on the heading displayed on the instrument panel a variation of about two degrees from the heading printed out on his flight plan.

The conclusion just expressed may be illustrated by the following information which was produced as part of the evidence at the inquiry: The great circle track from Cape Hallett to the Dailey Islands waypoint is 191.29° whereas the track shown in the flight plan (which would equate with a straight line drawn on a map from Cape Hallett to the Dailey Islands waypoint), is 188.9°. As will be observed, the pilot would read from his instrument panel the great circle track whereas the track shown on his flight plan would be more than 2° to the east.

Another point against the suggested necessity for an alteration to the flight track heading, if the flight track had been intentionally altered, was that the necessary alteration would only be from 188.5° to 188.9°. This slight difference may well have been thought to have been immaterial, bearing in mind that the flight plan track would always be on the final leg of the journey more than 2° different from the heading which the pilot would read from his instrument panel, and no pilot would take any notice of the difference between the two headings.

Then there occurred an event which gave me some cause for

anxiety. I was going away from the Court at the end of the hearing on one particular day and found myself accompanied in the elevator by a youthful reporter. He told me that a journalist was engaged in writing a book about the inquiry, and that the book was scheduled for publication in about four or five weeks time. He told me that the journalist in question had been led to believe by the reporters present that I was obviously treating the evidence for the airline, in particular the navigation evidence, with disbelief.

I could only say to my youthful informant that no matter what attitude I appeared to convey, I could not possibly make my mind up on any question of credibility until I had heard all the evidence. And I pointed out that there was a considerable quantity of evidence yet to come. And with this, we went our separate ways.

I have said that I was concerned at this disclosure and I had a very good reason for adopting that state of mind. In order to explain my apprehension over what the reporter had told me, it is necessary for me to make some allusion to another Royal Commission which was sitting in Auckland at the same time.

This Royal Commission had been set up to inquire into various allegations of police misconduct in the course of a prosecution for murder against a man named Arthur Allan Thomas who had been charged with murdering a farmer and his wife who lived in the same country district as himself. He had been found guilty by a jury. There had been an application to the Court of Appeal to direct a new trial upon the grounds that further evidence had been discovered and, although this application had been strongly opposed by the prosecution, a new trial had been directed. But the second jury again convicted Mr Thomas.

It had appeared, however, during the course of the second trial, that there was now some measure of doubt about the validity of a particular piece of evidence upon which the prosecution had always placed principal reliance. Mr Thomas had been alleged to have shot the two people through an open window of their home, and the crucial piece of evidence was the discovery by the police of an empty cartridge case lying in a small garden plot not far from that window. It was established beyond doubt that this cartridge case had come from a rifle possessed by Mr Thomas. It was assumed that, after firing the first shot, he had ejected this empty cartridge case and in the darkness had not been able to recover it.

But, at the second trial, the whole matter of this cartridge case had been closely examined by scientific experts retained on behalf of the defence, and they had discovered a remarkable fact. The bullets found in the bodies of the two dead victims of the shooting had been impressed in the course of manufacture with a numeral on the base of each bullet. But it was now said that the cartridge case found in the garden plot was of a type which had never been used in the manufacture of cartridges containing this particular numeral on the base of the bullet. This was an astounding discovery, if correct, for it meant that the ejected cartridge case found in the garden plot could not have fired any of the bullets found in the bodies of the two victims.

Following the second conviction of Mr Thomas, these inquiries into the empty cartridge case had been pursued further and a very large proportion of the public in New Zealand had come around to the view that Mr Thomas had been wrongly convicted, and that the empty cartridge case had been planted in the garden plot by the police. It was alleged that the case against Mr Thomas before the cartridge case was discovered had been not only circumstantial, but unsupported by any significant evidence. And it was alleged that this cartridge case had been found at a very late stage of the police inquiries, and in circumstances which suggested that without its discovery Mr Thomas would never have been arrested and charged. Mr Thomas had always protested his innocence. In addition, it appeared that the prosecution had never been able to produce any worthwhile motive for the shooting.

In due course the Government pardoned Mr Thomas on the grounds that the case against him had not been proved beyond reasonable doubt. But the public outcry still continued, and the Government decided to appoint a Royal Commission to inquire into the police conduct of the case and, in particular, to give an opinion whether the cartridge case had been planted by the police.

The Chairman of the Royal Commission was Mr Justice Taylor, a retired Supreme Court judge from New South Wales, and the other two members of the Commission were distinguished citizens of New Zealand.

When the police files were disclosed at the hearing of this Commission, there had been evidence to suggest that the courtroom explanations about discovery of this cartridge case had not tallied with the recorded information on the police files. This was only one of the indications which appeared to point to malpractice on the part of the police.

Mr Justice Taylor, so it appeared from the newspaper reports, was a very forthright man. He also came from a legal system which operated rather differently from our own; the conduct of litigation in New South Wales is far more robust than it is in either England or in New Zealand. If a judge comes to the conclusion that a witness or counsel is trying to mislead him, then the accepted practice in New South Wales is for him to say so in no uncertain terms and the level of criticism occasionally adopted by the Bench in that jurisdiction is of a type quite unknown in New Zealand.

Therefore, when Mr Justice Taylor discovered that the police files contained an explanation about the finding of this cartridge case which was materially at variance with the sworn evidence given by police officers at each trial, he strongly criticised the relevant police witnesses. He made no secret of his belief that either there had been a false report attached to the police file in question, or the police officers concerned had committed perjury.

These assertions were widely reported in the Press and they were deeply resented by the police and their counsel. As a result, the police lawyers had applied to the High Court in Auckland for an order of prohibition against Mr Justice Taylor's Royal Commission, which meant that they wanted the Court to stop the hearings on the ground of declared or apparent bias on the part of the Commission, and in particular, on the part of Mr Justice Taylor. The fact that these proceedings had been taken was also widely reported in the newspapers in July 1980.

I had all these considerations in mind as I reflected upon what the young reporter had told me in the elevator. What would happen if I announced in open hearing that I had considerable reservations about the credibility of some of the witnesses to whom I had been listening? Could this not be construed as exactly the same type of conduct as that of Mr Justice Taylor which was shortly to be considered by the High Court in Auckland? I was also aware, at this stage, that Mr Davis, the Chief Executive of Air New Zealand, had expressed an adverse view about the way in which counsel assisting the Commission and counsel for ALPA were conducting the proceedings. It will be remembered that in his confrontation with two of the ALPA representatives, he had denounced the aircrew as being solely responsible, despite the nature of the evidence which had so far been produced. I could see a distinct possibility that any open indication by me of provisional disbelief of airline witnesses might well provoke Mr Davis into instructing the airline counsel to adopt the same tactics as those which had been adopted in the case of the Thomas Commission. And during the cross-examination of Mr Thomson, when I had intervened to ask a question, counsel for the airline had launched a trenchant and carefully prepared criticism against my asking questions during cross-examination. This criticism had been advanced not long after the police had applied to the High Court for an order stopping the Thomas Commission.

Now I certainly had very deep reservations about the credibility of this navigation evidence, just as I had about the credibility of a number of executive pilots who had given the altitude evidence. But I had certainly not reached any conclusion. I had been in the legal business far too long to fall into the trap of coming to any final decision before all the evidence had been heard. I therefore decided that I had better make my position clear to counsel for Air New Zealand, and I decided that I would do so in chambers.

Consequently, at about the beginning of October when the navigation evidence had been concluded, I asked my secretary one evening when the day's sitting had been completed, to go into the courtroom and bring counsel assisting the Commission and leading counsel for Air New Zealand into my chambers. In due course she returned to say that counsel assisting the Commission had both left the premises, but that one of the senior Air New Zealand counsel was still there, so I told her to bring him along to my room. When he arrived, I said that I felt I was under an obligation to tell him that I was concerned at the possibility that he and the airline witnesses might think I had made up my mind against them on the issue of credibility. I referred to the executive pilots who had given evidence on the altitude question. I said that at this juncture, and especially having regard to the unexpected evidence of Captain Wilson, I had no option but to have doubts as to the credibility of those witnesses, or at least as to some of them. As to the navigation section witnesses, I again had no alternative but to maintain at the present time a considerable degree of doubt as to whether they were telling the truth.

However, I went on to say, it was axiomatic, as he and I well knew, that no final conclusion on matters like this could ever be reached until all the evidence had been concluded. There was evidence to be given, as I understood it, by other airline witnesses, including for example the Director of Flight Operations, and for all I knew some document might be produced which actually confirmed the very involved series of errors which had been deposed to by the navigation witnesses.

And I went on to say that because of the air of profound disbelief which was apparent throughout the courtroom when the navigation evidence was given, and because of some questions of my own which appeared to indicate that I might have made up my mind that I did not believe the navigation evidence, I was very concerned that the navigation witnesses might be going away from the courtroom believing that my mind was made up. I asked counsel if he would kindly advise particular navigation witnesses, whom I named, that I had not reached any final conclusion. They were clearly to understand that whatever the tone of cross-examination by counsel might have been, and whatever the apparent tone of my questions might have been, I had not yet reached any firm conclusion. I reaffirmed that I had considerable doubt at this stage about their credibility, but I could only repeat that these doubts might well be resolved in the light of further evidence. Counsel agreed that he would convey this information to the navigation witnesses I had named.

The hearing proceeded, and I heard no further from counsel on the topic which I had discussed with him in chambers. I assumed that he had carried out my directions with regard to conveying my views to the witnesses in question.

XIII

THE WHITEOUT EVIDENCE

It will be remembered that in his report, the Chief Inspector had given what turned out to be a brief quotation of an article dealing with whiteout conditions. That description had been entirely accurate, as later inquiries were to show. The term 'whiteout' is used in four different senses, but the sense in which it was used by the Chief Inspector was the accurate one in this case.

In this particular meaning the phenomenon has nothing to do with impaired visibility caused by snow showers or fog or cloud or the like. It occurs when an aircraft is flying over snow-covered terrain (which is perfectly white) and beneath a solid pale overcast. The effect is that the terrain in front of the aircraft appears to the eye to be uniformly flat for very many miles ahead. All hills and valleys disappear entirely. The reason for this is that, because there are no shadows or other indications that the ground is not entirely flat, the illusion becomes perfect when, as it was in the present case, the sun is shining from a position behind the aircraft. In those circumstances, the presence of a purely white snow-covered mountain right ahead of the aircraft will not be detected. It will flatten out as far as the eye is concerned, and will appear as only part of the flat white surface stretching interminably ahead. This optical illusion is known in polar regions and in Canada as the 'flat light' illusion.

By appropriate reading, I had ascertained the true effect of this type of whiteout, but we had now reached the stage of the inquiry where specific evidence was to be given by people who had studied the subject. The first of those witnesses was Captain Gordon Vette, a senior international pilot with Air New Zealand who had been an Air Force flier and had, in due course, obtained various qualifications as an instructor.

He had been with Air New Zealand since 1958. In that time he had become a command pilot on DC6 aircraft and then in 1964 he was appointed to be a Training and Check Captain on DC3s and

151

Lockheed Electras. In 1965 he was made a Training and Check Captain on DC8 aircraft and eventually he became a senior Training Captain within Air New Zealand.

In 1972 he had been appointed to be a Training and Check Captain for DC10 aircraft and in 1977 was appointed to the position of Senior Route Captain, North America. In 1979 he was appointed to be Line Superintendent, North America and as at the time of giving evidence, he was a Flight Instructor for DC10 aircraft and checked pilots at all levels of seniority.

Captain Vette therefore had an impressive background not only as an international pilot flying DC10 aircraft but also as a specially selected training officer in the operation of such aircraft.

Captain Vette had been the pilot in command of a flight to Antarctica on November 15, 1977. This was the flight on which Mr Brizindine, President of McDonnell Douglas, had been a passenger. Captain Vette described the flight in his evidence and then he turned his attention to the whiteout phenomenon.

After the accident was reported and before any accident report was published, he said he began to inquire into the question of why Captain Collins could have flown in clear air at low altitudes towards Mount Erebus without taking any avoiding action. It had been apparent from the passengers' photographs that visibility to the left and right of the aircraft had been virtually unlimited, under the overcast, right up to the point of impact. Captain Vette said that he was satisfied that the crew must have been totally misled in respect of the forward visibility. He explained the 'fail-safe' or 'crew co-operative' training which is the basis of modern pilot training in passenger jets and emphasised that the crew as a whole are flying the aircraft. In the case of a DC10 there are three crew members — the captain, the co-pilot and the flight engineer. Any matters which are drawn to the attention of one crew member by another must be responded to. This is known as the 'challenge' procedure and, apart from ensuring correct flying techniques, it is designed to detect any incapacity on the part of a crew member.

And here, of course, we had the heart of the problem. On the flight deck during the last few minutes of the flight were the two pilots, Flight Engineers Brooks and Moloney, and Peter Mulgrew. Not one of these persons had ever expressed any alarm or doubt as the aircraft closed at 260 knots on the mountain which lay directly in its path. Captain Vette had therefore been driven to the conclusion that the crew must have been confronted by a total optical illusion, and that no other explanation was possible.

Having explained the researches he had then made into this visual illusion factor, Captain Vette produced a paper which he had prepared on the subject of visual and optical deception, and he annexed this as part of his evidence. It was clear, in his opinion, that the 'whiteout' factor had been the ultimate cause of the disaster. Every aspect of the weather had been in conformity with that supposition. After levelling out at 2,000 feet, the aircraft had proceeded under cloud cover which at first had been scattered but which then had obviously become solid. The terrain ahead had been uniformly white and the underside of the cloud had been pale. The sun had been shining from a position directly behind the aircraft and at an angle of thirty-four degrees from the horizon. Under these circumstances, as all the published material demonstrated, the fact that the forward vista of snow-covered terrain was rising to meet the cloud would not be observable and the intersection of the cloud base with the snow-covered terrain would appear to be a horizon located in the far distance.

Then Captain Vette pointed to the content and the manner of the briefing of Antarctic crews and to the documentation with which they were provided which, in total, had led this crew, as it had with other crews, to the conclusion that the flight track would take the aircraft down the centre of McMurdo Sound. Indeed, until the co-ordinates of McMurdo were changed on the evening prior to the flight, that is precisely where the aircraft would have gone.

In addition, Captain Vette said that there would be evidence that Captain Collins had plotted his flight track on a map on the night before the flight left Auckland and at that time he would have relied upon the co-ordinates shown to him at the briefing. Captain Vette said that the final leg of the flight path, as plotted on Captain Collins' map or maps and probably on his atlas, would locate the aircraft as travelling down this corridor forty miles wide and that there could be no possibility of the track being incorrect. In addition, the snow-covered cape of Cape Tennyson far to the left and Cape Royds far to the right would coincide with the entrance to McMurdo Sound as depicted on the topographical map upon which Captain Collins had plotted his flight path. Thus it was, in the opinion of Captain Vette, that the DC10 had flown into the mountainside without any one on the flight deck ever seeing the ice slopes directly ahead.

In support of Captain Vette's view, there was called, as a witness, an expert in the person of Professor R.H. Day, who, since 1965, had held the position of Foundation Professor of Psychology at Monash University, Australia. Professor Day held various academic qualifications and was an expert on perception studies and it was accepted by all counsel present that he was a world authority in his field. He had special qualifications with regard to human factors in aviation.

Professor Day had studied the Chief Inspector's report and the brief of evidence to be given by Captain Vette, and he had discussed the general aspects of the disaster with Dr J.C. Lane, Director of Aviation Medicine, Department of Transport, Commonwealth of Australia. Dr Lane is regarded as one of the world's leading authorities on human factors in air accident causation. He too had studied the Chief Inspector's report and he had authorised Professor Day to say that he concurred with the Professor's views.

Professor Day had no doubt that the whiteout factor was present on the day in question and he gave his reasons in detail. He then directed his attention to what he termed the 'mental set' of the person afflicted by this optical illusion. Like Captain Vette, Professor Day had studied closely the photographic slides presented at the audio-visual briefing, which indicated the flight track passing to the west of Mount Erebus, and he had looked at the maps and the RNC-4 chart in the possession of the crew, all of which indicated a track to the west of Ross Island. Professor Day emphasised that the briefing and the documentation available to the crew would have coincided with what the crew actually saw as they approached Ross Island, in that the headlands far away to the left and right would be identified as the entrance to McMurdo Sound as depicted on the topographical map in the possession of Captain Collins. He emphasised the point that it was not the 'visual perceptual system' of one member of the flight crew that failed, but that of five persons, including the experienced Antarctic observer and commentator, Peter Mulgrew.

I could not help but reflect that, in spite of the worldwide resources of the airline and of Civil Aviation and their access to all information on this topic, neither of the two organisations had proposed to bring forward one word of evidence on this vital point. It had been left to the untiring industry of Captain Vette to unearth all this literature and detail, and to produce from Australia a world authority in the person of Professor Day.

But it was not only Captain Vette and Professor Day who gave valuable evidence on the whiteout question. One of the leading ALPA representatives to give evidence was First Officer Rhodes who had for five years flown DC10 series 30 aircraft. He had not flown on any Antarctic flight, but his evidence was given in his capacity as a qualified air accident investigator for ALPA.

The witness had originally been trained in flight safety and accident investigation duties by the Royal Australian Air Force and had been on various overseas courses connected with air accident investigation and flight safety procedures. He was a member of the International Society of Air Safety Investigators and was delegated by the International Federation of Airline Pilots to act as accident investigator for any member country. In particular, First Officer Rhodes had made himself familiar with the use of the electronic recorders (CVR equipment and the 'black box') as a function of aviation safety.

First Officer Rhodes went to the crash site as part of the investigation team and was responsible to the Chief Inspector for the carrying out of specified duties. He examined the air traffic control and meteorological aspects, and he also transcribed the Mac Centre tapes of the radio conversations between McMurdo and the Ice Tower and the aircraft in the area on the day of the disaster. After returning to New Zealand he assisted the Chief Inspector's staff with the analysis of the CVR and 'black box' data, and with the plotting of this information on a chart of common time base and scale.

The evidence of First Officer Rhodes was therefore limited to his air accident investigation, both on the site and elsewhere, and one of the most interesting parts of his evidence was his account of his own first-hand experience of the whiteout phenomenon in Antarctica. He said that although he had flown in snow and ice conditions as part of the crew of search and rescue flights in New Zealand's Southern Alps as a member of the Royal New Zealand Air Force, his flights in helicopters in Antarctica demonstrated quite unexpected flying conditions. This ocular illusion, he said, was always present, even in sunlight, but was very much worse when an aircraft was being flown over snow under an overcast. He made the following statement:

> The matt surface of the snow gives no depth perception even in conditions of fifty miles' visibility and causes the wall of snow ahead to appear as a flat plateau with a distant horizon.

This observation incurred the displeasure of the airline management, only because they were conscious of the failure to brief Antarctic crews regarding this ocular illusion in polar regions. Yet this statement was nothing more than a succinct and accurate confirmation of the very same point which had been made in the Chief Inspector's report, and First Officer Rhodes was testifying, it will be remembered, solely as an air accident investigator.

But there was yet another piece of evidence which created even more hostility on the part of the airline management, even though it was again restricted to air accident investigation procedures. First Officer Rhodes was critical of the manner in which documents at the crash site were collected and accounted for. He said he had seen Captain Gemmell with a considerable quantity of documents recovered from the crash site, that these documents had been taken away, and that the exact nature of this documentation appeared not to have been ascertained. It appeared to be the view of First Officer Rhodes that all documents recovered at the crash site should have been handed over to the Chief Inspector at McMurdo, whereas it appeared that the collection of documents which he had seen had been taken back to Auckland by Captain Gemmell. This expression of opinion, and it was a perfectly valid criticism from the air accident procedure point of view, subsequently involved First Officer Rhodes in considerable trouble with the airline management, a circumstance to which I shall refer later.

It only remains to say that the existence of polar ocular illusions was further checked by Baragwanath and myself when we later visited the United States. We interviewed Captain Arthur P. Ginsburg of the U.S. Air Force, stationed at the Wright Patterson airfield near Dayton, Ohio, who is a visual perception expert in the field of military aviation. We also interviewed Mr G.W. Shannon, a Canadian airline executive who is also a pilot with extensive polar experience, having flown in the Antarctic as well as the Arctic regions. Each of these experts confirmed every word of the whiteout testimony which I have been describing. Mr Shannon had himself flown in the McMurdo area and he spent some hours with us studying all the material we had brought with us and it was his opinion that Captain Collins had elected to fly away because he had not succeeded in establishing VHF contact with the Control Tower and particularly because he could not see anything ahead of him but a flat white plain running to the far distance when he should have been able to see without any difficulty the buildings and installations of McMurdo Base. Try as he might, Mr Shannon could detect no fault on the part of Captain Collins.

The literature on this subject is not precise as to the physical cause of this type of whiteout illusion. However, many scientists consider that the reason for the disappearance of any deviation in ground level under whiteout conditions is due to a complex process of light diffusion. The theory is that a large percentage of the light which penetrates the cloud cover is reflected back from the ground because it strikes the myriads of ice mirrors formed by the ice crystals which are tilted in all directions on the surface of the snow. The light rays are then reflected upwards and meet the white under-surface of the cloud and then reflect back again. This process of transmission and reflection is believed to be the reason why the forward vista of a uniform white surface, though usually visible in crystal clear air, will appear uniformly flat under an overcast even though the terrain may be tilted upwards at a steadily rising angle.

I will here quote an extract from Henry Longhurst's book, *My Life and Soft Times*. On pages 220-221 he describes travelling over a snow-covered plateau on his way from Teheran to Tabriz:

> A train had passed up just in front of us and, as it faded into the distance on its way up to Russia, there occurred an unforgettable optical illusion. The line rose slightly but the snow and the sky blended into each other, as they so often do from the air, and no horizon was visible to the human eye. We might have been specimens in some vast grey bowl. And so, as the train, vanishing, gradually absorbed itself into the grey landscape, it seemed quite distinctly to be climbing into the distant sky.

The Mount Erebus disaster certainly transcends in magnitude all past examples of aircraft disasters caused by whiteout phenomena. If the veil of cloud lying across the mountain at about 3,500 feet had parted — even for a second — and disclosed the black outcrop of rock (at about 4000 feet up the mountain slope) which it had hitherto concealed, then that outcrop would have appeared as a black object located high in the sky ahead, at an altitude at least 2,000 feet higher than the DC10. It would have looked just like Henry Longhurst's train. But the cloud base remained static. No visual sign appeared to warn the aircrew that they were looking at a snow slope and not at a flat snow plain.

XIV

INTERVIEWING THE U.S. NAVY WITNESSES

It had become obvious that it would be necessary to take evidence from any available members of the U.S. Navy who had been employed at McMurdo Air Traffic Control on the day of the disaster. My terms of reference required me to consider whether there had been any act or omission in respect of the air traffic control of the aircraft which had caused or contributed to the disaster.

The U.S. Navy would not permit any of those witnesses (who were now in the United States) to travel to New Zealand to give evidence, but it was agreed that Baragwanath and I could interview them in California, although only in the presence of a U.S. Navy lawyer, namely Lieutenant Commander E.A. Fessler, a member of the Judge Advocate General's Branch of the U.S. Navy.

Baragwanath and I duly interviewed these witnesses in California. They described to us the exact nature of the radio and radar facilities at McMurdo and they were adamant that the DC10 was at no time observed on the radar screen at the Ice Tower. However, neither the radio operator nor the radar operator on duty in the tower was produced for interrogation. As I recall it, one had left the Navy and the other had preferred not to give any evidence.

The significant evidence, as far as we were concerned, was given by Chief Warrant Officer C.R. Priest who was the Chief Traffic Controller and the Supervisor of Mac Centre at the relevant time. He could only say that he believed that the DC10 was not identified on the radar screen. But he said that if the aircraft had been picked up on the screen during its first orbiting turn, which took it well clear of Mount Erebus, then it would have been visible for only a short space of time and that, in view of the fact that the DC10 had notified Mac Centre that it was flying VMC, then no particular lookout would have been kept by the radar operator.

The Chief Warrant Officer also advised that if the McMurdo authorities had been aware of any proposal to programme the flight track of the aircraft over the top of Mount Erebus then they would have expressed disagreement with that proposal. They had no idea that the flight track proceeded anywhere but down the centre of the sound. No military aircraft was permitted to approach McMurdo from the north over the top of Mount Erebus and the Chief Warrant Officer was adamant that no civil aircraft would have been allowed to do so. His evidence, as in the case of other witnesses we saw in California, was eventually reduced into a sworn deposition prepared by Lieutenant Commander Fessler and the depositions were in due course sent to New Zealand and were lodged as part of the evidence before the Royal Commission.

I might also say that the U.S. Navy witnesses confirmed in every respect the dangers of the whiteout illusion and they also did not understand how it was that neither of the pilots who had been sent on this journey had ever been to Antarctica before. Prior familiarity with the Antarctic region is a vital prerequisite in the case of any U.S. Navy pilot flying in that area.

The primary purpose of our visit to California had now been accomplished, but there was another matter which had been exercising our minds and we decided to mention it to the Lieutenant Commander. It concerned the radar and radio facilities at McMurdo. On the control tower, situated close to the ice runway of Williams Field, were the radar equipment and a radio transmitter. The only frequency available at the control tower was VHF. VHF transmissions are dependent upon line of sight, but they are the common mode of communication with aircraft at relatively short range because they are almost always free from static.

At a distance of about one mile across the snow from the control tower is the large building which represents the nerve centre of all the U.S. Navy radio transmission in the Antarctic area, and this is known to the Navy as Mac Centre. Here there are located radio transmitters of different frequencies including VHF and HF. A transmission on high frequency is not dependent on line of sight, because the radio waves go upwards to the ionosphere and then downwards. It does not matter if there is high ground between the transmitter and the recipient of the signal. But HF transmissions are frequently subject to static; it depends upon the prevailing weather. On the day of the disaster, HF transmissions were perfectly clear, and Mac Centre had communicated with the DC10 on many occasions on HF during the approach of the aircraft to

Ross Island.

Also we had been told by the U.S. Navy witnesses that all transmissions to or from the McMurdo area are recorded on tape at Mac Centre, and in addition that all transmissions from the control tower are monitored constantly by a radio operator at Mac Centre. He listens to every transmission made from the control tower to aircraft in the area.

It was on record that the tapes at Mac Centre, which had been recording transmissions both from Mac Centre and from the control tower to the DC10, had been silent for a period of four minutes 42 seconds prior to the moment when the aircraft struck the northern slopes of Mount Erebus. This had been due to the fact, so it was understood, that neither Mac Centre nor the control tower had spoken to the aircraft over that period of time. It had not been necessary for any transmissions to be made, as the control tower was awaiting the announcement from the aircraft that it was about ten miles from Williams Field.

I related these facts to Lieutenant Commander Fessler. He said that this accorded with his own information on the matter. But I then went on to say that at one time there had been a different explanation for the silence of the McMurdo tapes over this final period of four minutes 42 seconds. Lieutenant Commander Fessler naturally wanted to know what other explanation had been brought to our attention. So I told him.

I said that when the investigation team from New Zealand had arrived at McMurdo after the disaster, one of the inquiries which had been undertaken was to see what transmissions from Mac Centre had been sent to the aircraft. The cockpit voice recorder of the DC10 had not at that time been retrieved. And even when it was retrieved, it was flown away to New Zealand and deciphered to the best extent possible at Wellington before being flown off to Washington. So one of the first tasks of the investigators had been to visit Mac Centre and ask for the ground tapes to be played.

It had then been discovered that the last four minutes 42 seconds of the Mac Centre tape was silent. The investigator in question, First Officer Rhodes, had inquired as to the reason for this silence and he had been told that this last portion of the tape prior to impact had been accidentally erased. Lieutenant Commander Fessler was astounded at this revelation. He said that his instructions from the Navy had not mentioned any such explanation. He wanted urgently to know more about it.

The explanation given, so I told him, was that the tapes at Mac Centre were changed over each day at a specific time and that the tapes in this case had been changed at a time roughly coinciding with the impact of the aircraft against the mountain and that, in the course of this process, the last few minutes of the tape had been accidentally erased.

Supposing that this had in fact happened, inquired Lieutenant Commander Fessler, then what was the inference to be drawn from it? I said the inference was that the missing four minutes 42 seconds may have contained transmissions from either the control tower or from Mac Centre, and that it was conceivable that the nature of those transmissions reflected some act of negligence on the part of the radio operators either at the control tower or at Mac Centre, and that when the tapes were played through by the U.S. Navy personnel immediately after the aircraft was found to be missing, someone had thought it prudent to erase this last part of the tape.

As might be expected, Lieutenant Commander Fessler was very disturbed indeed at this suggestion. He said he could not believe that the air traffic controllers at Mac Centre would do such a thing. I told him that there was no real evidence that this event had occurred but, unfortunately, it was by no means uncommon in civil litigation in the United States involving air crashes for the ground controllers to report that certain sequences of ground tape had been mistakenly erased. I said that the lawyers representing some American citizen on board TE901 might very well make the same allegation against the air traffic controllers at Mac Centre. The Lieutenant Commander then asked me, upon the assumption that the last part of the ground tape had been erased, whether accidentally or otherwise, what I supposed might have been contained on the tape in the form of transmissions to the aircraft. I then ventured the following possibility.

I said that so far as I was concerned, I had no view on the matter at all, and neither did Baragwanath. However, this is what some lawyer or other hostile party might say. First of all, it might be contended that the radar operator at the control tower had seen the DC10 on his radar screen. He would have observed a line of 'blips' travelling right to left from behind the mountain before turning away to the right again and disappearing. He would have told the radio operator at the tower. The radio operator might then have spoken to the aircraft on VHF and told the crew that, instead of being in McMurdo Sound, as both the crew and the control tower thought, the aircraft was behind Ross Island and consequently to the north of Mount Erebus. The radio operator might have warned the aircraft that it was about thirty miles off-course and was coming in on a collision course with the mountain. To this communication there would have been no reply, because of the fact that the aircraft was behind the mountain. The VHF transmission would not have been received. The radio operator would probably have repeated his warning and possibly given the warning a third time. There would still have been no reply. And then a couple of minutes later the aircraft had struck the mountain.

During these transmissions from the control tower, the radio operator at Mac Centre would have been listening carefully. He would have observed that there was no reply from the aircraft and he would have known why. It was ordinary everyday practice at Mac Centre to listen to VHF transmissions to helicopters and other low-flying aircraft which were frequently interrupted by the aircraft flying behind high ground. This was known to every radio operator at Mac Centre. When a VHF signal calling for a reply was sent and there was no reply, the standard practice was for the Mac Centre operator to repeat the message on his HF transmitter.

In this case, it might be suggested, the radio operator at Mac Centre had made the fatal blunder of not repeating on HF radio the warning which he had just heard on VHF radio from the control tower. Had he only taken the precaution of repeating the warning, then Captain Collins would immediately have heard the warning on HF and would have applied power and put the DC10 into a turning climb and flown away.

I then repeated the hypothetical allegation, which I had raised before, to the effect that after the occurrence of the disaster had become known, the Mac Centre air traffic controllers had played back the ground tapes and it had then been realised, as the operators listened to the unsuccessful transmissions from the tower, that this grave mistake had been made by the operator who had been monitoring the control tower transmissions. There would have been the highest possible motive to get rid of this piece of evidence, and this would have been done by the simple process of erasing that part of the ground tape.

Lieutenant Commander Fessler expressed not only alarm but resentment at these observations. I reminded him that this was mere speculation on my part. It was only an outline of what possibly could be alleged against the U.S. Navy in litigation brought in America by the representatives of the American passengers who had been killed. Nevertheless, it was certainly a sinister thesis, and the Lieutenant Commander clearly saw it in that light.

Lieutenant Commander Fessler then announced that the Navy still had the tapes in its possession, and he said that irrespective of any question of possible liability at law on the part of the Navy, he saw it as a matter of principle to have this allegation inquired into. He said that he was certainly not prepared to allow the possibility of this serious allegation against the Navy to be considered without full investigation by the Navy itself. I again reminded him that I was only propounding a possibility. However, the Lieutenant Commander was determined not to let the matter rest there. He said that he proposed to forward to Washington his recommendation that the ground tapes be examined by the Washington experts who had investigated the Watergate tapes, and who would be able to determine whether or not there had been any erasure of the tapes. He said he saw this as a paramount necessity having regard to the possibilities which I had mentioned.

I told him that Baragwanath and I had already given all this the most careful consideration. It seemed to us that no useful purpose could be served in my pursuing the possibility to which I had adverted. First of all, the Washington experts might report that there had been no erasure of the tape, and that the original explanation given to First Officer Rhodes had been wrong. If there had been no erasure, then this line of inquiry was obviously at an end. Nevertheless, I said that the Lieutenant Commander, being a lawyer, would realise that an explanation given at the time was usually to be preferred to an explanation advanced months later when the people involved had had the advantage of legal advice.

But suppose that the Washington experts did confirm that the last part of this tape had been erased? They would not be able to tell whether the erasure had been accidental or designed. And in any case they would certainly not be able to tell us, or rather tell Lieutenant Commander Fessler, whether or not there had actually been any recorded transmissions on the tape which had been erased. So, in the end, no conclusive answer would ever be obtained.

I then went on to say that, under these circumstances, I could not with any sense of responsibility raise this matter in the report which I was required to make to the New Zealand Government. I had decided that I would not support any factual proposition in the course of my report unless there existed some solid evidence warranting the occurrence of the event in question as a probability. I was certainly not prepared to raise this type of allegation on the basis of the evidence so far available, and when the most diligent scientific inquiries in Washington could take the matter no further. I therefore told Lieutenant-Commander

Fessler that, although I thought it necessary to warn him of this possible allegation, seeing that it would obviously be open in subsequent civil litigation, I nevertheless proposed not to refer to it in my report.

The Lieutenant Commander still insisted that it might be his official duty to pursue this matter further in the manner which he had suggested. I said that this was entirely up to him, but he knew my own attitude and I did not propose to take the matter any further or to make any further reference to it. On this note, our discussions with the Lieutenant Commander terminated.

We had now been working throughout the course of the day for a period of about twelve hours, and Baragwanath and I were driven back to Los Angeles on the coastal route which runs through Malibu. The sun was setting and we decided to stop at a restaurant for an evening meal. We sat together at the dinner table and looked out over the darkening sea of the Pacific. We discussed the events of the day, and we were both agreed as to the high intelligence and the co-operative courtesy of Lieutenant Commander Fessler. And we were impressed by his devoted loyalty to the U.S. Navy. We had not particularly wanted to raise this matter with him, but we felt that civil litigation against the U.S. Navy was at least a possibility. We thought we had been right to give him this warning, but what he did about it was no concern of ours.

In his report the Chief Inspector had described the type of airborne radar carried on a DC10 and how it could be set in either the 'weather' or 'mapping' mode. He had then gone on to express the following conclusion:

> The aircraft's radar would have depicted the mountainous terrain.

I must admit that this proposition seemed to me at first sight to be very sound. Everyone has a general knowledge of how radar works. A series of repetitive radio pulses are transmitted from the radar installation and, as the radio waves strike an object in the distance, they will be deflected back towards the radar screen, where the presence and location of the identified object will show up. The exact distance and the bearing of the object can be ascertained by looking at the screen.

I had seen the operation of radar on ships and aircraft some years prior to my involvement with the Mount Erebus tragedy. I had been on the flight deck of an international jet on two or three occasions and had been interested in observing the radar returns on the screen. I could remember, as I still do, flying right across the continent of Australia on the flight deck of a South African Airlines jet and, while following the progress of the aircraft from a map, watching the radar screen pick up, in the distance, features such as rivers and mountains.

But this preliminary view on my part came to be qualified by something said during the Royal Commission hearing by more than one of the pilots who gave evidence.

The most notable example came from evidence given by Captain Lawson who had been the original briefing supervisor of aircrews. He had held that position until January 1, 1978 and had been succeeded by Captain Wilson. Captain Lawson had been called as a witness by the airline for the primary purpose of explaining the briefing procedures.

Captain Lawson had been to Antarctica on two occasions, first on February 15, 1977 and again on October 18, 1977. He had not been briefed by the airline to say anything about the radar installation with which DC10 aircraft are equipped, but he was cross-examined on the point.

During this cross-examination he said that on the radar the presence of ice produced a misleading effect. Mount Erebus did not stand out on the radar screen any more than ordinary ground cover and would have appeared only as terrain. He said that the return on the screen would not indicate that it was high terrain as distinct from sea ice. This came as a very surprising revelation.

The same type of evidence was given by at least one other Antarctic pilot. It therefore seemed quite clear that there was something about terrain covered with ice which prevented the highly sophisticated airborne radar on a DC10 from producing identifiable returns of high terrain which was covered with ice. I could not think what the reason for this could be and I did not hear any evidence which explained it. I made an inquiry through counsel assisting the Commission as to whether they believed that either Air New Zealand or Civil Aviation intended to call any evidence on this point and I was told some time later that no explanatory evidence was intended to be given by either of the parties.

I had been advised by Mr Martin Foley, a Californian counsel appearing for McDonnell Douglas at the hearings, that my only course would be to visit the Bendix Corporation premises at Fort Lauderdale in Florida, the place where the Bendix radar installations are manufactured, and to interview the experts there to find an explanation for this unusual behaviour of airborne radar when confronted with ice-covered terrain.

After completing our inquiries of the U.S. Navy witnesses in California, it was then necessary for Baragwanath and me to interview a witness in Pensacola and also the Bendix witnesses in Fort Lauderdale. As time was running short, it was decided to divide these labours. Baragwanath went to Pensacola and I went to Fort Lauderdale, arriving there on October 31, 1980. Through the good offices of Mr Foley, an appointment had been made for me to see the two top experts at the Bendix factory — Wayne Shear and Daryal Kuntman. The former was the Director of Engineering at Fort Lauderdale, the latter, Manager, Radar Systems Design.

I spent the day with these two experts. They had read the Chief Inspector's report and we discussed its contents as far as the references to radar were concerned. When they saw the passengers' photographs I showed them they were astounded. They had assumed from the Chief Inspector's report, as indeed had been assumed by all the New Zealand public, that the aircraft had been flying in cloud. They could now see that the aircraft, right up to the moment of impact, had been flying in clear air. They asked why the Chief Inspector's report had not contained at least one of these photographs, as this would have dispelled the general understanding that the aircraft had been flying in cloud. I could only reply by saying that I had frequently asked myself the same question.

The two experts then explained to me the effect of ice upon radar returns. They pointed out that the weather radar installation on DC10 aircraft was a highly sophisticated piece of equipment. They said that radar could be programmed to look for particular items of information, and that, in the case of the system fitted to a DC10, it was set, as it was in most other jet airliners, primarily to look for cloud.

The importance of this is that when an aircraft enters cloud, it will almost always suffer from turbulence, caused by moisture in the cloud. Therefore, when a modern jet is travelling in daylight the crew will disengage the Nav track when they see cloud ahead so as to circumvent it, and will then re-engage it after they have made the detour. But at night time the cloud in the distance may not be observable. The radar therefore picks up at long range the presence of any cloud ahead because the radio pulses transmitted from the radar installation are programmed to detect moisture.

Consequently, when the radio pulses strike cloud, the moisture in the cloud causes them to rebound back to the radar screen on the aircraft. If the content of rain precipitation in the cloud is heavy then there is a strong return on the screen, and if the precipitation is light then there is a correspondingly lighter return. But in every case the radar screen will depict the outline of the cloud ahead, and will of course indicate its approximate distance from the aircraft.

Then the experts examined the question of the effect of ice when it is detected by the radar installation. Naturally, they had no experience of testing this radar equipment on big jets flying at low altitudes over ice terrain because such flights were unknown except where jets landed on snow-covered airfields. But they asked me if there was any moisture content in the ice in Antarctic. I replied in the negative — the Antarctic is almost devoid of moisture, even to the extent that, geographically, it is considered drier than the Sahara Desert. Consequently, the ice surface of the Ross Sea was totally dry as was the thick coating of ice on Mount Erebus. The experts then said that in these circumstances it was unlikely that the radio pulses emanating from the installation on the aircraft would provide any return.

Mr Shear produced for my inspection the technical booklets issued for the guidance of airline operators who used this type of airborne radar on their aircraft. One of these booklets had been produced at the hearing as one of the exhibits of Air New Zealand. In that handbook, Messrs Shear and Kuntman pointed to a printed warning relating to the possible presence of ice crystals in the air. The pilot may see on his weather radar a clear picture of cloud ahead, and he will estimate that he can climb over the cloud. But there is a danger that the area above the cloud may be filled with ice crystals formed by the freezing of raindrops as they are propelled upwards by the wind inside the cloud. Ice crystals in the air are productive of severe turbulence, but the radio waves from the radar will pass through the ice crystals because the crystals will be dry.

The radio waves will therefore travel on, disregarding the ice crystals, until they reach some cloud far ahead which is within its range. So, unless the pilot is alert to the ice crystal danger, he can fly into apparently clear air above cloud and encounter severe turbulence. The Bendix handbook also contained the following warning: 'Dry snowfall has not been detected with any success on weather radar'.

The result of all this was that, in the opinion of the Bendix experts, the accuracy of any radar return on Flight TE901 would be doubtful. If it were not for the preceding pack ice and the ice shelf, then the aircrew might see that there were some solid structures below the aircraft and in their path. But the prior returns off pack ice, calm water, and ice shelf, would mask any return received from the mountain because the latter would look like the previous returns from the pack ice.

These comments by the Bendix experts related to the radar being set in the 'mapping mode', and they were saying in effect that there would not be any noticeable difference in the return being received from ice on the ground and from high terrain covered with ice. It might be possible, so they said, for a pilot to note a slight change in the return from high ice-covered terrain as opposed to that received from the adjacent ice shelf and pack ice by reason of the 'shadow' effect produced by the presence of high ground ahead undetected by the radar, but the latter effect would be distorted and unclear. If the pilot had been in the area before, he might suspect that there was some type of high terrain covered with ice in the flight path of the aircraft. But he would only deduce this because he had flown over the area before. That is, although his eyes would see the same type of blurred return which he had been obtaining from pack ice, his pre-existing knowledge of the terrain would cause him to reject mentally those parts of the uncertain radar picture which did not resemble terrain which was known to him.

So the effect of the Bendix evidence was that not only would the DC10 weather radar (set in the 'mapping' mode) give a return hard to distinguish from pack ice, even though the return was being received from high ground, but that type of return would tend to confirm in the captain's mind that he was flying over pack ice in the centre of McMurdo Sound, if indeed that is where he believed he was.

We then discussed what the position would be if the aircraft had been flying directly at Mount Erebus at 2,000 feet with the radar set in the 'weather' mode, seeing that the 'mapping' mode would be of no assistance at that low altitude. If the radar set was switched on at all, it was more likely to have been in the 'weather' mode.

On this point, the Bendix opinion was that because the slopes of the mountainside were covered in snow and ice which was totally dry, then the return from the mountain would be nil. Even though this particular radar equipment was programmed only to detect moisture, it would nevertheless give a return off high terrain composed of rock or earth, but a thick coating of dry snow and dry ice on the northern slopes of Mount Erebus would cause the radar beam to be totally absorbed and make it impossible for any return to be received. This opinion was based upon the inability of the radar pulses from the radar to achieve any return once they penetrated the crystalline structure of dry snow and dry ice. The scientific basis for this was then explained to me.

If there is a water film on top of ice caused by some degree of melting, then the radar beam will give a reasonably clear return. If, on the other hand, the beam strikes ice which is totally dry then the beam, or rather the radio waves which comprise the beam, will be absorbed by the ice surface and will penetrate the dry ice. The more they penetrate the dry ice, the more power they lose. If the radio waves should strike a damp layer somewhere in the ice, then they would impart an immediate return to the aircraft's radar, but the return will be fairly weak. If however, there is no damp ice layer beneath the dry surface, then the radio waves will continue on into the ice and be absorbed by it.

The reason for the difference between a return from rock and a return from dry ice is that the radio waves act rather like light waves. A light wave will not penetrate rock, but it will penetrate ice. So with a radio wave. It followed, therefore, in the opinion of the Bendix experts, that there was nothing in the theory that the radar on the DC10, if set in the 'weather' mode, would have detected the presence of the ice-covered slopes of the mountain ahead.

During the course of the day I was taken over the extensive and very modern factory where all types of radio and radar sets are manufactured and saw many varieties of newly designed radar installations, which were all demonstrated to me. At the end of a long day, I returned to my hotel on the beachfront at Fort Lauderdale and in due course went for a swim in the tepid waters of the South Atlantic. Afterwards I lay on the beach and I reflected upon what I had been told that day.

This assertion by the Chief Inspector that the airborne radar would have depicted the mountain had been featured very prominently in the New Zealand press when his report was published. The radar reference had been printed in block type headlines and the same opinion had, of course, been distributed throughout the world. The immediate reaction of the public, I could have no doubt, had been the same as my own. The aircrew had failed to look at the radar screen when flying in impaired visibility and to see the clear and unmistakable outline of the mountain right in front of them. But now, as was painfully clear, this was a complete fallacy.

I remembered that during the day I had asked Mr Shear whether they had had any query from any quarter about radar returns which might have been received by this DC10 as it approached Ross Island. They said they had only had one query, and that had come from McDonnell Douglas and they had told them just what they had told me.

I remembered how the Chief Inspector had been cross-examined as to where he got the information that the radar on the aircraft would have depicted the mountainous terrain ahead. He said he had got the information from an 'expert' at McDonnell Douglas. But it appeared that the 'expert' had not made the position entirely clear. This was another example of the results which had been obtained by the Chief Inspector by virtue of a verbal discussion which he had used as the basis of a very serious finding in his report. I remembered that when he had been asked by counsel to identify the 'expert' from whom he had received this information, he had said that he did not recall his name. Such are the dangers of relying upon second-hand hearsay.

I left Fort Lauderdale and flew up to Washington where I was joined by Baragwanath. Our task in Washington was twofold. In the first place we had to interview one remaining U.S. Navy witness in the presence of Lieutenant Commander Fessler, and then we had to visit the offices of the National Transportation Safety Board and listen to the flight deck recorder tape through the listening and filtering instruments used for deciphering such tapes. This was to be done for us by Colonel Paul Turner who had supervised the original transcribing of the tapes.

The next day Baragwanath and I duly reported at the Pentagon and, after being cleared for security purposes by Lieutenant Commander Fessler, we were escorted down the labyrinth of corridors of that fabled structure to an interviewing room.

The procedure followed was the same as previously. We asked the witness the necessary questions and he answered them, and from time to time various points were elucidated by appropriate questions from the Lieutenant Commander. I need not recapitulate what we were told, as I have already given a condensed account of what all these witnesses had to tell us.

Baragwanath and I were acutely aware that we had not interviewed three particular witnesses who had been on duty at McMurdo Air Traffic Control on the day in question. They were the radar operator at the control tower, the radio operator at the tower, and the radio operator at Mac Centre who had been monitoring the transmissions from the tower and who had himself spoken to the DC10 on his HF transmitter.

We had discussed this point after concluding our conversations with the witnesses at Fort Hueneme in California. We had known before we left New Zealand that one of these witnesses had left the

Navy and was no longer subject to Navy jurisdiction. We knew that another had made a brief and not very informative statement at McMurdo not long after the disaster, and we had been told that he did not desire to add to what he had then said. As to the third witness, his position seemed to be a little obscure. The Lieutenant Commander said that this man was somewhere in the southern part of the United States, probably at Memphis, and he undertook to attempt to have him located, and to see whether he was prepared to make any statement to us. On the other hand, it was clear that this process was going to take some two or three days and Baragwanath and I were already running to a very tight schedule. For example, we were expected daily at Nepean in Canada for the purpose of interviewing Mr Shannon and we were very anxious indeed not to miss that interview.

Ultimately we decided, though not without some measure of regret, that we would not trouble the Lieutenant Commander further with requests to see any other U.S. Navy personnel. We were actuated in this decision by a fairly simple logical presumption. We knew that the radar operator at the tower would say that the DC10 had never appeared on his screen, and that there had been no transmissions from the tower to the DC10 over approximately the last five minutes before the crash. We were reasonably sure that the radio operator at Mac Centre would say that to the best of his knowledge those statements were correct, and we were certain that he would confirm that he himself had no cause to believe that the airliner was in any danger over that vital period.

There was another point which had given us some anxious thought. I was sure that there must have been a U.S. Navy Board of Inquiry at McMurdo not long after the disaster. It was inconceivable that this disaster could take place in U.S. Navy controlled airspace without some form of Navy inquiry as to the procedure of their air traffic control personnel on the day of the disaster. I was also fairly sure that the Board of Inquiry had made findings of culpability against one or more of the air traffic control personnel, but I was also aware that such findings, if they had been made, were likely to have been directed at non-compliance with specific Navy procedures laid down for air traffic control in that region, and might not necessarily have imputed any blame for the disaster on any member of the U.S. Navy. So the question was, should I raise with the Lieutenant Commander the question of whether there had been a Board of Inquiry? Should I endeavour, if the answer was in the affirmative, to inquire what the conclusions of that board may have been?

After due deliberation, I decided against it.

In the first place, I doubted whether the Lieutenant Commander would have any authority to answer even the first question. Whether or not a Board of Inquiry had been held was purely an internal matter affecting the U.S. Navy alone. We had already been given full co-operation by the Lieutenant Commander with regard to any information we wanted as to the air traffic control facilities at McMurdo, and how they were operated. He had gone to considerable trouble to assemble the necessary witnesses to suit our convenience, and he had also secured the attendance of Major Gumble to describe to us at first hand his approach to McMurdo in the U.S. Navy Starlifter which had been following the DC10 on the day in question. The Navy had been under no legal obligation to provide all this evidence. I was unwilling to press our inquiries any further.

I was sure that the Lieutenant Commander would never obtain authority from the Navy to reveal the findings of any Board of Inquiry which might have been established. And, to state my position with complete candour, I planned to seek authority, through Lieutenant Commander Fessler, to inspect the air traffic control facilities at McMurdo. Again I would be dependent upon U.S. Navy co-operation to be afforded this advantage. It was just possible that any questions directed at the hearings or findings of a Board of Inquiry might inspire some justifiable resentment on the part of the U.S. Navy and there was a risk of my not being given permission to set foot upon Navy installations at McMurdo.

With these considerations in mind, I then told the Lieutenant Commander that our inquiries of U.S. Navy witnesses could now be taken to be complete. Baragwanath and I both thanked him for his courtesy and co-operation.

I then raised the question of inspecting the air traffic control facilities in Antarctica and I said that I expected to go down there on or about November 28, being the first anniversary of the crash. I received a favourable response to this request and the Lieutenant Commander said that he would seek permission for such an inspection and he was sure that permission would be granted. He went on to say, however, that I would not be permitted to interrogate any member of the U.S. Navy at McMurdo without the Lieutenant Commander himself being present. In other words, the procedure would be the same as adopted up to this point. I said that I fully acknowledged the right of the Navy to have a legal officer present at any interrogation of Navy personnel in Antarctica, but, I pointed out that, since the air traffic control personnel who had been immediately connected with operational duties on the day were all now in the United States, I could not think of any person down there with whom it would be worthwhile to have any discussion. Mind you, I had not forgotten Chief Warrant Officer Choyce Prewitt, of whom I had heard from various sources. He had been in operational control of Mac Centre on the day of the disaster. I knew that he was still in Antarctica and I suspected that this might be the man the Lieutenant Commander had in mind when he stipulated that he would need to be present at any interview.

However, it was finally arranged that if I would notify the Navy of the actual dates when I would be in Antarctica, arrangements would be made for me to be shown around the U.S. Navy installations. But it was again specified that there was to be no interrogation of any Navy personnel otherwise than in the presence of the Lieutenant Commander who would fly down there himself if necessary for that purpose. I gave my undertaking that I would ask no questions of any Navy personnel in Antarctica.

Thus concluded our final discussion with Lieutenant Commander Fessler. We thanked him again for all he had done for us and he conducted us through the labyrinth of corridors and said goodbye to us on the Pentagon steps.

XV

LISTENING TO THE CVR TAPES

Our purpose in taking the flight deck tapes overseas was to listen to the relevant sections through the sophisticated listening devices available at the National Transportation Safety Board's offices in Washington. We also intended to listen to them again at Farnborough in the United Kingdom with the co-operation of Mr W.H. Tench, the Chief Inspector of Air Accidents there.

This planned investigation of the aircraft tapes had been inspired, as will be remembered, by the dissatisfaction expressed at the inquiry by Captain Arthur Cooper, who had been present at the Washington transcription, at the way in which the transcription had been presented by the Chief Inspector in his report. Captain Cooper had resented the insertion into the Washington transcript of two remarks which appeared to refer to bad visibility outside the aircraft. And it will be remembered that the Chief Inspector, who had not been at Washington, had said in evidence that he had taken the tapes at a later date to Farnborough which possessed, in his opinion, listening equipment which was superior to that available in Washington. The Chief Inspector had justified his insertion of these two remarks on the grounds that they had become decipherable at Farnborough when they had not been decipherable at Washington.

On the other hand, it was Captain Cooper's view that the Washington transcript had been the best available, and that there had been a specific agreement between him and the Air Accidents Investigation Office in New Zealand that the transcript so laboriously completed at Washington would not be added to or amended without his prior knowledge.

The two insertions made by the Chief Inspector and published by him in his report without further reference to Captain Cooper had been as follows:

Unknown Voice:	Bit thick here eh Bert?
Flight Engineer Moloney:	Yeah my . . . oath.

174

Then the next insertion which immediately followed the remarks quoted above had been:

Flight Engineer Moloney: You're really a long while on
                            instruments at this time
                            are you.

It had been the contention of Captain Cooper that these comments had not in fact been decipherable in that sense.

These were the remarks which were treated as having referred to the weather. The suggestion that the weather had been 'thick' had been seized upon by the news media in New Zealand and overseas, as suggesting that the aircraft was flying in cloud. And it was not only the public who had formed that impression — the avionic experts at Bendix had drawn the same conclusion. Yet all the available passengers' photographs had shown that the aircraft was flying in clear air. But, as I have said, the Chief Inspector's report had not included any of the passengers' photographs. So one principal purpose of our inquiry into these tapes was to find out whether Captain Cooper's criticism of these 'weather' inserts was justified.

Then there were the purported expressions of alarm said to have been uttered during the final stages of the flight. Again, these had been eagerly seized upon by the news media when the Chief Inspector's report had been released. The Chief Inspector had said, 'There were discussions on the flight deck indicating that some of the speakers believed they were to the west of Mount Erebus but the two flight engineers on the flight deck had voiced frequent queries about the procedure and expressed their mounting alarm as the approach continued at low level toward the area of low cloud.' On the other hand, as Captain Cooper had demonstrated at the hearing, if you eliminated from the transcript everything but the discussions between the two pilots, then it was obvious that neither pilot expressed any 'alarm' at all. And when the tape had been played over at Auckland in my presence it was evident that every word said by each pilot was unmistakable, in marked contrast to anything said by anyone else.

The foregoing comment on the discussions between the two pilots had been recognised by the Chief Inspector because he had also said this — 'The CVR record revealed that the pilots' demeanour was composed and confident during the aircraft's approach to the accident area which was covered by a low overcast.' The Chief Inspector had therefore suggested, though not stating the fact directly, that the pilots disregarded the 'mounting alarm' of the two flight engineers. Was this really so? I had by this time travelled on the flight deck of DC10 and other aircraft on several occasions. I had observed in operation the 'joint monitoring' system which in modern passenger jets is accepted by all flight crews. A co-pilot is entitled to express his opinion of any expressed intention of the pilot in command with reference to the handling of the aircraft. A flight engineer too is entitled to express his view. In the case of TE901 there had been two flight engineers on the flight deck. It would have been standard practice for either or both of them to have indicated their opinions to both pilots on the best way to handle or manoeuvre the aircraft. If they had plainly indicated 'mounting alarm' then why was it that neither pilot responded? That was the big question.

So we had decided to verify, as best we could, the suggestion that the flight engineers had been disagreeing with the decision of the pilot in command to descend through breaks in the cloud and then level out on an approach towards what the Chief Inspector obviously thought was low cloud.

It will be recognised that by this time, I was sufficiently acquainted with the 'whiteout' phenomenon to realise that there would be no 'low cloud' in front of the aircraft. In that case, what had the flight engineers been worried about? Why had neither pilot ever mentioned low cloud in front of the aircraft?

Then there had been that section of the published transcript which had read as follows:

> Where's Erebus in relation to us at the moment?
> Left about (twenty) or (twenty) five miles
> Left do you reckon?
> Well I don't know . . . I think
> I've been looking for it
> Yep Yep
> I think it'll be erh
> I'm just thinking of any high ground in the area that's all
> I think it'll be left yes
> Yes I reckon about here
> Yes . . . no no I don't really know
> That's the edge

Apart from the words 'Yep Yep' which were identified as being spoken by First Officer Cassin, none of these observations had been made by either pilot. But the section just quoted created the irresistible impression that the aircrew did not know where the aircraft was. Then within about half a minute there had been two unidentified voices speaking as follows:

What's wrong?
Make up your mind soon or...

Once again, these two unidentified remarks certainly pointed to lack of knowledge on the part of the speakers as to the location of the aircraft. But the speakers had not been identified as crew members and their supposed comments could not be verified with any precision.

The Chief Inspector had very fairly pointed out to us at Auckland, when the tapes were played, that apart from the discussions between the two pilots, the rest of the recording on the tapes had been indistinct and garbled and that there had been obviously many phrases and sometimes sentences which were part of two conversations simultaneously taking place between people behind the pilots. These people would have included not only the flight engineers, but passengers on the flight deck. And when we had heard the tapes in Auckland we had all been alarmed at the extent to which all remarks, other than those of the pilots, had been inaudible except for occasional groups of words.

So, in due course, Baragwanath and I kept our appointment with Colonel Turner, who had a room full of sophisticated sound apparatus. He had a variety of filters which could be operated so as to suppress background noise, to some extent, and to bring out as clearly as possible words which were being said. At our request, he played over those portions of the tapes in which we were interested. They were played through different filters and were replayed over and over again so that we could do our best to relate what was in the transcript to what we were hearing.

It was all too clear that the Chief Inspector's reservations about garbled crosstalk were highly valid. Identifiable words and phrases had been written out by the transcribers and, where possible, the identity of the speaker had been specified. But there was no doubt, even where the identity of the speaker had been verified by Captain Cooper or his companions, that the words which could be heard were only in sequence in so far as they amounted to phrases, and were obviously in many cases the product of simultaneous conversations being carried on by people in the flight deck and behind the two pilots.

I could see now why it had taken seven days to attempt to produce some type of record of what had been said on the flight deck over a period of thirty minutes. On the other hand, the transcribers had been under a duty to record whatever identifiable words or phrases had been said. And it had been understood by all parties that, with the exception of the remarks of the pilots, a good deal of the transcript was the result of agreement between the transcribers to set down a consensus of opinion as to what had probably been said. The transcribers could have done no more.

I knew by this time why it was that only the remarks of the pilots could safely be relied upon. The flight deck microphone was installed in the roof immediately above and between the heads of the two pilots. But, unfortunately, that location did not prevent the recording of remarks made by other persons behind the two pilots and indeed extending as far back as the galley which is located just behind the flight deck. And I had also observed that if the commentator on a flight had been sitting in the 'jump seat' directly behind the pilot in command, and if he had leaned forward to the left of the pilot in command so as to make some remark to him, then the commentator's remark might not only be garbled, but perhaps entirely inaudible because the pilot's body would be directly between the commentator and the microphone.

As to the two alleged remarks about the weather, Colonel Turner was quite unwilling to accept that they had been made. First there was the unknown person who was supposed to have said 'Bit thick here eh Bert?'. We found upon listening repeatedly to this segment of conversation that the word 'here' was not in fact said. This was a disturbing revelation. It was the word 'here' which made all the difference. Colonel Turner's interpretation of this remark was that a speaker was in fact saying, 'This is Cape Bird'. And, of course, this meant that the purported response by Flight Engineer Moloney, 'Yeah my . . . oath' was not an affirmative response, as it appeared to be on the transcript, to someone saying that the weather was a 'bit thick here'. In addition to all this, we knew that there had been no crew member on the flight deck by the name of 'Bert'.

Then there was the reference by Flight Engineer Moloney to being 'a long while on . . . instruments'. Colonel Turner was again definite that this remark about 'instruments' really comprised two sections of an interlocking conversation, and that no reference to the DC10 being flown on 'instruments' on its approach to McMurdo could be inferred.

We eventually completed the process of playing and replaying the tapes. It seemed at this stage as if nothing had been said about the weather being 'thick'. It was also clear that the remarks of the two pilots had never disclosed any element of concern. The 'mounting alarm' of the flight engineers was, in our view, not evident at all from what we could hear through Colonel Turner's listening devices.

It was also clear that the great majority of the transcription of what was said by persons other than the pilots was, at the best, only guesswork and that it was certainly not possible, when listening to the tapes under these circumstances, to infer that any member of the flight crew was uncertain of the aircraft's position. All one could say was that there had been more than one question by a flight engineer and probably also by one of the pilots as to verifying the aircraft's position, but these remarks had been unquestionably associated with a reference to a map. You could hear the rustling of a large map when these comments were being made. And, speaking for myself, it was obvious that the computer track of the pre-existing flight path had indeed been plotted by Captain Collins on a large map and that remarks of this kind represented a comparison between the readout on the instrument panel of the miles to run with an indication on the map of that point of the plotted computer track which corresponded with that particular distance from the destination waypoint.

It was apparent that the interpretation by one person of the sequence of disconnected remarks on the transcript would certainly be controlled by the state of mind of the interpreter. Suppose that someone had formed an initial impression that the aircrew were uncertain of their position. It would then be all too simple to read and re-read the transcript and interpret the document more and more in that sense. But suppose that someone else, satisfied that the computer track had been plotted on a map, and knowing that the pilot in command had consistently locked the aircraft back on to Nav track after each orbit, had been sure that it was not possible for either pilot or either engineer to have been 'uncertain' of the aircraft's position at any given moment, which would certainly be the approach of anyone familiar with the operation of a modern wide-bodied passenger jet. How would such a person interpret the transcript? Again, his approach might be determined by his state of mind. He would unquestionably disregard all the words and phrases which appeared to indicate any uncertainty by the aircrew as to where they were. He would treat any remarks of that kind as being casual discussion between people on the flight deck who were not members of the aircrew.

The playing of the flight deck recorder tapes at the Royal Air Force Station at Farnborough had been arranged for us by Mr W. H. Tench, the Chief Inspector of Accidents at the Department of Trade in the United Kingdom. After long experience as a military pilot and later as an airline pilot for KLM Royal Dutch Airlines, he had in 1955 been appointed an Inspector of Air Accidents and he had served in the Accident Investigation Branch ever since.

Mr Tench had given evidence before the Royal Commission at Auckland some weeks previously as he happened to be in New Zealand for an international conference, and counsel assisting the Commission had taken the advantage of his presence to procure evidence from him as to the English investigation procedures.

Mr Tench took us out to Farnborough where we met Mr Shaddick, and also the voice recorder technician. Then we went through the same process as at Washington — the relevant portions of the tape were played through various types of filters. We came to the same conclusion as we had at Washington. As far as the two alleged comments involving the weather were concerned, we found once more that we could not discern the word 'here' as following the word 'thick'. It appeared that the technician had been unaware that there was no person called 'Bert' on the flight deck, and we assumed that the Chief Inspector from New Zealand had also been unaware of this fact when discussing the transcript with the technician at Farnborough. As to the other sentence involving the word 'instruments', we came to the same conclusion as at Washington.

I was tempted to enquire as to how the technician came to agree with the New Zealand Chief Inspector about inserting these two extracts, if indeed he had done so, but decided not to pursue that inquiry. I had to bear in mind that the Chief Inspector had not been at Washington, and he had believed, evidently, that the sound equipment at Farnborough was superior to the equipment at Washington, and he had apparently gone to Farnborough in an attempt to improve the quality of the transcript. However, it appeared that since the original transcription in Washington, the equipment available to Colonel Turner had been improved by the acquisition of a highly sophisticated new model of listening device and, of course, in Washington, Baragwanath and I had had the advantage of this new equipment.

But all this did not get over the thrust of the objection by the Airline Pilots' Association that these two significant additions to the Washington transcript, with their obvious appeal to the public and the news media, had been accomplished and that the amended transcript had then been revealed to the public in breach of the clear understanding reached with the pilots who went to Washington that no amendment would be made or considered without their consent.

We felt obliged to raise with Mr Tench the truly appalling sound quality of the flight deck recording system installed in

DC10 aircraft. We pointed out that, with the exception of statements made by the two pilots, the majority of the rest of the words which could be deciphered were so inaudible and so disjointed that it was almost impossible for anyone to prepare a reliable record. We found that Mr Tench agreed with this criticism and went on to explain the different equipment installed in British aircraft. The British sound system enables the separate statements or remarks of each member of the flight deck to be separately recorded. The main tape contains the voices of each member of the crew but the voices are reproduced with perfect clarity, and if it is desired to concentrate attention on what one particular crew member was saying, then, by adjusting the listening mechanism, one can shut out all other voices and listen to that voice alone.

By way of example, Messrs Tench and Shaddick played over a flight deck tape recording involving an incident when a BOAC VC10 was climbing away from Kennedy Airport in New York when one of the engines caught fire. The various instructions and responses of crew members were just as clear as if the crew members were sitting around the table in our room at Farnborough. Baragwanath and I were deeply impressed by the completely unperturbed voices of the crew as the pre-determined emergency drill was carried out. We noticed that the Captain's announcement to passengers on the PA system was almost casual in its urbane presentation. He did not seek to mask the nature of the emergency but made the simple announcement, in terms of deprecating simplicity, that one of the engines had caught fire, but that the fire had been put out and that the aircraft would be returning to Kennedy Airport.

One major difficulty in interpreting tapes such as we were dealing with lies in the fact that many remarks may have been made to the accompaniment of a gesture towards some land feature and, without the advantage of knowing these additional facts, it is not only possible, but probable, that a phrase thought to convey one meaning may, in fact, have been conveying another.

There were some examples of phrases or part sentences which were clearly audible and some of them were without any doubt made with reference to the view being obtained from the flight deck. To take just one example, there was the sentence 'Those conditions don't look too good do they?'. This might justifiably have been a reference to weather conditions. But what conditions were they? Where were they located? The speaker was almost certainly pointing in some direction. Did he mean the weather conditions forward of the aircraft, or was he pointing left or right?

And were the 'conditions' close at hand, or fifty miles away? This is only one example taken at random from the transcript. There were many others.

I could understand the resentment of the Airline Pilots' Association at the publication of the entire thirty-minute transcript with all its manifold opportunities for mistaken interpretation. But the Chief Inspector had been obliged, in terms of the settled format of his report, to include the best possible transcript of the flight deck recorder tapes.

Later, in his London office, we talked with Mr Tench about air accident investigation in the United Kingdom. As Chief Inspector of Accidents, he is part of that branch of the Department of Trade dealing with aviation. However, as Chief Inspector, he is not responsible to any individual official within the Department of Trade and has direct access to, and must report to, the Secretary of State himself.

Where a serious accident involving heavy loss of life occurs, the Chief Inspector will either inform the Secretary of State verbally of the details or write a short minute to the Secretary within a day or two of the occurrence. Thereupon the Secretary of State will decide whether to order a public inquiry. If it is to be held, the Accident Investigation Branch of the Department of Trade investigates the facts of the accident and then the reports from the various inspectors in charge of different aspects of the disaster are passed over to the office of the Attorney General and copies of the reports are passed also to representatives of all interested parties. Those reports then form the basis of evidence which will be prepared by the Attorney General's legal staff and by lawyers for interested parties in preparation for the forthcoming inquiry.

However, where there is to be no public inquiry, the procedure is much the same as in New Zealand. An inspector prepares a draft report and gives interested persons the right to submit their views upon it. He then prepares a final report and the Chief Inspector submits it to the Secretary of State. The form of accident reports of this kind, as in New Zealand, follows the form specified in Annex 13 of the Chicago International Convention on Civil Aviation.

As will be seen, it is not possible under the United Kingdom system for the Air Accidents Branch to prepare and then publish its own opinion when a public inquiry has been directed. In New Zealand, it is possible in terms of the statute law for this to be done. As described already, the publication of the report of the New Zealand Chief Inspector when a Royal Commission had been directed, had been the occasion of widespread criticism in

New Zealand. The New Zealand Chief Inspector in his report had recommended that the United Kingdom practice as described by Mr Tench be adopted in New Zealand.

Because Mr Shaddick had been present in Auckland for some weeks from the commencement of the Royal Commission hearing, we had arranged for his London office to be provided with the transcripts of evidence as they became available. For that reason, Mr Tench's Accident Investigation Branch had been in close touch with the progress of the inquiry. We were not sure at that stage exactly what further evidence would be produced to the Royal Commission by Air New Zealand, because Baragwanath and Harrison had been experiencing the customary difficulty in obtaining any advance knowledge of their intentions. But we told Mr Tench that, in addition to the hearing of further witnesses, we also intended to visit Antarctica and that we hoped that all the evidence would be completed some time in December.

Before I left Mr Tench he said that there were some observations he would like to make. He said that he was not referring to any specific air disaster in what he had to say and would only speak in general terms.

Mr Tench then developed his thesis. His experience of air accident investigation both in the United Kingdom and on the Continent had been very wide and, of course he was familiar, as one might expect, with the detailed aspects of all serious air disasters in the world over previous years. He said that it had often been a matter for regret that aircraft operators and aircraft manufacturers had frequently thought it advisable to make an attempt to conceal some fact or occurrence which it was thought might be damaging to the particular company concerned. He had seen this at first hand, and other international examples were well known to him.

Mr Tench said that these misguided attempts were nearly always unsuccessful. If there were any form of inquiry, whether under the English system or the other inquiry systems operating on the Continent or in the United States of America, then the long process of evidence and cross-examination inevitably uncovered the secret fact which the airline operator or manufacturer had been seeking to conceal. In the result, the final determination reached by the inquiry tribunal was almost always highly critical of the vain attempt to conceal damaging evidence.

Mr Tench said that he believed that as a result of the policies of his own branch, there had been a very much needed reform in this aspect of air accident investigation, at least as far as the United Kingdom was concerned. He said that he believed that airline operators in the United Kingdom, and in many countries on the Continent, were now convinced that the best policy was to admit at the outset some error or malfunction which might have been a contributing cause to the accident under inquiry. He said that his branch seldom encountered these evasive tactics which were sometimes fairly common in aircraft disasters. He went on to say, however, that there had been recent incidents of such tactics being employed overseas. He did not refer to specific cases. Neither did I, but I knew to what he was referring. He had in mind the Windsor Incident of 1972, the Turkish Airlines disaster at Paris in 1974, and I suspected that he was well informed about the American Airlines disaster at Chicago in May 1979 about which I had ascertained the details myself while in the United States.

I asked whether, in his experience, these concealment tactics by aircraft operators or manufacturers were sometimes the result of pressure by the insurance companies which carried the indemnity liability for claims arising out of a disaster. Mr Tench said that he thought that this was a conceivable view (it crossed my mind that he would have made an excellent diplomat) but went on to say that he believed that insurance companies had now recognised that the exposure of attempts at concealment was almost inevitable when litigation went to Court, and was very likely to inflame the feelings of juries when it came to formulating awards of damages. I had the impression that this might have been a discreet reference to the state of California in the United States, where awards of damages in aircraft litigation are notoriously exorbitant.

Therefore, Mr Tench held the clear view, based on his long and wide experience, that it was far better for errors contributing to aircraft disasters to be freely admitted from the outset. A false case presented at an inquiry or in litigation was invariably exposed. The public image of the airline or manufacturer was damaged as a result. Far better to tell the truth at the outset and secure immediate public approval of the honest disclosure that there had been some avoidable malfunction, either administrative or mechanical, which had been the prime cause of the disaster.

I carefully noted these opinions which certainly came from an expert source. Mr Tench was closely familiar, as I knew, with the transcript of evidence so far given at the Commission hearings. But he had been speaking only in general terms.

Baragwanath and I later agreed, after we had said our farewell to Mr Tench, that we had been dealing with a supremely intelligent Government official, who was a complete master of his field of expertise.

XVI

THE ANXIETIES OF MR MARTIN

The purpose for which we had gone to the United Kingdom was now accomplished and Baragwanath and I booked a flight for New Zealand leaving in about thirty-six hours. But I then received a telephone call from Martin Foley, who was in London for several days discussing various aviation insurance claims with Lloyds for whom Mr Foley's firm acted in California. Mr Foley told me that there was someone who wanted to see me urgently before I left London.

It turned out that this was a London solicitor by the name of Peter Martin. It appeared that Mr Martin was an aviation law expert who did a great deal of legal work for Lloyds underwriters in the aviation field. Indeed, he was a joint editor of one of the leading English text books on aviation law and had, in fact, been in New Zealand to deliver a paper on that subject at the New Zealand Law Conference held in Auckland in 1978. But I had not been at the conference and Mr Martin's name was unknown to me.

Martin Foley said that Mr Martin would make himself available at any time so as to have a few words with me in connection with the Royal Commission hearings. It seemed to me discourteous to decline this request. Lloyds underwriters were not a represented party before the Royal Commission, but their Auckland lawyer had been supplied, with my approval, with the daily transcripts of evidence at the end of each day of the hearings in Auckland, and I was aware that his reason for wanting the transcripts was to send them across to the appropriate department of Lloyds underwriters in London. I therefore said that I was willing to see Mr Martin, but had only a limited time available.

Martin Foley discreetly intimated that he thought it very likely that Mr Martin wanted to find out something and I said that I had already reached that conclusion myself and that I would take the precaution of having Baragwanath with me at the meeting. It might, of course, have been that Mr Martin only wanted to

arrange a meeting purely as a courtesy to the Royal
Commissioner, but I felt that Martin Foley's opinion of the reason
for the meeting should be kept carefully in mind.

It was arranged that Baragwanath and I would meet Mr Martin
at the main office of Lloyds underwriters. First he took us on a
tour of the operational part of the building where we saw the
scores of brokers' agents busy recording insurance transactions in
their respective cubicles and watched the process by which a
placement of insurance over the telephone was accepted and the
appropriate cover note drawn up. All this was very interesting.
The rapidity and the volume of business being transacted was a
striking example of the worldwide activities of Lloyds in all fields
of insurance.

Then Mr Martin escorted us upstairs to Lloyds Coffee House, a
celebrated institution in London city. Many are the transactions
informally completed there over a friendly cup of coffee.

So far, Baragwanath and I had received no hint as to Mr
Martin's purpose in desiring this urgent meeting. However, I had
noted the interesting and courteous prelude to the proposed
discussion. When I was in practice at the Bar I had had a great deal
to do with big companies, including some big American
corporations, and I was familiar with the process by which an
atmosphere of friendly hospitality was first cultivated before some
anxious consultation was embarked upon. These seemed to be the
methods being assiduously employed by our host.

Once seated around the coffee table Mr Martin lost no time in
revealing the reason for the meeting. He said that he had been
receiving the daily transcripts of evidence from New Zealand and
that these had been carefully studied as they arrived, not only by
him, but by his aviation clients at Lloyds. Mr Martin said that
both he and his clients were becoming alarmed at the nature of the
evidence being produced before me by Air New Zealand.

He then ventured upon the delicate task of endeavouring to find
out whether I agreed with him. He need not have troubled to be so
circumspect. I had already warned the Air New Zealand lawyers in
Auckland that their altitude and navigation evidence was very
plainly of suspect credibility, and that everyone at the hearing
viewed these two branches of evidence as being carefully
concocted by the two groups of witnesses so as to conceal, if
possible, the real facts of the alleged 16,000 feet minimum safe
altitude and the real facts behind the shift of the destination
waypoint nearly thirty miles to the west of its original position. I
therefore had no hesitation in expressing the same doubts to Mr
Martin.

I should mention that before Mr Martin made any reference to the subject-matter of our discussion he had first stated that everything that passed between us was to be 'without prejudice'. In other words, he meant that everything said would be off the record. At this point Baragwanath had immediately intervened. He said that any discussion involving the inquiry was to be very much on the record. Our discussions could not on any account be regarded as being 'without prejudice'. This warning was, of course, perfectly correct. I had power under my warrant as Royal Commissioner to make such inquiries as I thought fit and nothing said to me could be concealed from my ultimate report to the Government unless for good reason I felt it should be.

Mr Martin then immediately reversed his standpoint and agreed that I was at liberty to use, as I thought fit, anything that passed between the three of us at the discussion.

As soon as his opening remarks and my response had taken place I was, of course, aware of what it was that Mr Martin wanted to know. He wanted to know whether his own anxiety as to the evidence being produced before me was shared by me. He now knew the answer.

But I took care to express the same stipulation as I had expressed to the airline's lawyers in Auckland. I pointed out that the evidence was not yet concluded. Having regard to the unexpected evidence of Captain Wilson, the suggestion that the aircrews were not permitted to descend below 16,000 feet on the approach to McMurdo had now been destroyed. But, as to the navigation evidence, with its almost incredible basis of multiple and concurrent errors committed by top experts in the navigation field, there was still evidence which might show that my current impression was wrong. Other witnesses from the Operations Division of the airline were to be called. There might well be evidence, perhaps documentary evidence, which ultimately could confirm the fact that the western waypoint had originally been fixed by mistake, and that no one in the Navigation Section had ever been aware of the mistake. This was all distinctly unlikely, as I had already pointed out, but my years in the courtroom had warned me that one must never adopt a final conclusion until all the evidence is known. I particularly pointed out that there might emerge some document supporting the navigation witnesses. Air New Zealand documents were popping up here and there at the hearing like rabbits out of a hat, though mostly because of the industry of counsel for the passengers' consortium, counsel for the Airline Pilots' Association, and counsel assisting the Commission.

Mr Martin readily accepted all these observations. And then he told us why he had felt it necessary to impart these views to me before I left London. He said that he felt it likely that in the end I would be compelled to make adverse findings against Air New Zealand as to the credibility of their evidence. He said he wanted it clearly understood that Lloyds had played no part in the concocting of these false explanations.

Mr Martin said that he feared that if I made findings of credibility against the airline, I might at the same time suggest that Lloyds must be deeply involved in the way the facts had been presented. Mr Martin went on to say that such a comment would be unwarranted and would be deeply resented by Lloyds. He said that the circumstances of the disaster were unique, that the occurrence of the computer mistake was unprecedented in airline disasters, and that he had left the control of the inquiry in the hands of Air New Zealand. He then ventured upon a bitter criticism of the Air New Zealand management and used a particularly vituperative epithet with regard to Mr Davis. He said it had been a great mistake to leave the presentation of the case solely within the control of the Air New Zealand management.

Mr Martin then went on to justify the allegations he was making. He said that he would like it to be clearly understood that he had made it clear to Air New Zealand on his visit to Auckland in the early part of 1980 that Lloyds would be paying out all claims without reference to the $42,000 limit of liability. He said that this notification to Air New Zealand surely made it certain that Lloyds had no possible motive for being involved in the type of evidence which I had been listening to. He asked that I should bear this carefully in mind.

By this stage Mr Martin had made his point. He plainly regarded the altitude and navigation evidence which I had listened to as being false, but he wanted it clearly understood that neither he nor Lloyds were in any way implicated and that when findings of credibility were made against the airline, as he clearly thought was inevitable, it would be unfair for me to make any statement suggesting that the airline's insurers must necessarily have been involved.

Then there occurred, as the final phase of our discussion, a disquisition by Mr Martin on the general nature of aircraft disaster inquiries. He spoke, as I was now well aware, from a wide background of experience. I had discovered from his conversation that it was part of his duty to travel regularly to all parts of the world inquiring into aircraft disasters in which Lloyds were involved. He was very clearly a highly experienced lawyer with vast experience in this field and he was, moreover, a man of singular fluency. By and large, he was a very impressive individual. He proceeded to describe the dangers which always were present when there was a public inquiry into an air disaster and in general, his remarks were almost identical to those made to me previously by Mr Tench, except that the latter had been speaking in general terms. Mr Martin did not purport to be speaking in general terms.

Mr Martin said that, when an airline was confronted with the occurrence of a disaster involving loss of life and an inquiry was convened, its first step was always to retain the best counsel available. This, of course, was an entirely natural thing for an airline or an aircraft manufacturer to do. Unfortunately, so Mr Martin went on to say, the counsel so selected were always successful trial counsel, and they tended to see every such inquiry as a court case. Their whole careers had been bound up with the concept that success at the Bar depended upon winning cases. Airline counsel in such situations always tried to 'win the case' for their clients. The fact that the hearing was an inquiry to ascertain the true facts very seldom crossed their minds. They only saw it as a courtroom battle between one side and another.

Mr Martin said that he thought this attitude was highly regrettable. It was the responsibility of counsel in such circumstances, so he said, to advise their clients that if there had been an operational blunder or a technical malfunction or a failure to observe proper aircraft maintenance procedures, then those facts should be admitted. If they were not admitted and the issues were fought out as contentious issues and the airline or the manufacturer was ultimately declared by the inquiry to have been negligent, then the only possible result was that there must be findings of credibility made against the airline or the manufacturer, as the case might be.

Mr Martin made it clear that such a result was unfortunate in the extreme from the point of view of the company held to be at fault, and its employees. In other words, he was telling me what Mr Tench had told me. If there had been a blunder then the airline or the manufacturer should admit it at the outset. By doing so, it enhanced its own reputation and incurred the sympathy of all people associated with the consequences of the disaster.

Mr Martin's thesis was persuasively presented, and I knew that he was speaking against a background of very wide experience of air disaster inquiries and litigation. He was speaking very much from the insurance point of view when he deprecated, with such emphasis, the tactics of airline operators and manufacturers who presented false evidence or concocted false explanations so as to exculpate themselves from blame, because of the tendency of juries, especially in the United States of America, to express their dissatisfaction of such malpractices by awarding exorbitant amounts by way of damages.

On this note the interview ended. I had no doubt in my own mind that, apart from the unfavourable impression made upon Mr Martin by reading the transcript of the altitude and navigation evidence, he had also been informed by the legal advisers for Air New Zealand that the initial attempt to place all blame on the aircrew did not look likely to succeed. And I also had no doubt that he had been warned from New Zealand that I was plainly not impressed by this evidence. What he had done, probably, was merely to obtain confirmation of the doubts which he knew I must have about the credibility of the airline evidence on these two topics. There was nothing improper in his approach to me. I was perfectly willing to tell him what I thought about the evidence at this particular stage and I was fully aware of the fact that he would report my views to Air New Zealand.

During the journey from London to New Zealand I gave a great deal of thought to our interview with Mr Martin. I hoped that he did not really think that we would take him seriously when he inferred that the conduct of the airline's case before the Royal Commission had been left solely in the hands of the airline management.

I was perfectly well aware of the position taken by aircraft insurers in relation to a formal inquiry into a major air disaster. Their practice was to monitor very closely indeed every stage of the inquiry and this was one of their legal rights created by the contract of insurance. I knew that Lloyds had estimated its ultimate liability for passengers' claims at a maximum of $50 million.

I had no doubt at all that Mr Martin would have been fully aware, at all stages, of the details of the evidence which the airline was proposing to tender. And, although I could not be certain, I thought that he might have been supplied in advance with the written statements of the evidence which the airline proposed to give. If there had been some aspects of the evidence which he considered potentially harmful to Lloyds, then he would not have hesitated to intervene. It was Lloyds who would have to pay in the end, not Air New Zealand. He would without doubt have studied and approved the nature of the case which the airline was proposing to advance and he would have been quite right in giving his approval.

The statements of witnesses would have, at first sight, made convincing reading. But as he studied the transcripts of cross-examination progressively sent to London by his Auckland representative, he would have become alarmed, and not without cause, at the way in which the interlocking altitude and navigation defences had been broken down in cross-examination. The looming probability of adverse findings of credibility against the airline had caused him such disquiet as to attempt to find out from me whether I shared his view. And I had told him without hesitation that my professional views as to credibility were identical with his own. I could only presume that he foresaw, as an experienced aviation lawyer, that there was no possibility now of undoing the damage which had been done. Hence his anxiety to ensure that findings of credibility against the airline witnesses would not be publicly associated with Lloyds.

XVII

FOLLOWING THE FLIGHT TRACK OF TE901

It had previously been arranged that I would be taken to McMurdo Sound to look at the scene of the accident and the Antarctic environment, and it had been proposed that I should go there on the first anniversary of the disaster so that the northward extent of the pack ice would be at about the same latitude as it had been on November 28, 1979. After Baragwanath and I returned to New Zealand from London these arrangements to visit Antarctica were finalised.

We were taken there in a Royal New Zealand Air Force Hercules aircraft commanded by Wing Commander Ken Gayfer, and were accompanied by Mr Harrison, Air Marshal Sir Rochford Hughes (technical consultant to counsel assisting the Commission), Air Commodore David Crooks of the Royal New Zealand Air Force, Mr Bob Thomson and Mr J.E. Davies (director of administration and general services for Air New Zealand). The party also included Mr John Macdonald (aviation reporter for the *Auckland Star*) and Miss Carmel Friedlander who was visiting Antarctica on behalf of Radio and Television New Zealand.

Having been equipped with the appropriate Antarctic clothing we boarded the Hercules at Christchurch Airport early on the morning of November 26, 1980 and flew away to the south on our long journey.

Like all turbo-prop aircraft, the big Hercules seemed to sit in the air; it was as steady as a rock. We sat on webbing seats surrounded by our packs, alternately dozing and waking as the slow hours crept by. We were all provided with earplugs so as to deaden the roar of the engines, a circumstance which certainly inhibited any tendency towards conversation, and from time to time various members of our party would get up and walk a few paces back and forth in the restricted space between the big containers of supplies and the area where we were sitting. The containers weighed seventeen tons, so we were told, and between them and the high wall of the fuselage there was about two feet of space, so it was possible to extend our short walks by venturing now and then down these narrow corridors towards the rear of the aircraft.

From time to time I looked out the windows. We were travelling through the night, and you could see the distant stars above, but below all was dark. Then someone came aft from the flight deck and reported that we were at the parallel of 60° south latitude, the point of no return, and that McMurdo radio had reported clear weather, so we would fly on to the south according to schedule.

Over the later stage of the journey the flight crew gradually lowered the temperature inside the aircraft with the object of arriving at McMurdo with a cabin temperature somewhere near the outside temperature which would be below freezing point. We had begun the flight wearing lined boots and thick trousers and shirts, and as we went onwards through the night we put on our thick woollen jerseys and some of our number donned their padded anoraks as well.

The distance from Christchurch to McMurdo is about 2,500 miles, and after we had travelled something over 2,000 miles, Wing-Commander Gayfer came aft and suggested that I go up to the flight deck for the remainder of the journey. I climbed the steep staircase and went forward to a position behind the pilot, Flight Lieutenant Russell. For some time the darkness of the air, as seen through the fuselage windows, had been fading as we approached the region of perpetual daylight where, at that time of the year, the sun circles the Pole for twenty-four hours each day, and we had been entering what might be called the light of dawn. But now, looking forward from the flight deck, the view to the far south was sharp and clear in the sunlight. We were flying over the northern tip of Victoria Land, and there below us was the northern edge of the continent of Antarctica. I looked at the altimeter — we were flying at 31,000 feet. Below us there were patches of cloud but, as we flew on, the clouds receded backwards, the view below became as clear as the view ahead, and I found myself looking at one of the most striking panoramic scenes the world can provide.

On our right was a long sequence of mountain peaks stretching far away to the south, dwindling unbroken into the horizon towards the South Pole. The sun was shining on the snow and ice of the mountain tops, and the peaks glittered and shone as if touched with white fire. Far away to the west were further ranges and valleys, forming a white tableau which extended in clear air to the very limit of vision. Over to our left was the dark blue expanse of the Ross Sea, and straight ahead on the horizon I could just see the vague white haze which marked the coast where the Ross Sea ice-shelf began. The sheer immensity of this limitless expanse of sea and snow seemed almost unreal.

We flew out over the eastern coast of Victoria Land and over the Ross Sea. As we crossed the coast we could see Coulman Island on our left. Coulman Island is twenty miles long and rises to 6,000 feet at its highest point. I remembered the letter I had received from a New Zealand cartographer who had been in this region in 1962 on an aerial mapping survey. He had given me a remarkable example, which he had seen himself, of the rapid weather changes in Antarctica. The sky had been quite clear and then banks of cloud had assembled over and descended upon Coulman Island and, within four minutes, the whole of the island had disappeared from view, with the cloud at sea level.

We were about 275 miles from the TACAN at Williams Field. Now we could see the ice floes of the pack ice, and between them were strips of sea water of varying widths. These sea 'leads', as I was told they were called, became ever more narrow as we travelled south. By contrast with the dark blue sea further north, the strips of sea between the ice floes gleamed darkly, as if washed with black light. They were indistinguishable, at this distance, from the strips of black rock which marked at intervals the coastline of Victoria Land, so that when looking towards Victoria Land I could not tell if the shallow black strips along the coast were rock faces or sea water.

Soon I was able to identify, far away in front of us, the outline of Ross Island and the entrance to McMurdo Sound. Wing-Commander Gayfer moved forward and occupied the co-pilot's seat. I put on the headphones and listened to our radio transmission to Mac Centre as the Wing-Commander notified them of our intentions. He would fly on track towards the Byrd reporting point, turn left over Ross Island so as to fly over the wreckage of the DC10, and then turn back to the north before turning around again and flying towards Lewis Bay. In the meantime, the Hercules was descending from its cruising altitude. We levelled out at 18,000 feet and after a while descended further in preparation for the left-hand sweep over the lower slopes of Mount Erebus.

The mountain was now plainly in view. From its flat summit there flowed a long plume of steam which drifted away to the east until it dissipated in the cold air. I could see the horizontal shallow strips of rock — two or three of them — lying at the foot of the ice cliff, 300 feet high, which formed the edge of Ross Island. The pack ice had given way to solid ice, covered with snow, at about the entrance to Lewis Bay, but these strips of black rock looked very like sea leads until we got closer. The entrance to McMurdo Sound grew near and as Cape Bird came up on our left, the Wing-Commander directed a left-hand turn.

As the aircraft rolled to the left and crossed the saddle between Mount Bird and Mount Erebus, there came into view the surviving remnants of the wreckage of the DC10. The drifting snow had covered everything except the three engines and two or three large sections of the fuselage. They each carried a dusting of snow but were clearly identifiable in the dazzling sunshine. They lay almost in line up the mountain slope. After we had flown over the crash site we turned left again and flew away to the north. On our left there came into view the distinctive outline of Beaufort Island, a rock outcrop protruding through the snow-covered pack ice. The island was covered with snow except for its southern face of perpendicular black rock. We flew on until we reached a point about forty miles due north of the crash site and then the pilot turned 180° and reversed his course. On the northern run we had been climbing steadily and when we turned to the south we were at 17,000 feet. The Wing-Commander then directed a course of 357° grid. We were now at the same altitude and on the same heading as Captain Collins would have been when he saw the cloud break below him, and decided to orbit downwards to 2,000 feet and take the DC10 towards McMurdo under the cloud base which lay ahead.

Thus we commenced our approach to Ross Island, following the exact track of the disaster aircraft. The Wing-Commander had in front of him a map of the area and upon it had been overprinted the approach path of the DC10, complete with all data as to speed, altitudes, rate of descent, turning angles, and the like. Then there followed a series of orders to the pilot. We flew straight on, gradually descending, until we were about eleven miles from the crash site which was clearly visible ahead. At this point the Wing-Commander directed a right-hand 180° descending turn. As we completed the turn I could see the edge of Cape Bird down below us. We flew north and descended to 9,000 feet, and then the Wing-Commander, continually checking the C-130 instruments against his map, ordered the right-hand 180° turn which would bring us back to our original course towards the crash site. The heading of the Hercules was checked and a slight correction was made so as to resume our heading of 357° Grid. Thus we had completed the first orbiting sequence, following faithfully the exact track and descending altitude of the DC10.

We flew on to the south. When we were about eight miles from the crash site, and now at 8,000 feet, a left turn of 180° was ordered, and this was the start of the second orbit. The turn completed, we again flew to the north, gradually descending as we did so. About twenty-eight miles north of the crash site, and now at 7,000 feet, another left-hand turn of 180° was carried out. Again the Hercules was brought back to a heading of 357° Grid. Once satisfied that we were exactly on course towards the crash site, the Wing-Commander directed a descent to 2,000 feet at a specified rate of descent. He directed an air speed of 260 knots. So now we had completed the two orbits and, at a point twenty-eight miles north of the crash site we were following the track of the DC10 as it flew to the south with about five minutes remaining before its destruction on the thick glacial ice of the mountainside.

The Wing-Commander said that he would hold his course until the latest moment consistent with a reasonable margin of safety. He then instructed Flight Lieutenant Russell that, upon the order being given, he was to execute a left-hand 180° turn. The Flight Lieutenant pre-set the banking angle on his controls. The Hercules continued on — course 357° Grid, altitude 2,000 feet, speed 260 knots.

When I had listened to the garbled sounds of the voice tapes at Washington I had believed, in accordance with Colonel Turner's opinion, that Peter Mulgrew said, 'This is Cape Bird'. He had been sitting directly behind Captain Collins, and judging from the sound of his voice on the tape, probably leaning forward. Knowing the exact time of impact, and the exact time when the remark was made, and taking the speed of the DC10 to have been 260 knots, it had been possible by a simple calculation to fix the geographical point at which Mulgrew had spoken. He had made his remark when the DC10 had been about thirty-seven miles from the TACAN. I wanted to see whatever Mulgrew had seen when he spoke, and with thirty-seven miles to run I was going to be at the same location in the air as he had been when, as I thought very probable, he had identified Cape Bird.

The Hercules does not have a digital DME readout and I asked the navigator our position. He said it was forty miles from the TACAN. From my position just behind the pilot I looked forward and to the left. Twelve miles away to the left there came into sight, through the narrow cockpit window, the western coastline of Cape Tennyson. This was the moment when Mulgrew had spoken. After making allowances for the better sideways vision from the flight deck of a DC10, it seemed to me that Mulgrew had spoken within half a minute or so of first seeing the shoreline of Cape Tennyson. And if he had been speaking to Captain Collins, as I thought was possible, then Collins would have seen from the map in front of him that Cape Bird was forward and to his left, thus confirming Mulgrew's identification, and Collins would have known that Mulgrew was pointing out what to him was a familiar feature. So what we thought originally seemed now to be verified. Mulgrew had seen Cape Tennyson appear, and had identified it as Cape Bird.

By now we were rapidly closing on the crash site. I looked at the rock outcrop located higher up and to the left of the crash site. On the day of the disaster the cloud base of about 3,000 feet had been lower than the rock outcrop. So all the terrain in front, once the pack ice had terminated, had been white, with one exception, and that had been the two shallow strips of black rock running along the base of the ice cliff. From further back these had looked like strips of sea water at the base of the cliff but now, in the sunlight, with the edges of the ice cliff sharply defined, I could see that they were strips of rock. But, on the day of the disaster, so Mr Shannon and Professor Day and Captain Ginsburg had each assured me, the forward terrain would have been flat, the ice cliff non-existent, and the strips of rock at sea level indistinguishable from sea leads. And apart from that, the DC10 had been flying with a nose-up attitude of 5°, which meant that the black strips would have been observed by the crew only at long range, disappearing below the forward windows when the aircraft was still several miles off. I could see what Captain Ginsburg had meant when he said that no one on the flight deck could have identified the black rock as anything but isolated thin strips of sea water in a long flat expanse of snow-covered ice.

I looked forward at the approaching mountainside. When Collins said, 'We're twenty-six miles north, we'll have to climb out of this' the actual position of the DC10 had been twenty-eight miles from the TACAN, the Navigation Computer Unit displaying a two-mile forward error. He had spoken those words when the airliner was two miles from impact. Wing-Commander Gayfer also spoke when the Hercules was about twenty-eight miles from the TACAN. He said, 'Turn now'. Flight Lieutenant Russell rolled the big aircraft over to the left, and turned away to the north. We had been about twenty-five seconds away from the ice slopes of Mount Erebus.

The Hercules flew north, then turned left into McMurdo Sound, flew over the Byrd reporting point, and then began its descent to Williams Field along the military flight path. After a perfect landing, which Flight Lieutenant Russell modestly attributed to the wheels touching the ice runway and sliding along it, we clambered stiffly out of the aircraft to be greeted by American and New Zealand officials and a battery of cameras. The snow was dazzling white in the bright sunlight. There was a slight but icy breeze. We had been in the air for 8 hours and 18 minutes.

Later, as I rested on my bunk in the warmth of the Scott Base building, I reflected on the aviation exercise which I have just described. I had seen the dark-edged shore of Cape Tennyson on the left and the dark-edged eastern shore of Cape Bird on the right, and that was what the crew of the DC10 had seen. I had seen the dark-edged shore of Cape Bird as we flew into McMurdo Sound and over to the right the shore of Cape Bernacchi, and these were the shorelines which the DC10 crew believed they were looking at. The flight track plotted on their map had shown the two capes to the left and right. They were seeing just what they expected to see. And when we had entered McMurdo Sound, the terrain beyond the two capes had extended forwards for forty miles as a flat white plain, and that was the sight which the crew of the DC10 had seen as they flew onwards in clear air under the low overcast.

I had been particularly struck with the similarity between the coastline of Cape Tennyson, as seen from Lewis Bay, and the coastline of Cape Bird, as seen from McMurdo Sound. They each had the same rounded linear formation. When Peter Mulgrew had looked forward and to his left, and had seen the coastline of Cape Tennyson, identifying it as Cape Bird, he had been looking at what was nearly a facsimile of the Cape Bird coastline as seen from McMurdo Sound.

The Hercules had turned away to the left about twenty-five seconds before impact. I kept thinking of Captain Collins' decision which he announced twenty seconds before impact, 'We're twenty-six miles north, we'll have to climb out of this.' But he did not turn away. He and First Officer Cassin then discussed whether they would turn to the right or to the left. Cassin suggested turning right, but Collins eventually decided to turn left. He adjusted his controls so as to pre-select the power increase and the rate of climb, and then disengaged the Nav mode by pulling out the Heading Select knob. Just as he turned the knob to the left, so as to turn the DC10 through the auto-pilot, the GPWS sounded, and it was then too late to turn away.

As was evident from listening to the voice tapes, there was no element of anxiety or urgency in the discussion between the two pilots as to which way they should turn the DC10. They were no doubt scanning the terrain in front of them. They certainly saw nothing to cause them alarm, and neither did anyone else on the flight deck. There can be no doubt as to what they saw. They were flying in clear air under a cloud base of not less than 2,500 feet, and the edge of the cloud lay horizontally and evenly across the white slope of the mountain. With the snow shadowed by the cloud, the ocular illusion characteristic of polar regions had sprung into life. The 300 feet high ice cliff had vanished, and the horizontal edge of the cloud base, lying across the rising white terrain, had appeared as a horizon many miles away. Hence the casual discussion as the DC10 flew on at 260 knots over the 3,500 yards between the aircraft and the mountain slope.

When Wing-Commander Gayfer gave his order to turn away, we were also 3,500 yards from the mountainside, and were also travelling at 260 knots. But in the light of the sun, and with no cloud in the sky above, the ice cliff and the rising ground beyond were sharp and clear. We had looked, and the crew of the DC10 had looked, at the same slope of ice and snow. Both aircraft had been flying in clear air, but we had been looking at different things. We had seen the white terrain as it really was. They had seen it totally and fatally disguised.

Suppose that there had been no discussion between Collins and Cassin about which way to turn. Suppose that Collins, having decided to fly away, had merely applied his power and climb settings, pulled out the Heading Select knob, and turned it left. His big aircraft, extremely manoeuvrable and highly powered, would have rolled into a left turn about 2,000 yards before the ice cliff and climbed safely away to the east and then to the north, just as we had done.

The discussion which had taken place between Collins and Cassin represented normal procedure. The direction of turn did not really matter because, on their assumed track, they were almost in the centre of McMurdo Sound which is a flat corridor nearly forty miles wide, and a 180° turn would involve a lateral sweep of only six miles. But a change of plan required discussion, in conformity with established inflight procedures, and the discussion lasted for only a quarter of a minute. But that quarter-minute delay was fatal. Such are the inequalities of chance.

But, equally significant, was the view I had seen from the Hercules of Beaufort Island. Again I had seen exactly what the crew of the DC10 had seen and from the same height and angle of vision. And I thought I had discovered why the crew never identified Beaufort Island, and I was sure now that I knew why Peter Mulgrew had not realised that Beaufort Island was on the wrong side of the aircraft.

One of the criticisms levelled at the aircrew of Flight TE901 had been their failure to identify Beaufort Island. During the orbiting sequences it had been plainly visible and it showed up very clearly in the passengers' photographs. It was certainly many miles to the west of the flight track plotted on the map, when it should have been many miles to the east. The island was clearly marked on Captain Collins' atlas and also, no doubt, on the map which he had procured on his own initiative for the purposes of the flight.

Before I went to Antarctica I must admit that I could see no answer to the allegation that the aircrew should have seen that they were on the wrong side of Beaufort Island. Of all the criticisms advanced so assiduously by the management against the aircrew, this alone had seemed valid. But, as so often happens, there is nothing like visiting the scene and making your own observations.

It was when I first saw Beaufort Island from the air on our approach to Lewis Bay that I realised why it had not occurred to the aircrew of the DC10 that they were looking at Beaufort Island. There it was, about twelve miles to our right. But then I looked further away to the right, towards the mountains of Victoria Land, and I knew that the flight track on Collins' map showed a flight path which would be nearly thirty miles to the right of the flight path of our Hercules. I visualised Collins flying in what he thought was the centre of McMurdo Sound, and looking at an island which he would have seen was unmarked on his map. From his point of view the island he was looking at was therefore nearly thirty miles to the west of Beaufort Island. The display on the HSI panel verified that his aircraft was flying exactly on course, therefore Beaufort Island was far away to his left. It could not be anywhere else. What Collins and Cassin were looking at, in their minds, was an anonymous island lying some distance off the coast of Victoria Land.

I could see now why there had been no fault on the part of the aircrew in failing to detect the identity of Beaufort Island. On the atlas and on the maps, Beaufort Island is marked as a distinctive black dot on a green background. But there are no green areas in Antarctica. What we actually saw from the Hercules, as I have said, was a rock outcrop protruding through the ice, the outcrop being almost totally covered by snow. It was quite a different visual situation, as I could see, from an aircraft flying over blue sea with every island, covered with bush or trees, easily discernible at long range. Those who had criticised the failure of the aircrew to identify Beaufort Island seemed to me to be people who did not understand the vast white immensity of the terrain. But, in particular, they clearly had not mentally placed themselves in the centre of McMurdo Sound and then asked themselves what they would think if they saw this snowy outcrop over to their right and knew, by reference to their map, that Beaufort Island was miles away to their left, and was probably another snowy mound in the bleak white landscape. Neither pilot had mentioned the island, either before, during or after the orbiting sequences, and when I surveyed this white landscape myself I could see why.

So much for the Beaufort Island theory and the simple unimaginative attribution of fault to the aircrew for not identifying that feature. But what about Peter Mulgrew? He had been to Antarctica on several occasions. He must have known what Beaufort Island looked like. Why had he not pointed it out to the aircrew? Before we left for Antarctica I had been giving this question careful consideration. Was it possible that for some reason, Mulgrew had never seen the island as the aircraft passed it by?

As we flew north in the course of the second orbit, I kept in mind the fact, ascertained from the transcripts of the voice tapes, that Mulgrew had been absent from the flight deck during the first orbit, and had not returned until the aircraft was about to turn left and complete the second orbit. According to the voice tapes, he first spoke at 0042:59 GMT and almost immediately afterwards, at 0043:20 GMT, Mulgrew got into his seat behind Captain Collins, a fact verified by a brief discussion, omitted from the official transcript but referred to in the draft prepared in America as an 'irrelevant conversation relative to installing commentator in his seat'.

Where was the DC10 when Mulgrew walked on to the flight deck, made his first remark, and then settled down in his seat? By calculating the air speed and the time interval between 0042:59 GMT and the impact time of 0049:50 GMT, it could be estimated that the DC10 had about thirty-four miles to run when Mulgrew arrived on the flight deck, and with thirty-two miles to run the aircraft was just beginning to roll to the left on its final turn.

So as soon as the Hercules commenced to roll to the left in completion of its final orbit I had looked forward and to the left at Beaufort Island, and from my position on the flight deck, which had been Mulgrew's position, Beaufort Island had immediately disappeared from view as the aircraft banked left at a 25° angle. It was clear from the voice tapes that Mulgrew had been looking for some physical feature to mention on the PA system, but I could see now why he had not pointed out Beaufort Island. While the passengers on the left side of the DC10 had been photographing the island, Mulgrew had been making his way forward to the flight deck, and just as he arrived the DC10 began its left turn. And, as the passengers on the right side of the aircraft began to photograph the island, it had then disappeared from the view of those on the left side of the aircraft, including Mulgrew.

It seemed to me that this sequence of events, supported as it was by our knowledge of the time when Mulgrew arrived on the flight deck, answered one of the major queries of the investigation. Mulgrew had been to Antarctica on previous occasions and he would have identified Beaufort Island without hesitation at low altitude during the orbiting sequences. But he had not seen it. During the first orbit and for most of the second orbit he had been somewhere in the cabin section, walking along, as apparently was his habit, talking to the passengers of whom the majority, as the passenger movie films had shown, were standing in the aisles. And then, as the time for his commentary approached, he had walked forward and entered the flight deck at the moment already described. It would not have been possible for him to have seen Beaufort Island whilst he was standing up, with the forward flight deck windows at waist level and, by the time he sat down, the DC10 was rolling left and the island was far away to his right and out of view.

As the aircraft straightened up and resumed its Nav track, Beaufort Island was now about four miles behind, and there could be no doubt, on this reconstruction, that as the DC10 flew onwards to disaster, Mulgrew had never had the chance to see that Beaufort Island was on the right of the aircraft instead of on the left, and to realise, with his past experience of the region, that they were flying directly at Ross Island. Even at an earlier stage, when the DC10 had first approached Beaufort Island at 18,000 feet, Mulgrew had still been in the cabin area, and unless bending down and looking out a right-hand window, which is unlikely, would not have seen Beaufort Island far below, especially as the northern aspect of the island is snow-covered and hard to detect against the pack ice and the snow.

In later days, I thought over again what I have just described. I tried to imagine Peter Mulgrew making his way forward along the aisle, moving a little slowly with his artificial legs, anxious to reach the flight deck and to take his seat so as to begin his main commentary of the flight — namely, a description of the landmarks and other features of McMurdo Sound and Scott Base, and the Black and White Islands, and principally, of course, the towering volcano which is Mount Erebus. Perhaps as he neared

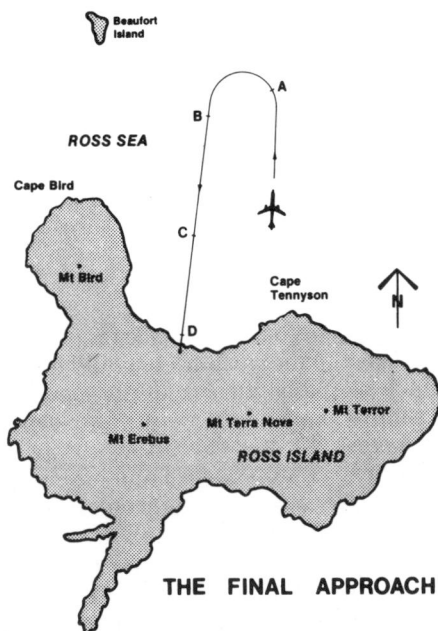

This diagram illustrates the author's reconstruction of the sequence of events on the final approach:

A — Mulgrew enters the flight deck and is helped into his seat

B — Mulgrew says, 'Taylor (the Taylor Valley) on the right now '

C — Mulgrew (pointing to Cape Tennyson) says, 'This is Cape Bird '

D — Collins says, 'We're 26 miles north — we'll have to climb out of this '

THE FINAL APPROACH

the flight deck a passenger detained him for a minute or two. Perhaps he stopped to converse with a group of people standing in the aisle. We know that there were passengers standing in the galley, just aft of the flight deck. Did he pause to answer their queries?

If only Mulgrew had reached the flight deck two minutes earlier, and taken his seat behind the pilot, with the DC10 still travelling north, he would have seen out of the window by his side the unmistakable outlines of Beaufort Island about seventeen miles away to his left. He would certainly have pointed it out to Captain Collins, and the latter, with one glance at his map, would have made the astounding discovery that the computer flight track plotted on his map was nearly thirty miles to the west of the flight track which had been typed into the DC10 computer.

I could not escape the conclusion that a delay of only two minutes in reaching the flight deck, a random chance for which Mulgrew was not responsible, had prevented him from averting the disaster. And I reflected, as I had done so often before, upon the malignity of the hovering fates which had shadowed throughout its journey the flight path of TE901.

XVIII

MY VISIT TO THE CRASH SITE

Arrangements had been made for me to be flown to the crash site, or as close to the crash site as could be managed, on November 28, which would be the first anniversary of the crash. However, the feasibility of the flight was going to depend upon the weather. On November 27, the day before the projected visit, a northerly weather front approached and enveloped Ross Island, bringing with it a low overcast. Vision out towards the north-west was clear but over to the true east, that is to say looking into the distance to the right of Ross Island, the overcast had now caused the snow to blend with the horizon so as to make it invisible, and it was impossible to say where the snow ended and the cloud began.

If these conditions persisted on the following day it was going to be difficult to fly to the crash site. With the low overcast covering Ross Island the helicopter pilot would probably not be able to tell whether he was flying into or over the slopes of Mount Erebus. However, it was hoped that the weather might clear and a programme was scheduled whereby the helicopter would leave at 11 a.m. the next day.

On the following morning, however, the low overcast still persisted and had now spread over Scott Base and well out to the true north. Over McMurdo, a little to the left of true north, visibility was still clear, and in particular towards the eastern borders of Victoria Land.

In these circumstances the helicopter flight scheduled for 11 a.m. had to be cancelled. The low overcast and the cloud covering Mount Erebus made it impossible to approach the mountain from the true south. But as the day went on we were advised that visibility over Lewis Bay was thought to be improving. We still had the low overcast and cloud between us and Mount Erebus, which was twenty miles to the north, but north of Lewis Bay and the northern slopes of the mountain were free from cloud. Thus it was worth an attempt to land on the black outcrop of rock about 4,000 feet up the slope and a little to the left of what had been the line of approach of the DC10. The helicopter therefore took off at 4 p.m. The passengers were myself, Baragwanath, Air Marshal Sir Rochford Hughes, Bob Thomson, and Edward Davies of Air New Zealand. Mr Davies was to place a wreath at the base of the cross which had been erected on the rock outcrop.

We flew away towards the north and the pilot, a highly experienced American, aimed at the saddle which runs between Mount Bird and Mount Erebus. Mount Bird was on our left, Mount Erebus on our right. Once over the saddle, which is about 3,000 feet high, we would be in Lewis Bay and crossing over the slopes of Mount Erebus which would be towering upwards to our right.

As we approached the saddle, heavy cloud surrounded Mount Bird and cloud was drifting in a general easterly direction across the saddle, but there were certain thin breaks in the pale cloud revealing occasional strips of sunlight on the snow.

The pilot first attempted to fly through the cloud breaks but we soon became engulfed in cloud, and were forced to turn back into the clear air. The pilot then decided to attempt to fly over the saddle but under the cloud base. The gap appeared to me to be minimal, but there proved to be enough clearance between the cloud base and the top of the saddle for the helicopter to fly through.

It had been decided that, if Lewis Bay was found to be either in cloud or covered by low overcast, we would have to fly away to the true north and then make a wide circling turn to the true south and return to McMurdo. However we found that the weather over Lewis Bay was free from cloud and there was bright sunlight. The helicopter then flew towards the true north and turned, coming back again on the same heading as had been adopted by the DC10.

As we approached the ice shelf at about seventy-five knots, it could be seen as clearly as it had been two days before, and the rising ground which began at the ice shelf was also clearly apparent in the sunlight. But then a disconcerting freak of the weather suddenly developed. The pale cloud drifting from Mount Bird towards Mount Erebus unexpectedly increased in height and within a minute or so the massive structure of Mount Erebus totally disappeared. This was certainly a striking illustration of the unpredictable weather patterns of Antarctica.

Then we noticed an ice fog lifting off the solid ice in front of us. It was drifting over the ice shelf and entirely concealing three or four miles of it to our left. But, further over to our left, we could see a narrow strip of black rock at about the level of the sea ice. This marked the western border of Cape Tennyson. Over to our right we could see a similar narrow strip of black rock which marked the edge of Cape Bird.

We flew over the crash site at low altitude and made several passes back and forth. The pieces of wreckage could now be seen more exactly. We then flew on to the black outcrop a little further up the mountain and to our left, where we landed after some delicate manoeuvring of the landing gear so as to avoid boulders. We all disembarked and I was able to look at the whole of the area surrounding the site of the disaster. We were between 3,000 and 4,000 feet up the mountain slope. The pale cloud kept drifting towards us from the direction of Cape Bird. Sometimes it was thick enough and high enough to blot out the sun. When this happened, the even white slope which ran down from where we were standing towards Cape Bird imperceptibly became almost level. It was hard to tell that the ground was sloping away before us.

Then the sun would penetrate the cloud again and illuminate the lower slopes of Mount Erebus. As soon as this happened the slope became clear in all its detail. But when the drifting cloud was high enough to obscure the sun, and when I looked upwards at the towering bulk of the mountain, the whole of this massive land figure would disappear.

I took some photographs and Mr Davies placed a wreath at the foot of a small cross which was embedded in the black rock not far away. He also had with him four containers of ashes of victims which the relatives desired to be scattered on the mountainside. With these solemnities concluded we walked back over the rock and snow to where the helicopter was waiting. Its engine had been prudently left running.

The two pilots had been keeping a wary eye on the drifting pale cloud. It was not far above our heads, and they had been prepared for the eventuality that we might suddenly be enveloped in it. If that occurred, then it was planned that the helicopter would lift off and fly north for something like twenty miles before turning to the left into McMurdo Sound. Then the pilot would turn left again and wait until he was picked up by the McMurdo radar. However, the cloud continued to stream slowly past above us and the base was high enough for us to fly away to the true west and to cross again the saddle between Mount Bird and Mount Erebus. We then were able to descend and return home in clear air at low altitude across the ice shelf. After the homeward flight of about twenty miles we landed once more at Scott Base.

I suppose the most striking feature of this visit to the crash site was the variation in surface contours which took place whenever the cloud obscured the sun. We had been looking in sunlight across the snow-covered slope of Mount Erebus towards the distant headland of Mount Bird about fifteen miles away. In sunlight, the descending slope or slopes were bright and clear, but the moment the sun disappeared the sharpness of the contour disappeared also, and it had seemed almost as if we were looking across practically flat white terrain.

These sudden fluctuations in the even white slopes in the foreground, with their shifting contours, had been a disconcerting and sinister revelation. We had been only onlookers at a dangerous peaceful scene, but for a polar aviator it was something else again. With a pale overcast above him obscuring the sun, and with clear air all around, the sloping contours of the snow would disappear. In every drifting bank of cloud lay the presence of death, silent and unseen. Such was the environment into which the airline management had arranged, so it seemed, for its airliners to fly, not only at low altitude but piloted by crews who had never flown in polar regions before.

I and my companions had already visited various parts of the Scott Base area and I had stood in the snow close to the control tower and looked for a long time to the north across twenty miles of snow at the southern slopes of Mount Erebus. It was there I came to the conclusion, as I stared at the mountain in the sunlit clear air, that the approaching airliner must surely have been visible on the radar at the tower as it turned away to the west on its first orbit. The track of the aircraft, as it emerged from behind the mountain and flew out to my left almost to the coastline of Cape Bird, must have shown up as a series of 'blips' on the radar screen at the tower, because, as I could see from where I stood, the line of sight between tower and aircraft had been uninterrupted. I could see no alternative to that conclusion.

I would naturally have been interested in looking at the radar screen in the tower, but I would have been even more interested had I been permitted to ask a few simple questions. But my arrangement with Lieutenant Commander Fessler had to be honoured. I was not to be allowed to ask anyone at the tower anything at all. I could only listen to what they chose to tell me.

I had been taken for a tour through McMurdo Centre shortly after arrival in Antarctica and had been impressed by the singular brevity of the technical descriptions given to me, Baragwanath, Harrison and Air Marshal Sir Rochford Hughes by a senior warrant officer who had conducted us throughout this big radio communication complex. I had also been impressed by his courteous hostility. I knew that this would have stemmed from a long signal from Washington warning the warrant officer of the possibility, which I had revealed in Washington, that the last few minutes of the ground tape might have been erased. The probability of such a signal from Washington had been made certain, so I thought, when the warrant officer had pointed to the banks of revolving reels of tape and had made the announcement that they recorded 'each and every word' of all radio transmissions to and from McMurdo base. He had particularly emphasised the quoted phrase and his tone had been unfriendly.

In addition to all this, on the previous evening when having a cup of coffee in the canteen, I had been favoured with some unauthorised information from one of the Americans. It had been apparent from the time he sat down on the opposite side of the table that he had spent the last couple of hours at one of the bars available at the American base. He was loquacious and confidential and alluded in humorous terms to a very long signal which he said had been received from Washington prior to my arrival. The warrant officer in charge of McMurdo Centre knew more about me, so my informant reported, than I did myself. He was vastly amused at this recollection, and repeated it more than once. 'They told us loud and clear, sir,' he said. 'They told us — don't tell him nothing.'

Under these circumstances, it seemed to me of only limited value to be escorted into the radar room at the tower. I had watched radar screens on previous occasions — on the ground, in the air and on one occasion aboard a ship. I could not help but feel that if any information would be gained by looking at the radar set and observing its capabilities, then that could safely be left to Air Marshal Sir Rochford Hughes.

During these cogitations I was approached by Bob Thomson and told that he and Air Commodore Crooks and Mr Davies were leaving that same night for New Zealand on a Royal Australian Air Force Hercules which was flying out at about 6.30 p.m. local time. I decided that I would fly out with them. I could see no further purpose in my remaining in Antarctica and waiting another day for our departure. I therefore arranged to fly out that night in the Australian aircraft and notified my companions accordingly.

When I boarded the Australian Hercules the flight captain asked me to stay on the flight deck during take-off. He said that there was something the flight crew would like me to see. The overcast was still low over the whole McMurdo area and the navigator, who had been at McMurdo that day last year, told me that the conditions were identical to those prevailing on the day of the fatal flight. The pilot in command then told me what he intended to do. He would fly out to the true east and attain a height of 1,000 feet, and then he would turn back and fly to the true west and pass Scott Base at 500 feet, before commencing the climb away to New Zealand. He asked me to look out for a snow ridge which we would encounter as we approached Scott Base.

Near the left-hand top edge of this ridge was a black outcrop of rock. The snow ridge then ran off to the right so that it would lie directly across our path. It was about 300 feet high. The purpose of the Australian flight crew in asking me to note in advance the position of this snow ridge was to demonstrate the visual illusion which they said I would observe as we approached the snow ridge from the air. I knew that the snow ridge was present, and had seen it on the previous two days in bright sunlight, and it was a very discernible feature, but the flight crew were aware that, with a low pale overcast of the kind then present, it would be difficult to distinguish.

We took off and flew away to the east. After a few miles, and at 1,000 feet, the pilot banked the aircraft to the left and we straightened up on a westerly course, with Scott Base ahead and on our right. The Hercules dropped to about 600 feet. The pilot pointed out the snow ridge across which he proposed to fly. It branched out to our left from the high ground near Scott Base, and at its top left-hand edge, at the point where the ridge terminated, there was a small black outcrop of rock. I could just make out the top of the ridge, even though it was white against the white panorama of the flat snow running away for miles beyond the ridge towards the distant peaks of Victoria Land.

Then I remembered something Captain Ginsburg had told me in Ohio. He had said that a single dark point of reference in the snow can relay to the brain a slope or a contour which the eye cannot distinguish. I lifted up my left hand and blocked the small black outcrop from my view. The top of the snow ridge disappeared instantly and I was now looking at a flat expanse of snow. As the Hercules flew over the top of the snow ridge I looked down out of the left-hand window behind the pilot and, as the white terrain fled swiftly below us, I caught a momentary glimpse of the top of the ridge just as we were directly overhead, whereas on the approach, with the black rock not visible, the ridge had not been there.

The crew told me that the overcast then subsisting at Scott Base was approximately the same as it had been one year before, and that the visual illusion to which I had been subjected was characteristic of what happened when flying over uniformly white terrain with an overcast of that nature. The flight captain and the navigator said that, in their opinion, this would be an exact replica of the visual deception to which Captain Collins must have been exposed as he flew under the same level of overcast when approaching Mount Erebus one year ago.

This had certainly been a striking demonstration of the whiteout phenomenon. I had known the location and the appearance of this snow ridge and I had seen it on the two previous days in bright sunlight. Its exact configuration had been clear and unmistakable, with the sun shining down on it out of a blue sky. But with a low overcast — despite the clear vision which extended for something like 100 miles in all directions — all slopes and undulations in the terrain ahead of the aircraft had disappeared once I had visually obliterated the single point of reference created by the small black rock outcrop standing about 300 feet above the ground.

After flying over Scott Base the aircraft flew out into the sound, maintaining a steady climb, and then turned to the north and continued its climb to its cruising altitude. I had kept an eye on the altimeter, and noticed that we entered the bottom of the cloud base at 3,000 feet and that we emerged from the pale coloured cloud at 5,000 feet. I looked over to the right. The top 7,000 feet of Mount Erebus stood out sharply in the clear air and the eternal thick high plume of steam and gas drifted slowly away to the east, ascending some thousands of feet. I moved forward between the pilot and co-pilot and looked backwards to my right as the mountain receded from view. I knew I was unlikely ever to see that majestic sight again.

I climbed down the vertical stairway from the flight deck to the cargo deck of the aircraft and sat for a while in one of the webbing seats which ran along the sides of the fuselage. Air Commodore Crooks was standing motionless, reading a book with close concentration. Now and then he would go for a brief walk towards the rear of the aircraft and back, but he would then resume his reading. I ventured to enquire as to why he did not sit down. The Air Commodore said that the light was better if you stood where he was standing, and that in any case he could concentrate better when he was standing up. I could only admire his stamina.

After a while I climbed up the stairs and resumed my position on the flight deck. By this time we had flown out of the daylight and into the night. The big aircraft kept steady on its course to Christchurch. Some time went by and then the pilot turned around, tapped me on the shoulder, and pointed out to his left. I looked out the window and, far away in the night sky, in the direction of the South Magnetic Pole, I saw an arresting sight. In the distance the sky was lit with long pale green streaks of fire. 'The Aurora Australis,' said the pilot laconically. I stared for a long time at this phenomenon as it gradually receded from view. I knew that such a display was associated with magnetic storms and frequently disrupted radio communications.

As we flew on through the night I reflected upon the singular whiteout phenomenon which the aircrew had demonstrated. I remembered the words of Professor Day. Apart from describing the 'flat light' illusion as an extreme optical deception, he had laid great stress upon the 'mental set' of the observer and had emphasised that, given a pre-conditioned mental picture in the eye of the observer, the failure of the visual system could not be said to be the cause of the error. Nor was it a result of a failure to be vigilant. It was simply a failure of the visual system itself.

I knew now what Professor Day had meant. I had known that the snow ridge was there. When I had seen that piece of black rock about 300 feet off the ground to my left it was my brain and not my eye which had intruded the barely perceptible white ridge running from left to right. But once I had removed the 'point of contrast' described by Professor Day and by Captain Ginsburg and when the apparently visible snow ridge disappeared it was because I was now dependent upon sight alone with no visible cue to inform me that the flat snow ahead was running abruptly uphill and was not flat at all.

As the Chief Inspector had said in his report: 'Those who have not been exposed to whiteout are often skeptical about the inability of those who have experienced it to estimate distances under these conditions, and to be aware of terrain changes, and the separation of sky and earth.'

I must express my gratitude to the intelligence and initiative of this Royal Australian Air Force flight crew who knew that the conditions were substantially identical to those prevailing on the day of the fatal flight, and who saw the opportunity to demonstrate this weird optical phenomenon which is difficult to understand unless it has actually been seen.

XIX

THE EVIDENCE
OF THE FAMILIES OF
THE TWO DEAD PILOTS

After our return to New Zealand I prepared a written account summarising the Antarctic trip and had it distributed to all counsel, just as Baragwanath and I had done in relation to our inquiries in the U.S.A., Canada and England. A date was then set for the final hearings of evidence before the Commission, there being a number of witnesses still to be heard.

I was notified by counsel for the Collins' estate that it was proposed to call the evidence of Mrs Collins, the widow of the dead pilot and of her two oldest children. They were going to testify, as I understood it, that, on the night before the fatal flight, Captain Collins had been working with maps and plotting instruments on a table in the dining room of their home and that he had spent a very considerable time on this task. It was to be established, in other words, that Captain Collins had procured his own large topographical map of the general McMurdo Sound area, and probably of the whole of the northward aspect as far as New Zealand, and that he had plotted on this map the flight track as laid down by the list of co-ordinates appearing on the flight plan produced at the briefing which had taken place nineteen days before the fatal flight.

Mrs Collins gave evidence. A quiet, composed witness, she was not overly articulate. Not the type of witness who volunteered anything, she would patiently await the question and then give a brief and clear answer. She maintained this studied composure throughout her evidence and her cross-examination.

If I had been advised correctly of the content of her evidence and that of her two daughters, then what they collectively had to say was of the greatest importance. If it was a safe inference from their observation of Captain Collins as he worked on his maps that he had indeed plotted the flight track either from New Zealand to the bottom of McMurdo Sound, or only from the Balleny Islands or Cape Hallett to the bottom of McMurdo Sound, then this evidence was vital because it explained, without any qualification, the persistence with which Captain Collins had flown on his computer track from Cape Hallett southwards, and why he had meticulously rearmed the Nav mode of the aircraft at the conclusion of each of his two descending orbits.

It was this latter precaution which had emerged as probably the most significant factor of the last few minutes of the aircraft's flight. The fact that the Nav mode had been rearmed at the conclusion of each orbit had of course been faithfully recorded by the 'black box'. And the aircraft had therefore been locked into its Nav mode and thus on to its computer track, right up to the moment just prior to impact when Captain Collins had disengaged the Nav mode upon his decision to fly away.

I remembered how this pre-flight plotting of the computer track had been raised with the Chief Inspector in cross-examination. He had agreed that this information had been known to him. It had been pointed out that he had not referred to this information in his accident report. He had replied by saying that this information was not 'evidence' as he understood that term. It had appeared that the Chief Inspector only treated something as 'evidence' if it was recorded in some document which he had seen or was otherwise recorded on a map in some irrefutable form. I had thought at the time that this simplistic view of what amounted to 'evidence' would have some surprising results if applied to the ordinary litigation process where juries and judges were required to draw fixed conclusions that something had happened because of other factors which pointed unmistakably to the occurrence of some fact or incident, despite the fact that no direct evidence of the occurrence was available.

As I have said, this evidence from the Collins family was going to be of prime importance. If Captain Collins had indeed plotted his track, and he was a qualified navigator, then during the last few minutes of the flight he had been certain of the aircraft's position at every stage. He had only to glance at the distance-to-run indicator on his instrument panel and then compare that with the map spread out in front of him. He could then see that his position lay on the plotted track at a distance of exactly so many miles from the destination waypoint. All this, of course, made nonsense of the Chief Inspector's persistent opinion that the crew were 'uncertain' of their position. I therefore paid very close attention to what Mrs Collins had to say.

She first of all referred to her husband's copy of the hardback limited edition of the *New Zealand Atlas* which had been given to her husband by her parents in April 1977. He would frequently refer to it to illustrate to his children various geographical features in New Zealand which he had seen during his various flights. Mrs Collins said that in addition to this and other atlases her husband had a varied collection of maps from all over the world. In other words, he had his own library of maps and atlases.

Mrs Collins said that on the evening of November 27, 1979 her husband had been working at the dining room table in their home in preparation for the Antarctic flight on the following day. He had been working with a number of maps and other materials which were spread out over the table. He had evidently spent between one-and-a-half to two hours working on these maps and materials on the table. At 10 p.m. he had completed his mapping preparations for the flight and had then packed up the maps and materials and placed them in his black flight bag in preparation for the following morning.

Mrs Collins said that, following the disaster, she had given no further thought to the *New Zealand Atlas* until December 19, 1979 when she had been visited by the Chief Inspector. Unknown to Mrs Collins, her husband had taken the atlas with him to the briefing nineteen days before the fatal flight. The Chief Inspector had evidently found this out; hence his visit. The Chief Inspector asked Mrs Collins if she had the atlas. She looked for it in its usual place on the bookshelf, but found that it was missing, as was its dust cover. She made an extensive search of their home but the atlas was not found. She then became aware, for the first time, that her husband had taken it with him on the flight.

A copy of the atlas referred to had already been produced in evidence as Exhibit 46. Page 185 (which in the original is about 30 by 25 centimetres) depicts the area from Beaufort Island at the top to a point about ninety miles south of McMurdo at the bottom. The map provides a large scale and closely detailed reference to every topographical feature in McMurdo Sound, with something like twenty place names clearly indicated alongside the respective features. A pilot would only have to look at the scale at the bottom of Page 185 and then look at the distance-to-run readout on his panel to see at a glance his exact position.

I was under no illusion as to why the Chief Inspector had been so anxious to see the atlas. He wanted to see whether the destination waypoint had been plotted by Captain Collins when he attended the briefing. But the atlas had gone with Captain Collins on the aircraft.

Then Mrs Collins referred to her husband's diary. This was a small personal diary about ten centimetres long by six centimetres wide, red in colour, and he always carried it in his jacket pocket. He used it to note flight numbers, departure and arrival times, and personal memoranda.

Mrs Collins said that her husband was an habitual note-taker. He had a black ring-binder notebook for the recording of technical information and she said that, when she last saw it, it contained its customary collection of looseleaf pages. But when it was returned to her by the airline, the pages were missing. She said she had seen her husband place this ring-binder notebook in his flight bag from time to time. In view of the fact that her methodical husband would have been unlikely to have taken in his flight bag a ring-binder notebook with all the pages missing, it seemed clear to me, from her evidence, that the pages had been removed from it by someone prior to the empty cover being returned to Mrs Collins.

Mrs Collins also said that, since the disaster, as well as not being able to locate her husband's *New Zealand Atlas*, she had not been able to find the collection of maps which he had also kept on the bookshelf in close proximity to the atlas.

Then there came the evidence of the two Collins' daughters. They had sworn and signed affidavits, as it was believed that their evidence could not possibly be contested by counsel and because it was hoped to spare them the ordeal of going into the witness box. These girls were seventeen and fifteen years of age respectively.

I was not content with this arrangement. After I had read the affidavits of the two girls, I could see how important their evidence was. I was, of course, reluctant to make them appear in the witness box unless it was necessary. Following the publication of the Chief Inspector's report, their mother had been subjected to abusive telephone calls and the like, and these girls had been vilified by the children at their school. This was because of the Chief Inspector's conclusion that their father had been responsible for this massive disaster.

I decided to interview the two girls in my room. They were alert, obviously of high intelligence, and to all outward appearances, quite composed. I went carefully through their affidavits with them and checked the contents line by line.

I could not help but observe that the affidavits had been most scrupulously drafted. Neither girl said that she had actually watched her father as he laid off any leg of a flight track from one point to another and drew the respective lines on a map or on his atlas. All they said was that they had seen him working, with 'a ruler or some measuring equipment', on a large chart of the Antarctic Ross Sea region. But it was obvious, or so it seemed to me, that Captain Collins had in fact been plotting the computer track. There could be no other reason for the 'ruler' or 'measuring equipment' which he had been using when working on the chart.

The older daughter had asked her father about the flight scheduled for the next day. He then opened the *New Zealand Atlas* and looked at it with her. He then referred to another larger map which was not the one he had been working on when his daughter interrupted him. This larger map was 'quite big' and rather than open it out on the table, Captain Collins had spread it out on the floor so as to demonstrate the flight track to Antarctica. He showed her that the aircraft would fly down McMurdo Sound past the coast of Victoria Land. He made no mention of Mount Erebus and did not indicate its whereabouts to his daughter.

Then there came the affidavit of the younger daughter. She said that she had seen her father working with a copy of the *New Zealand Atlas* and a map which was open on the table. She said that she had spoken to her father before her older sister and had enquired about the journey. Captain Collins had said that the DC10 would not be landing on the ice shelf which she could see on the map, but would be returning to Christchurch without landing.

Captain Collins then showed his daughter where the aircraft would be going on the journey south. He pointed out the ragged edge of the coastline to the right-hand side of the Ross Sea and ice shelf (looking south), and he had said to her, 'We keep fairly close to this bumpy lot.' She had later heard him explaining the flight to her older sister.

The witness said that she had been shown a large number of maps in an attempt to identify a map of the type which her father had used to explain the flight, but she had not been able to recognise the particular map which her father had been using. She said that, as she remembered it, the sea on the map was a green colour and that purple colours were used in respect of the land. She said that the map was quite large and indeed was too large for the dining room table which was why her father had placed the map on the floor. She remembered that when her father had pointed out the southward track to McMurdo, indicating that they would be travelling close to the Ross Sea coast, it was on quite a large-scale map.

The affidavits of the two daughters had, of course, been circulated among all counsel and were also available to the Chief Inspector. I asked Baragwanath and Harrison to check with all counsel as to whether they wanted the girls in the witness box and I made it clear that the two girls were quite willing to appear if necessary. But all counsel replied that they did not require the girls to give oral evidence; they said that the affidavits would be sufficient. I understood that the same view had been expressed by the Chief Inspector, although I did not receive direct confirmation of that fact, either from him or his counsel. This meant that all counsel at the inquiry conceded the fact that Captain Collins had been plotting the flight track to McMurdo on a map or maps on the night of November 27.

It was now clear, as I have said, that Captain Collins had indeed plotted his computer flight path at least for the last leg of the journey and in all probability from Auckland right down to the Dailey Islands. In order to achieve the latter task he would need either to have listed in his black ring-binder notebook all the co-ordinates shown on the flight plan produced to him at the briefing, or, and I thought this more likely, he probably obtained his own flight plan printouts from the Computer Section some time before November 27.

So, in the end, the evidence of these members of the Collins family was accepted by all parties without demur. And the significant point was that Captain Collins had not merely been looking at a map or maps and his atlas. He had actually been using his plotting instruments. And he could only have done that if, in his meticulous way, he had been plotting the computer flight path to the Dailey Islands.

Within two days of the disaster, Mrs Collins had notified one of the senior pilots of the airline that her husband had apparently been engaged in plotting his flight track on a map or maps on the night of November 27, 1979, and this pilot had immediately reported that fact to the Director of Flight Operations. The company therefore had known about this within forty-eight hours of the disaster. Whether they ever entrusted the Chief Inspector with this piece of information is not quite clear. It certainly did not appear in his report. And of course, on the question of causation, it was the major decisive fact.

It had always been a simple logical deduction that Captain Collins had before him, on the approach to Ross Island, a map with the computer flight path plotted on it. Otherwise, why re-arm the Nav mode at the conclusion of each descending orbit? But, as far as I could see and until there was any evidence to the contrary, the evidence of his family confirmed that Captain Collins had taken these precautionary steps. The airline had not provided him with any large scale topographical map with the flight track to McMurdo printed upon it. So he had obtained such a map and had plotted the flight track himself.

On the morning after the disaster Mrs Cassin had been visited at her home by a pilot who was said to have been acting on behalf of the Airline Pilots' Association and who was undertaking the task of giving assistance to the relatives of employees of the company who had died in the crash.

He made his visit but he did not see Mrs Cassin. However, he said that some days later he did see Mrs Cassin's brother-in-law who had arrived at the Cassin home in order to be of assistance in this time of need. It appeared that the visiting pilot had asked for any flight documents which might be in the house. There had been a folder of flight documents in that same room and, according to this pilot when he gave evidence, he had obtained the consent of the brother-in-law before taking possession of the folder. The pilot had then gone away and had apparently handed in the documents to some member of the company management.

Mrs Cassin had been quite unaware of this transaction. She knew that some documents, such as flight manuals and the like, were the property of Air New Zealand and that the company was entitled to recover them from her possession. But the briefing documents would in the ordinary course be the property of her late husband, and she was at a loss to understand how all the flight documents in the house had been removed by an employee of Air New Zealand on the morning after the disaster, for that is when she said it had happened.

Subsequently she complained to her lawyers about this conduct on the part of the company. It appeared that there had since been returned to her the cyclostyled briefing documents which she had seen in her husband's possession before he departed on the fatal flight, but she said three pages of handwritten notes which she had seen and which had been written out by her husband were not returned.

Mrs Cassin is a qualified pilot herself and she remembered quite well looking over the flight documents when they were in her husband's possession and seeing these three handwritten pages. Her complaint was: Why had the handwritten notes, which were plainly her late husband's property, not been returned to her?

Needless to say this allegation sparked off an immediately hostile response from the airline. They pointed out that the pilot who made this visit to the Cassin home had done so on behalf of ALPA and the airline had nothing to do with his visit. Indeed, when it became obvious that this pilot would have to testify, the airline refused to call him and insisted that he be called as an ALPA witness.

The pilot said that he had been offered the flight documents by Mrs Cassin's brother-in-law and had delivered them to someone in the management of the company. He said he did not remember any handwritten pages. He said that this was merely part of his duties as the person nominated to render such assistance as might be required in the case of relatives of the dead aircrew. It further appeared that no one in Air New Zealand had ever seen the three handwritten pages to which Mrs Cassin had specifically referred.

It was very evident, as this conflicting testimony was received, that both counsel for the Cassin estate and counsel for ALPA were very hostile towards this sequence of events, and to the explanation which the pilot had given. They were obviously placing great significance on the point that every flight document in the Cassin household had been recovered by the company at the first available opportunity after the disaster had occurred, and they naturally fully accepted the evidence of Mrs Cassin, denied by the airline, that the documents had contained these handwritten notes which she had described.

In view of the bitter feelings which obviously prevailed over this incident I arranged at a later stage for further inquiries to be made of Mrs Cassin. It had been said that when the pilots assembled at the Flight Despatch Office on the morning of the fatal flight, First Officer Cassin had said that he had left his briefing documents at home. The pilot who had visited her had certainly called at the Cassin home on November 29, but he had said that he was given no documents at that time and that it was not until about nine days later that the brother-in-law had referred to flight documents or company manuals. He denied that any documents relating to Antarctic briefing had been sighted by him or shown to him at any time. He said that all he had taken to Air New Zealand were flight manuals, but he was later told there had also been an envelope of miscellaneous papers which had been in a cardboard box with the manuals. He said that these papers had not included any of the notes or pages relating to the Antarctic briefing.

But if First Officer Cassin had said at the Flight Despatch Office that he had left his briefing documents at home and if this statement had been correct, then where had they gone? And where were the three handwritten pages which Mrs Cassin had seen?

All this was very confusing, especially when it was ascertained that First Officer Cassin's briefing documents issued to him on

November 9 had in fact been returned to Mrs Cassin, though not the handwritten notes.

So all this was left in a state of indecision. The brother-in-law of Mrs Cassin gave the airline a letter in which he verified that it was on his own responsibility that he had handed over flight documents to the pilot who had visited the home. But the airline did not call the brother-in-law as a witness.

So the position remained that the airline denied outright that it had ever received from the Cassin home any flight document belonging to or written out by First Officer Cassin which they had not in due course returned to Mrs Cassin.

I had, therefore, to leave the matter there but, as I have indicated, the whole incident was seen by the counsel opposing Air New Zealand as being an immediate attempt by the company to recover from the Cassin home the flight documents which had been said by First Officer Cassin to have been left behind by mistake when he went out to the airport to embark upon the fatal flight. It was clear beyond doubt that, in spite of the evidence of the pilot who had visited the home after the disaster, briefing documents had indeed been handed in to Air New Zealand and only some of them had been returned. It was no doubt incumbent upon the company to recover documents such as these as soon as possible, but it had certainly seemed a tactless procedure for the flight documents to be removed from the Cassin home without Mrs Cassin's knowledge or personal consent.

Mrs Cassin was very upset indeed at the failure of the management to return to her the handwritten notes of her husband which she had seen. In addition, and this has been specifically confirmed by interviews with her for the purpose of writing this book, she was resentful at the nature of the inquiries made of her by the airline pilot who had originally taken the flight documents away from her home and who had been assisting her thereafter in relation to her immediate family problems arising out of the loss of her husband. Helpful though this pilot had been, he also appeared to be intent on discovering what information she might have in her possession with regard to the fatal flight and she very soon found that everything she told him was very shortly within the knowledge of the airline management.

XX

THE CHIEF PILOT TESTIFIES AGAIN

The time had come for the Chief Pilot's reappearance in the witness box. When he had given evidence previously, Captain Gemmell had confined it to the processes of setting up the planning for the Antarctic flights. On this occasion, however, he produced a 29-page brief of evidence accompanied by two appendices. It was his intention to advance his own view as to how and why the disaster took place.

I was not very interested in the theories of witnesses on the cause of the disaster, because this was not a case where some esoteric technical cause may have been the basis of what occurred. This was merely a case where, looking at all the evidence available, an inference had to be drawn as to what caused the accident. This was a matter for the person conducting the inquiry and, although theories were of course of assistance, they could be no more than someone's view of a task which the Royal Commissioner alone had to perform. In addition, I had always to bear in mind the particular interest or motive of the person who might testify on such topics.

The first thesis of the Chief Pilot was that, in view of the weather known to be prevailing at McMurdo, namely a low overcast, the flight crew would have flown on at 18,000 feet and have passed across the top of Mount Erebus, had it not been for the offer from Mac Centre to offer a radar letdown. In the Chief Pilot's view, this was the initiating factor which prompted the ultimate decision to descend and approach McMurdo at low altitude.

I was not at all sure about this. No mention had ever been made of what had been said to or by the flight crew at the Flight Despatch Office just before the aircraft left Auckland. As far as I could see, the position was simply that the crew had known throughout that, unless weather conditions changed, they would be approaching McMurdo under a static overcast of about 3,000 feet. And there would be nothing abnormal or unusual about descending to that height and approaching under the overcast. This is done by all pilots flying jet aircraft right throughout the world as they make landing approaches, and occurs daily on hundreds of occasions.

I do not want to do any injustice to the Chief Pilot's long and comprehensive statement of his opinions as to what the aircrew thought and did in those final minutes before impact. It had been thought out carefully, in relation to various known facts, and it had certainly been expressed in a most clear and detailed manner. But there was a recurring theme which ran through everything he had to say.

This theme was that there was a minimum safe altitude of 16,000 feet and that it could in no circumstances be departed from. Over and over again the insistence on an MSA of 16,000 feet was referred to and there was use of the phrase 'total disregard of the company's instructions'. In other words, the Chief Pilot was stressing, as often as he could, that the aircrew had no authority to fly at any altitude less than 16,000 feet on the approach to McMurdo.

Another theme which dominated the whole of this evidence was the thesis that the crew were uncertain as to their position. However I noticed that the Chief Pilot did not use the garbled crosstalk from the voice transcript to attempt to establish this opinion. I think he was well aware by then that no responsible person could attach any definite meaning to the great majority of the words and phrases used by anyone on the flight deck other than the two pilots. And I was also well aware that the Chief Pilot knew, just as I knew, that in the very clear reproduction of the conversation between the two pilots there had not been the slightest hint of any doubt as to their actual position. And I was also fairly sure that the Chief Pilot recognised that, with a map in front of him and the last leg of the southward journey plotted thereon, Captain Collins would have known his exact position, from minute to minute, merely by comparing the distance-to-run indicator on his panel with the map which indeed could be heard rustling from time to time as one listened to the voice tapes.

So why was it that the Chief Pilot kept inferring, but not stating directly, that the crew were trying to 'establish their position'? The answer to this, as it seemed to me, was that the whole thesis of having to rely upon visual ground references, and the whole basis of the theory that identification of ground features was not made, depended entirely upon the previous supposition that the crew were uncertain as to where they were. But, as I have said, it was simply not possible for the crew not to be certain as to where they were. And in that respect, the evidence of Captain Vette, so I thought at the time, was simply not open to rebuttal. The known track of the aircraft and the obvious similarity between the approach to Lewis Bay and the approach to McMurdo Sound had confirmed the knowledge of the crew as to their position as revealed to them by a glance at the map in front of them.

At this stage of the Chief Pilot's evidence I once again became slightly concerned, as I had been so many times before, at this apparent assumption that I was unable to follow or understand perfectly clear and simple facts. How could the crew ever have been 'uncertain' as to where they were without one single word on that topic having been exchanged between the pilot in command and the co-pilot? That was the single question. And of course, it was the stumbling block against which the Chief Pilot's theory and the Chief Inspector's theory inevitably had to collapse.

It was significant, I thought, as I reflected upon the Chief Pilot's written statement of evidence, that he had been careful to make no reference to any one of the following three factors:

1. The clear and undisputed inference that Captain Collins had plotted his flight track on a map on the night before the flight.
2. That evidence had been given by a number of pilots that they had been specifically briefed to descend to any altitude authorised by American Air Traffic Control and that they had done so. This had been a specific briefing by the senior briefing officer of the airline and this, of course, meant that the 16,000 and 6,000 feet flight level MSA was a myth.
3. Not a word was said by the Chief Pilot as to why Civil Aviation dispensed with the requirement that an aircrew must have been to Antarctica before, even though he was the person who was said to have asked for this dispensation.

The Chief Pilot had given, in a very expert and comprehensive manner, only another version of the theory relied on throughout by the Chief Inspector. He had merely repeated the Chief Inspector's evidence, but he had done so as a person fully familiar with commercial jet aviation and with the inertial navigation system.

Therefore it was clear that the airline was still adamant in its attitude that the cause of the accident was that announced by the

Chief Inspector of Air Accidents. And now, at this very late stage of the inquiry, they had not departed one inch from that position, maintaining it in spite of all the evidence which pointed so directly in the contrary direction. I could only marvel at their implacable attitude.

Next in the witness box was the Director of Flight Operations, Captain Eden. I had heard a good deal about him — he was one of the tough, aggressive individuals the Chief Executive liked to have around him. As it turned out, his evidence was principally devoted to the details of the operational organisation of the airline because this aspect of the inquiry had for some time been the subject of continual questioning and probing by Baragwanath.

It was the responsibility of the airline to supply Civil Aviation with details of the exact organisation of the company with particular reference to flight operations, and to describe all the job specifications allotted to the persons holding the many and varied titles in the airline. It was also known that although the merger of NAC and Air New Zealand had been effective as from April 1, 1978, Civil Aviation had not yet been provided with an up-to-date description of the airline's organisational structure as required by law. Indeed, as I had ascertained by demanding production of the Civil Aviation files, the Director of Civil Aviation and his subordinates were still engaged, as late as December 1980, in fruitless attempts to obtain from Air New Zealand a settled organisation chart setting out all this information. And it was to this aspect of the matter that the evidence of the Director of Flight Operations was principally directed. His explanation of the delays was backed up by the production of voluminous copies of correspondence and the like.

However, he also referred to the evidence which had just been given by Captain Gemmell regarding operational features of the fatal flight. The Director of Flight Operations merely said that he had read this detailed brief of Captain Gemmell's evidence and he agreed entirely with all the opinions which had been expressed.

Captain Eden's evidence did not therefore add very much to the principal question: What was the effective cause of the disaster? But if he was prepared to state his agreement with the opinions of Captain Gemmell as to the cause, then, like Captain Gemmell, he was simply endorsing the Chief Inspector's original opinion and was clearly disregarding the mass of evidence which had so clearly shown the invalidity of that opinion.

In his prepared brief, the witness made no allusion to his conversation with First Officer Rhodes as a result of which

Rhodes had been constrained to withdraw his allegation, if indeed he had made the allegation, that documents had been recovered from the crash site by Air New Zealand and appeared not to have been seen again. I did not ask him about the conversation. If Rhodes had no hard evidence to support his allegation, supposing that he had in fact made an allegation, then it was well within the power and responsibility of the Director of Flight Operations to advise Rhodes that no such allegation should be advanced, or even suggested.

XXI

THE CHIEF EXECUTIVE GIVES EVIDENCE

Baragwanath and Harrison had been attempting to discover for some time whether or not the Chief Executive was to be called as a witness but they had met with no success. At one point it had been suggested to them that he would be called and then, at a later stage, the airline counsel had been non-committal. But it now appeared that the decision had finally been made. Mr Davis appeared in the courtroom, and went into the witness box and read his brief of evidence. As it turned out, he was to be the last witness to testify before me.

Needless to say, I paid close attention not only to the evidence of Mr Davis, but also to his demeanour. Like most other New Zealand citizens, I had seen him from time to time on television when he gave one of his very infrequent press conferences. His large spectacles with their thick black rims and his pugnacious features were familiar to nearly everyone in the country. His aggressive and sometimes abrasive responses to television interviewers were well known. He was obviously a highly dedicated servant of the airline. His personal characteristics as Chief Executive had been relayed to me throughout the inquiry by various informed persons over and over again. I knew all about his aggressive personality and his peremptory orders and his dictatorial attitude in the management of the company's affairs.

I knew about the violent confrontation which had taken place between him and First Officer Rhodes when the latter, accompanied by Captain Cooper, had tried to remonstrate with him some weeks before as to the way in which the case for the company was being progressively broken down in the courtroom. They had been very concerned, as representatives of ALPA, about the company's public image.

But the figure which now presented itself in the witness box seemed far removed from those public appearances which I had seen on television in days gone by, and even farther removed from the dogmatic and intractable Chief Executive who had so violently rejected every criticism by ALPA of the way in which the company's case was being presented. He was subdued, highly co-operative and apprehensive.

I need not spend too much time in describing his evidence. He was, of course, never closely associated with the operational details of the Antarctic flight proposals. He was the administrative head of the company and he neither knew, nor could he be expected to know, all the operational plans and procedures which were adopted on the Antarctic flights.

Naturally he was in some difficulty over the absence of company documentation as far as the Royal Commission was concerned, but he explained this by saying that he was in daily contact with senior executives and was kept informed of all developments throughout the company. He said that the interchanges between himself and the various divisional heads of the company were seldom reduced to writing, and he said that he believed that verbal communication rather than written communication was rather typical of the procedure adopted in international airlines generally. I was not at all sure about all this. I was very concerned about the total absence of files which in the ordinary way must surely have been kept within the various operational branches of the company.

The Chief Executive referred to the article which had appeared in the *Air New Zealand News* and which had described the experience of Captain Keesing on one of the Antarctic flights. He confirmed that all members of the company received copies of this publication but said that he did not remember reading it. He said he believed that if he had seen the reference to 2,000 feet terrain clearance, he would have investigated the matter.

Then he referred to the production before the Commission of a copy of the magazine article written by Mr Brizindine of McDonnell Douglas. He remembered that he had been sent a copy of the article by Mr Brizindine, but he had not read it. Seeing that this eulogistic article clearly referred to an approach down the centre of McMurdo sound at an altitude of 3,000 feet, the question naturally arose as to why the Chief Executive had been unaware, as from the end of 1977, that the suggested MSA of 16,000 feet was not being complied with.

When cross-examined, Mr Davis replied to the effect that he received considerable quantities of mail and that it was his practice not to read many of the attachments annexed to his correspondence. I asked him myself whether this philosophy applied to the President of the McDonnell Douglas Corporation, one of the largest manufacturers of aircraft in the world. He replied in the sense that even correspondence of this major importance was not immune from his practice of not reading all attachments to his letters.

However, there had appeared at a late stage in the inquiry the publication *Travelling Times*. It had been found that the airline itself had arranged for the distribution of this circular — which included Mr Brizindine's article — and that distribution had been effected by an advertising company on September 9, 1978. It had been further discovered that about one million copies of this circular had been prepared and it was quite plain that the object of the airline had been to ensure, as far as possible, that a copy of the publication reached every home in New Zealand. Counsel assisting the Commission had ascertained that a total of 978,620 copies had been distributed throughout the country at a total cost to the airline of $16,008.30.

This revelation had been greeted with some measure of surprised protest by counsel for Air New Zealand and it had been apparent that, in this matter, as in various other matters which arose during the inquiry, they had not been informed by the airline of the existence or distribution of this circular.

The Chief Executive was naturally closely cross-examined by counsel on a matter which had not been referred to in his typed brief of evidence. This was his instruction, almost immediately after the disaster, that all 'surplus copies' of documents were to be destroyed. Mr Davis explained that, in giving that instruction, he was concerned only to see that unwanted copies of documents were not left lying about, and that his intention was to bring together all relevant documents and put them into one file. He felt, so he said, that spare copies of documents might be handed by some employee to the news media. So it was that he had instructed that 'surplus copies' were to be destroyed through the company's shredder.

It so happened that an instruction in identical terms, referring to 'surplus copies', had been the distinguishing feature of the celebrated Windsor Incident in 1972, and had also been given by the airline in the case of the American Airline's massive Chicago disaster in May 1979. I was aware of all this but I did not raise the matter with Mr Davis. His selection of that particular phrase may well have been entirely coincidental, but it was distinctly unfortunate, as I saw the matter, that he had used the exact phrase which had twice before been employed in America to facilitate the concealment of documentation which would detrimentally have affected McDonnell Douglas in 1972, and American Airlines in 1979.

Again, the hostility of the ALPA contingent, and their counsel, and counsel for the estates of the deceased pilots, could almost be felt in the courtroom.

As I saw it, it may well have been that Mr Davis's explanation for this very unfortunate instruction may have been perfectly valid. His aversion to the news media was well known; indeed it was a matter of record in one of the company reports which had been produced before the Commission. But the instruction may well have had effects which he had not foreseen. There were various people in the airline who, by virtue of that instruction, were obliged to hand over to a designated officer of the company such documents as they felt complied with the Chief Executive's instruction, and it was that officer's duty to destroy those documents. And indeed it was the very existence of this instruction which led to the creation of a whole series of allegations by various parties against the airline to the effect that significant documents had, at different times and places, disappeared. It was the 'document destruction order' which inspired the wide-ranging allegations of suppression and destruction of evidence which had been either made or suggested during the inquiry.

After the Chief Executive had been cross-examined by counsel I asked him a few questions myself. One of my final questions was how the airline could have published one million copies of the *Travelling Times* without his knowledge. To this he gave no verbal answer. He simply turned towards me and spread his arms outwards in a despairing gesture. He was indicating his total lack of comprehension that such a thing could have happened. I knew the feeling.

I was very tempted to question Mr Davis about his confrontation with Captain Cooper and First Officer Rhodes, but decided against it. They had their careers to consider, and I was not at all sure of the treatment they would get from the airline management if the angry denunciations of Mr Davis were publicly disclosed.

There were one or two further areas of inquiry, so far not directly raised during the hearings, which I had contemplated raising with the Chief Executive. But I thought better of it. I did not envy him his position. He stepped down from the witness box and left the courtroom. Thus the evidence before me came to a close. All that remained was to arrange for a lengthy adjournment so that counsel for all parties could prepare their submissions.

XXII

CLOSING SUBMISSIONS
OF COUNSEL

I do not need to elaborate to any extent on what was said by counsel for the various parties in their closing submissions. Attacks were made on the evidence given by executive pilots to the effect that they were unaware of the altitudes at which flights were being conducted in the McMurdo area, and the evidence of the navigation section witnesses was similarly criticised, it being contended that it was simply not possible for such a sequence of errors to have been made by such a number of people in that particular area.

Strong submissions were made that the true cause of the disaster was the reliance placed by Captain Collins on the computer track which had been displayed to him at his briefing and which he had obviously plotted on his own map or maps on the night before the flight. It was pointed out that the evidence of Mrs Collins and her daughters as to Captain Collins' working with maps and plotting instruments had not in any way been disputed by any party to the inquiry. And it was therefore contended that, although the aircraft had been flying in clear air from Cape Hallett right to the very point of impact on the mountainside, it was obvious that the classic whiteout illusion which can occur in clear air had in fact been present as the aircraft approached Ross Island, with the result that no one on the flight deck had ever seen that the rising, white slope of a mountain was directly in front of the aircraft. It was also pointed out that the crew had been carefully monitoring their position in relation to the ground because it was obvious from the voice tapes that they were identifying the headlands to the left and right as being the headlands of the approach to McMurdo Sound which was where the computer track on the map was taking the aircraft.

In the submissions by counsel for the Collins estate a particular attack was made upon the conduct of the Chief Inspector with regard to the flight deck recorder tapes, it being asserted that he had without authority introduced those two expressions calculated to make people believe that the aircraft was flying in poor visibility.

I must describe here an incident which occurred during the final submissions for ALPA.

As the end of the inquiry approached it had been evident for a long time that there had been a very bad breakdown in the communication systems between various branches of the Flight Operations Division and this had been conceded by different airline witnesses. There could be no other explanation for such things as the total lack of adequate written confirmation between one department and another in relation to the Antarctica flight track being changed. Another example had been the failure of the airline to comply with the Flight Under Supervision requirement contained in the Operations Specifications.

I had the impression that many of these communication gaps arose from the airline's delay in complying with repeated requests from Civil Aviation for a clear designation of all the various job responsibilities within the company, but I had been assured on more than one occasion that steps had been taken to rectify these deficiencies.

Consequently it came as a very considerable surprise to everyone at the hearing when, during his final submissions, Mr A.F. Macalister, senior counsel for ALPA, produced a xerox copy of an internal company memorandum which demonstrated that there had been yet another computer mistake. This document, handed in by Mr Macalister, had obviously been 'leaked' by someone within the airline to one of the ALPA representatives. The document comprised several pages and it represented the report of a small committee appointed by the airline to inquire into an incident which had occurred as recently as December 4, 1980.

It appeared that someone had been preparing sample flight plans with the aid of the Air New Zealand ground computer. There had been prepared a fictitious sequence of weather reports giving wind velocity at different flight levels, and this data, complete with the associated fuel planning figures, had been typed into the ground computer. All this work had been purely experimental.

But it appeared that, through an error on the part of some unknown person, the fictitious data had been inserted into the standard operational flight plan from Auckland to an overseas destination and that when the flight plans for the impending overseas departure had been delivered to the Flight Despatch Office, they had contained not the actual data for that day's flight but the fictitious data prepared by way of experiment. As a result, the fuel loading for the flight was grossly wrong.

The fact that an erroneous flight plan had been delivered to Flight Despatch had been picked up by an alert Flight Despatch officer who had seen that the code number for the flight plan appeared to be wrong.

Upon being informed of this very serious error I had not been unduly concerned about what might have happened if the Flight Despatch officer had not noticed something wrong with the code number of the flight plan. I was well aware that the crew would have checked the fuel calculations for the journey and they would immediately have seen that they were inadequate. So there was no problem about that — the mistake would have been discovered by the flight crew itself before the entry of the flight data into the aircraft computer.

But what very much concerned me was that here was yet another example of the lack of checking and the lack of communication which had been the distinguishing feature of the Flight Operations Division as revealed by the evidence at the inquiry. I had been told that these communication difficulties had long since been attended to and rectified.

In all this I could only see once more the intractable attitude of the airline towards any criticism about the administrative side of its operations. It was almost as if someone had said, 'We are not interested in all these attacks upon our system — the system will proceed exactly as before.'

Not unnaturally there was a strongly vocal objection from the airline counsel at the production of this document. They complained that they had not seen it before. I had no doubt about that. It was certainly not the first document produced at the inquiry about which the airline had failed to notify its counsel. All I could do was to ask senior counsel for the airline if he would look into this matter urgently the same evening and let me have the airline's explanation on the following day. He agreed to do so.

But when the hearing began the next day, senior counsel for the airline merely advised that he had been unable, in the time available, to clarify the matter. He then resumed his seat and remained silent, and no explanation was ever given to me.

I could not help but contrast this lack of information with the remarkable speed previously shown by the airline management in the overnight adjustment of various bits of evidence given during the day which had appeared to require reassessment by the same witness. On the other hand, I had no doubt that no adequate explanation could possibly be offered. Here was a document which recorded the findings of a committee in relation to this incident and, in the committee's view, there had been a disastrous breakdown within the communication systems of the company. The committee had urged the very reforms which I had already been assured had taken place many months ago.

On the night of this disclosure which had been reported in the newspapers, an airline spokesman was interviewed on television. He explained how there was a series of checks as to the accuracy of every flight plan and that the first check had shown that the flight plan was wrong. He made it clear that, in the opinion of the airline, I had not really understood this when making my comments on the incident during the course of that day.

I could see from this that the airline was still maintaining its stance that everything to do with civil aviation was a deep mystery capable of being understood only by those who were professionally engaged in that industry. I must say that I was amused as I watched this earnest attempt on the television screen to invest the simple checking of a flight plan with an air of impenetrable expertise, and the studied inference that the Royal Commissioner was out of his depth.

I had not been at all concerned with the possibility that the flight plan would not be checked. I was concerned about the point which the airline spokesman had conspicuously left out of his public explanation. That point was that I had been assured, by no less a personage than the Chief Executive himself, that all these communication gaps had been closed and that, in particular, verbal decisions to update flight plans would be confirmed in writing. But more than one year after the disaster, there was still a series of verbal instructions about updating a computer flight plan with no confirmative memorandum required for each step.

That was my only interest in the matter. I had made that quite clear at the hearing. Here was a persuasive airline spokesman, reading no doubt from a hurried memorandum prepared by the management, giving a voluble explanation which did not once refer to the vital flaws in the airline planning which this memorandum had again demonstrated.

I now return to my summary of the closing submissions. Counsel assisting the Commission presented a detailed review of the whole case and indicated that for all practical purposes, the notion of 'pilot error' had disappeared and then the validity of the altitude and navigation evidence was challenged in detail.

The submissions of counsel for Civil Aviation were based upon the primary consideration that, from the departmental point of view, the minimum safe altitude of 16,000 feet on the approach to McMurdo was an official flight level which could not be departed from and that if the crew had maintained the flight level of not less than 16,000 feet, there would have been no disaster. This, of course, was self-evident. But the official view, as represented by Civil Aviation, was that the aircrew had had no authority to descend below 16,000 feet. On this point the evidence was very clearly to the contrary. The officer in charge of the Route Clearance Units of the company was plainly authorised on behalf of the company to brief the aircrews, as he had in fact done, by indicating that the aircraft could approach McMurdo at any altitude authorised or directed by the air traffic controllers at the American base.

Of course it was essential for Civil Aviation, in the interests of its almost certain involvement in civil litigation, to cling like a leech to the proposition that descent below 16,000 feet was the sole effective cause of the disaster and this was a reflection of the view of the Chief Inspector.

The submissions for Civil Aviation were therefore fairly predictable, but they also included an explanation of a particular fact which had emerged fairly late in the inquiry. It had been discovered that the flight manual which is required to be carried by all civil aircraft had not contained the minimum safe altitude sectors, nor the track and distance information laid down in respect of the Antarctic flights. The law required that such information be contained in all flight manuals, but it was open to argument that the statutory requirement only applied to 'scheduled' flights.

When this omission from the airline's flight manual had been belatedly revealed during the inquiry — though not by the airline — there had been an immediate attempt by the airline to suggest that the Antarctic flights were 'non-scheduled' flights and that the legal requirement did not apply. In fact, when the Chief Executive had given his evidence he had kept referring to these flights being 'non-scheduled'.

However, it was plain that Civil Aviation took another view of the matter and were of the opinion that the company's flight manual was deficient in that this vital information about minimum safe altitudes and track and distance was in breach of the law. Consequently, the closing submissions of counsel for Civil Aviation were devoted to a considerable extent to explaining that it was the responsibility of the airline to prepare a proper flight manual and that Civil Aviation officials could not be expected to monitor every word of that manual. They were entitled, so it was said, to rely upon the highly-skilled technical people at Air New Zealand to supply a correct manual.

This defect in the company's flight manual, whether a legal defect or not, certainly caused me some uneasiness. There had always seemed to me to be a gap in the evidence in respect of the flight planning for Antarctica and the approvals obtained from Civil Aviation. I had for a long time been of the opinion that there may have been some informal arrangement between the airline and Civil Aviation about which I had never heard. This arrangement, as it seemed to me, might have amounted to an agreed deviation from the ostensible 16,000 feet MSA and the flight track over Mount Erebus which was formally recorded in the archives of Civil Aviation. I had never believed that Civil Aviation were unaware, as a specific Government agency, of the real operating altitude into McMurdo and of the fact that the computer flight track from 1978 onwards had been directed not at the TACAN or the NDB, but at the Dailey Islands waypoint which was twenty-seven miles to the west of McMurdo Station.

Every Government department maintains files of press clippings relating to reported activities in which its own administration is involved, and it was impossible to accept that all the published material about the true operational altitudes into McMurdo had escaped the attention of Civil Aviation. Its position with regard to the flight track was perhaps not quite so clear but, if the aircrews from 1978 onwards had known all about the altered computer flight track and if the American authorities had always known that over the same period the flight track terminated at the Dailey Islands position, then it certainly seemed unusual that Civil Aviation had not also known.

But no matter what the truth of these strong possibilities may have been, I could not help but believe that there might have been communications as to altitude and computer tracks between the airline and Civil Aviation about which I had not heard. And I could only treat this serious omission in the flight manual of the airline as being to some degree confirmatory of my own belief.

I had no difficulty in guessing why Civil Aviation, in its evidence and in its final submissions, were still sticking to the 'pilot error' theory as being the sole cause of the disaster, and were denying the 'whiteout' phenomenon. If indeed the airline had authorised the approach to McMurdo at less than 16,000 feet and if indeed there had been a ghastly computer mistake which was an effective cause of the disaster, then in civil litigation it would be alleged that Civil Aviation had been at fault in the way in which it carried out its statutory duty of monitoring civil aviation in New Zealand. So they wanted no part of these errors or blunders. They were for Air New Zealand to answer, and Civil Aviation was contending that it had no knowledge of these occurrences and was therefore protected from all civil liability by non-compliance with the 16,000 feet MSA. Such was their position as advanced before me. I could not blame them but, as I have already explained, their agreement to dispense with the previous Antarctic flight experience seemed to me to be fatal within the context of liability for damages at a later date.

Finally, there were the closing submissions advanced on behalf of Air New Zealand. They comprised 135 pages of close typescript. Once again, these submissions were predictable.

The airline submissions had been most skilfully prepared and they were so lengthy that no useful purpose would be served in attempting to describe them in detail. The lack of knowledge of the actual operating altitude into McMurdo was repeated. The long catalogue of mistakes made by the navigation section was recounted and justified at every point. Broadly speaking, Captain Gemmell's review of the circumstances of the disaster, as produced to me in his final appearance in the witness box, was asserted to be correct in every particular. The computer mistake was denied as being a cause of the disaster.

It was contended that the 'whiteout' phenomenon in its clear air meaning had not existed and it was submitted that the aircraft had in fact been flying in and out of cloud with the crew 'hoping' to obtain VMC conditions. It was contended that it was essential for an aircrew to have a visual fix before descending to low altitude.

It was suggested that Captain Collins should have checked on the morning of the flight that the destination waypoint on his flight plan was the same as had appeared on the flight plan showed to him at the briefing. In this respect, no explanation was given as to why any aircrew would check all the figures in a standard computerised flight plan for any particular route. I could only assume that the airline was unaware that I knew that such a process was quite unknown and indeed not even conceivable because of the rigid rule, operating among all airlines in the world, that there must be no change to a standard flight plan without the aircrew being told.

Then, of course, the same insistent theme was harped upon, namely that adherence to a minimum flight level of 16,000 feet would have prevented the disaster.

It was submitted by counsel that the company had come to the inquiry in order to see that all relevant facts were revealed to the Royal Commission. This was certainly an astonishing submission. The documentation produced by the airline at the inquiry had been meagre and unsatisfactory. Complete files which obviously had been held by the airline had never been produced. Their disappearance had never been accounted for except in one instance. Captain Johnson, who had been in charge of the simulator briefing, had been asked where his file was. He said he had handed it in to the management the day after the disaster and he had not seen it since. And, apart from all that, not one fact had ever been volunteered by the airline unless it was in support of the airline's case. All adverse facts, and there had been very many, had been uncovered by the diligence of counsel for the passengers' consortium and for ALPA. Baragwanath, in his capacity as senior counsel assisting the Commission, had, in particular, probed incessantly all the inconsistencies and evasions in the airline's case. The general tone of the submissions for the airline was distinctly hostile to Baragwanath. It was also clear that the airline had resented various questions which I had asked which indicated scepticism at some of the stories I had been told.

So, in the end, the airline's submissions simply reflected its original position before the hearings ever started. There may have been one or two minor deficiencies in the briefing procedure and there may have been one or two slight defects in the communications system between the various departments. But, overall, the airline itself, treated as an organisation, had been in no way responsible for the disaster. Counsel were very careful not to say explicitly that the aircrew alone was to blame, but on the thesis which they were putting to me then no one could have been blameworthy except the aircrew.

In other words, the position of the airline had not changed one iota throughout the course of this long hearing. The fact that their case had irretrievably collapsed was simply disregarded. The fanatical determination of the management to show that the company was not responsible for any aspect of the disaster was being maintained just as strongly as it had been from the outset.

I have described previously the hostile confrontation between the Chief Executive and the two representatives of ALPA, Captain Cooper and First Officer Rhodes, when they saw him in September 1980. During the period between the close of the evidence in late December 1980 and the commencement of counsels' submissions some weeks later, there had been a further confrontation. This time it involved Captain Vette.

Captain Vette had been seeing the Chief Executive on some different matter and the course of the inquiry had again become the subject of discussion. Captain Vette had made no secret of the general belief that the defensive case for the airline had broken down at all points. Once again, the Chief Executive had violently denounced the dead aircrew and had again asserted that they had been 'wholly culpable'. Captain Vette, as reported to me during this interval, had been dismayed at the intractable attitude of Mr Davis. Evidence had been heard by the Commission over a period of seventy-five days, but the Chief Executive's attitude had not varied one iota.

This attitude on behalf of the airline was dramatically illustrated by a specific submission which they made and which was without doubt the most surprising I have ever listened to in a courtroom. It was strongly urged upon me that I should make no finding as to blameworthiness on the part of any person. It was urged upon me, by reference to the combined philosophy of the ICAO Air Accident Regulations and the New Zealand Air Accident Regulations, that the main thing was to avoid attribution of blame. This submission, I need hardly say, was in direct opposition to the terms of reference with which I was compelled to comply as part of my duties as Royal Commissioner. I was specifically required to find 'whether the crash was caused or contributed to by any person in consequence of an act or omission which that person had a duty to perform or which good aviation practice required that person to perform'.

Counsel for the airline, while knowing that I was required by law to answer this question, had not the slightest hesitation in suggesting that I disregard it and that I abstain from any finding of blameworthiness. I had no difficulty in defining the motive for this extraordinary suggestion. Without doubt, it had originated with the management of the airline. They well knew that their attempts to evade responsibility for the disaster had failed. If I acceded to this submission, which they had very clearly pressed upon their counsel, then the way was clear, once my report was published, publicly to denounce the aircrew as being solely to blame. In this respect they would have a free hand, because I had not attributed blameworthiness to anyone. They could therefore assert, without fear of contradiction by anything in my report, that the Chief Inspector's view and their own view had always been right.

But I had no doubt that the intelligent senior counsel for the airline must have warned the management that I would never accede to such a foolish submission. They would have pointed out that I was required to make findings as to the cause of the accident and as to whether acts or omissions by any persons had contributed to that cause.

It was perfectly obvious to everyone in the courtroom that any finding which I might make which inculpated the airline management, and in particular the computer mistake, as being responsible for the disaster would be publicly attacked by the airline the moment that my report was published. I could foresee all that.

Such was the nature of the final argument submitted on behalf of the airline. As I say, nothing had changed.

I should conclude this chapter by referring to one of the many documents which the airline kept to itself notwithstanding a formal order issued by me for production of all documents. This was the report of a meeting of directors held shortly before the hearings of the Royal Commission began. Its existence was not disclosed until after my report had been published. It had been officially decided by the management, and duly recorded by them, that the case for the airline was to be founded upon the breach of the 16,000 feet minimum safe altitude, and that the report of the Chief Inspector was to be the foundation of their case. So much for the assertion by the airline counsel, in the course of final submissions, that the airline had come to the inquiry with the devout and sincere intention of simply producing all the facts and not with the intention of advancing any specific case. On the contrary, the way in which their case had been presented followed exactly their recorded decision and that decision, simply translated, had been to place the whole blame upon the aircrew. This might not have been the most significant document concealed by the airline from the Commission, but it was certainly highly revealing.

My final task was now to review the 3,083 pages of evidence, the 284 documentary exhibits, and the written text of the closing submissions of counsel which comprised 368 pages. From this mass of material I would be required to reach the conclusions on the matters upon which the Government desired to be informed.

XXIII

MY FINAL CONCLUSIONS ON THE ALTITUDE AND NAVIGATION EVIDENCE

There were two issues which were central to my inquiry into the cause of and the culpability for the crash. The first was the question of why the aircraft was flying at 1,500 feet at the time of impact having regard to what was claimed by Air New Zealand to be a rigidly maintained minimum safe altitude of 16,000 feet.

Having considered the evidence, I was satisfied that in fact 16,000 feet did not represent the minimum flight level on the approach to McMurdo. It was regularly departed from on Antarctic flights with the authority of the briefing officers and flights below the so-called minimum safe altitudes of 16,000 feet and 6,000 feet had been widely publicised in newspapers and in publications issued for and on behalf of Air New Zealand itself.

It was obvious that the altitude evidence given by the executive pilots and by the management was interlocked with the navigation evidence. The reason can be easily stated. If it were known within Flight Operations Division that the actual operating altitude into McMurdo was about 2,000 feet, then any alteration in the flight track would be a matter of paramount importance. But if everyone in Flight Operations Division, including the Navigation Section, believed that no aircraft on previous flights had ever approached McMurdo at less than 16,000 feet, then a change in the computer track, whether intentional or accidental, would have been of no consequence. Admittedly, any change in a standard flight track must as a matter of practice always be notified to a crew, but even this omission would not involve anyone in Flight Operations Division in any culpability, provided they were ignorant of the true operating altitude into McMurdo. In other words, the navigation 'defence', if I may call it that, could only succeed if the altitude 'defence' also succeeded.

Hence the insistence, as I saw it, of the management and of Flight Operations Division that they were totally unaware that the real operating altitude into McMurdo was about 2,000 feet.

The second issue central to my inquiry was the question of why the aircraft was flying at this height on a track which took the aircraft on a collision course with Mount Erebus. As to this, I was satisfied that the evidence pointed overwhelmingly to the fact that:

1. on all previous flights in 1979 and on all the 1978 flights the route lay, and was known by those concerned in the company to lie, not across mountainous terrain but across the flat sea ice of McMurdo Sound;
2. that crews, including the crew of the fatal flight, were briefed on the basis that their route lay along McMurdo Sound;
3. that on the night before the fatal flight the route was changed to one across Mount Erebus in consequence of an alteration made by members of the Navigation Section;
4. that through a major blunder someone failed to ensure that the crew were told of the change.

On the first central issue of low-flying, the company had produced a series of executive pilots and finally called the Chief Executive and one after the other they denied knowledge of low-flying. They denied to a man ever seeing any of the newspapers recording the occurrence of low-flying; they denied to a man any knowledge of the fact that low-flying had been publicised in the company's own internal newsletter or in publicity material put out by the company itself and distributed to a million New Zealand homes; they denied to a man ever hearing reports of low-flying, apart from one or two vague rumours which it was said were not worthy of being pursued.

In the teeth of the wealth of external evidence establishing that low-flying was not only common knowledge but common knowledge disseminated by the company itself, I believed myself compelled to reject the evidence of witnesses from Flight Operations Division that they never knew the actual operating altitudes.

The greatest difficulty in assessing the credibility of Flight Operations Division witnesses on the navigation question, had occurred with reference to the evidence of the Chief Navigator. I have described the evidence which he gave. The series of errors which he said he had made seemed to be unusual having regard to his great expertise and his meticulous procedures. But once it was accepted that he had mistakenly adopted the wrong destination waypoint when preparing the computerised flight plan for Antarctica, then the error in pressing one wrong key and then failing to ascertain that he had done so, was a credible explanation. And the shifting of this waypoint twenty-seven miles to the west by accident was certainly reinforced by the omission to make a corresponding alteration to the track. The latter procedure would have been carried out by using not the main computer, but a small spheroid trigonometry computer called the NV90. The operator types in the co-ordinates for Point A and then the co-ordinates for Point B and the NV90 computer will then print out the heading of the track which an aircraft will fly as it proceeds from Point A to Point B. The failure to alter the flight track was relied upon strongly by the airline as demonstrating that the destination waypoint had been altered by accident because it was submitted that a meticulous man like the Chief Navigator would not have made that omission.

The reader may remember that after I had listened to the navigation evidence I had reflected upon a theory of my own as to what might really have happened with regard to the alteration of the destination waypoint. This theory had been simple enough. At about 2 a.m. on November 28, 1979 it had been the duty of someone to call up the current Antarctica flight plan on the computer, to type in the latest weather data for the various sections of the flight to McMurdo and back, and to insert the estimated wind velocities at various altitudes and the corresponding fuel calculations. If the computer contained various experimental McMurdo flight plans — which I was sure it would — then there may have been one showing the TACAN as the destination waypoint and the operator had selected this flight plan in error and had inserted into it the weather and fuel data which he thought he was typing into the standard Antarctica flight plan with its destination waypoint at the Dailey Islands.

I thought it might be instructive to reconvene the inquiry so as to put this possibility to the navigation witnesses. But quite apart from the possibility of such an explanation, I was still concerned with a question which I had raised during the inquiry, namely whether the Dailey Islands waypoint might not have been fixed merely by extending to the south one or other of the military flight tracks.

These flight tracks are overprinted on long topographical maps showing the southern part of New Zealand at the top and the

McMurdo area at the bottom. I had noticed that one or more of the military flight tracks, which all terminated at the Byrd reporting point and then became one single track turning to the left towards Williams Field, seemed likely to have intersected the McMurdo latitude somewhere about 165° longitude east if they had been projected straight onwards instead of turning left at the Byrd reporting point. Hence my question to the navigation witness during the inquiry.

After the evidence and final submissions were concluded and I was writing my report, I asked the Air Force to supply me with one of these long maps with the military flight tracks overprinted thereon, and I asked if their navigators would be kind enough to plot on this map the exact position of the Dailey Islands waypoint.

This map was delivered to me with commendable promptitude, and there were three military flight tracks. They led respectively from Melbourne, Dunedin and Christchurch. As already stated, they all terminated at the Byrd reporting point and they then merged into one track travelling south-east from the Byrd reporting point to Williams Field. By using a ruler, I projected each of the Dunedin and Christchurch tracks straight onwards through the Byrd reporting point and I now saw that they intersected the McMurdo latitude (77°53 minutes), just to the west of the longitudinal meridian of 165°; in the other words, at about 164°48 minutes longitude east.

We had already heard at the inquiry of the nature and function of the NV90 computer used by the airline. I was fairly sure that this computer could be used in order to fix the exact position at which each military flight track would intersect the McMurdo latitude if projected straight forward through the Byrd reporting point, and I made an independent inquiry which confirmed this supposition.

Once again I had to ask myself whether I should have the navigation witnesses recalled so that this aspect of the matter might be reviewed. I could direct that the great circle headings of the military flight tracks from New Zealand be inserted into the NV90 computer and the necessary calculations made under the supervision of Air Marshal Sir Rochford Hughes. In addition, I had also been supplied with another map of a similar kind which showed the origin of the Invercargill military flight track to McMurdo, so it would be possible to check each one of the three New Zealand military flight tracks in this manner. I was sure that the computer would print out a longitudinal position at the McMurdo latitude of somewhere about 164° 48 minutes south in each case if the military tracks were extended in the manner described.

I had also observed something else by studying the long topographical map supplied by the Air Force. The southernmost extremity of McMurdo Sound is a narrow 'V' shaped bay with the point of the bay pointing approximately to the south. I noticed that the Dailey Islands waypoint as fixed by the Air Force was located some little distance north of the southernmost point of the bay, but lay almost exactly between the eastern and western sides of the bay. I could see that if anyone wished to plot the last leg of the Air New Zealand flight track down the very centre of McMurdo Sound, then, upon looking at the map to which I have been referring, that person would select this triangular bay (it is called Salmon Bay) as being the destination waypoint, the bay being located just to the west of the Dailey Islands. A waypoint selected on the McMurdo latitude and in the approximate centre of Salmon Bay would result in a longitudinal position of 164° 48 minutes east, allowing for a few seconds of longitude one side or the other. And Salmon Bay is the most distinctive mapping landmark at the head of McMurdo Sound. It is twelve miles long and about nine miles across at its entrance. So here was another method by which the 'Dailey Islands' waypoint might have been selected.

There was no difficulty in recalling the navigational witnesses in order to hear what they had to say about these possibilities that the Dailey Islands waypoint had been plotted intentionally, and also to ask why it had not been described as the 'Salmon Bay waypoint'. But I could also foresee the torrent of hostile cross-examination which would be directed at the navigation witnesses and possibly at other officials of Flight Operations Division if I brought up these queries for examination at a reconvened hearing.

I finally came to a decision. Within the broad ambit of my inquiry, it did not really matter whether the Dailey Islands waypoint had been deliberately or accidentally plotted. Even if accidentally plotted, I was satisfied that its position was in fact known to the airline and had long been adopted by the airline as the standard destination waypoint for Antarctica. So I kept my views to myself. After all, these indications of an intentional plotting of the Dailey Islands waypoint were only marginal so far as the main thrust of the inquiry was concerned. It was the alteration of the waypoint which really mattered, and I decided to leave things as they were, my main reason being that I had reached the conclusion that I should accept the Chief Navigator's evidence that he had altered the waypoint by mistake.

However, for the purpose of writing this book I made the further inquiries which I had contemplated making at a reconvened hearing. I found that if the great circle tracks from the three New Zealand beacons were projected forward in the manner described, then a spheroid trigonometry computer such as the NV90 would print out within fractions of a second the three longitudinal positions at which they intersected the McMurdo latitude. I also found that if you selected the military headings proceeding south from the Invercargill and Dunedin beacons, and if you asked your computer to print out the average or mean of the two longitudinal points at which the McMurdo latitude was intersected, confining the answer to the closest minute of longitude, then the computer printout would read: 77° 53 minutes S. to 164° 48 minutes E. This of course is the Dailey Islands waypoint.

So, even accepting in full the explanation of the navigation section that the Dailey Islands waypoint had been accidentally altered, there was certainly evidence demonstrating the manner in which that waypoint could deliberately have been established had Flight Operations Division decided to take that step.

In my report to the New Zealand Government I declined to make any positive finding that the Dailey Islands waypoint had been deliberately selected. But I said that I was satisfied that the airline had in fact adopted the altered waypoint and had used it thereafter as part of the standard Antarctica flight track.

On this issue as to whether the Dailey Islands waypoint had been adopted by the airline, the company had produced a set of witnesses mainly from the Navigation Section. Each member of that section asserted that he always believed the flight track to have lain across Mt Erebus. They were of course confronted by the fact that at the briefing of the Collins and Simpson aircrews there had been produced no less than three separate charts or diagrams each depicting a flight track down the centre of McMurdo Sound. One of these diagrams, prepared by some other division of the airline for passenger information, had obviously been prepared by reference to the track and distance chart Exhibit 164, and either the Navigation Section or some other branch of Flight Operations Division had supplied Exhibit 164 for that specific purpose. And what about Exhibit 164 itself, which although cut off at the bottom so as not to include the complete semi-circular turn around the south of Ross Island, clearly showed the south bound track from Cape Hallett as being plotted down the centre of the Sound? This chart, as previously explained, had actually been supplied to aircrews as part of their flight despatch documents at the commencement of the 1978 flights, and it had come into existence contemporaneously with the establishment of the Dailey Islands waypoint. None of the Navigation Section witnesses had been able to give any satisfactory explanation as to why aircrews had been supplied with Exhibit 164 to take with them on their flights. And if you looked carefully at the last outward leg of the flight track plotted on Exhibit 164 it could be seen that the track passed just to the east of the Byrd reporting point before disappearing off the edge of the diagram. I knew that the computerised flight track with its heading of 188.9° terminating at the Dailey Islands waypoint also passed just to the east of the Byrd reporting point. During the evidence of the navigation witnesses I calculated with a protractor the heading of the last southward track of Exhibit 164. Making allowance for the small and indistinct photocopy of Exhibit 164, and for the fact that the track did not appear to start exactly at Cape Hallett, the track appeared to be just to the east of 190°. In other words, despite the denials of the airline that Exhibit 164 was associated with the Dailey Islands waypoint, the southward track led either directly or approximately to that very position.

The clear statement of Captain Simpson, which so clearly notified Flight Operations of the position of the Dailey Islands waypoint, was said, in terms which I was compelled to reject, to have been misinterpreted. It was not only Captain Simpson who had noted the Dailey Islands waypoint position in the course of his flight. Other pilots on the Antarctic flights were said to have done the same thing and it will be remembered that the flight crew of November 7 had underlined in ink the Dailey Islands waypoint co-ordinates on their flight plan, this being the very flight plan produced to the Collins and Simpson aircrews at the briefing of November 9. If other flight crews had known the actual location of the destination waypoint in 1978 and 1979, then how could some responsible officer or officers in Flight Operations not have also shared this knowledge? I was unable to accept that the highly skilled members of Flight Operations, or at least some of them, had not known and approved of the twenty-seven mile shift on the destination waypoint, especially when it was a location both sensible and prudent for aircrews which could be letting down to low-level altitudes on the McMurdo approach.

For all these reasons I was satisfied that the error made by the Chief Navigator had been ascertained long before Captain Simpson made his report, and because of the operational utility and logic of the altered waypoint it was thereafter maintained by the airline as the approved destination waypoint. I accordingly reported to the Government in these terms.

I also could not overlook the fact that, in the false accounts given, each group of witnesses sought to persuade me to reach a different view as to causation and culpability from that which I in fact took. The executive pilots sought to persuade me that the crew were at fault in flying low, and Flight Operations Division sought to persuade me that their culpability in failing to advise the crew of the change of co-ordinates was slight.

It will be remembered that Mr S. J. Macfarlane, in his appendix to Captain Vette's book, had counted a total of fifty-four errors which, on the basis of the airline evidence, had been made by various personnel with regard to the navigation procedures adopted for the Antarctica flight. Using the same method of counting all consequential checking mistakes which had followed the basic mistakes, either of omission or commission, he had demonstrated a total of one hundred and seventy-seven 'altitude' mistakes. When I came to appraise the whole of the altitude and navigation evidence, I calculated the total of the basic errors, whether of omission or commission, which on the basis of the airline's case, had been made by various people in the airline who were all experts in their particular fields. I found that fifteen witnesses had made between them thirty-five such errors, and I was quite unable to accept that all these mistakes could possibly have been made. This factor, coupled with the demeanour of those witnesses, was probably the principal reason why I felt myself obliged to reject the interlocking altitude and navigation explanations, even allowing for occasional valid errors.

I had to give particular consideration to the position of Mr Davis with regard to the conclusion which I had reached as to a preconcerted plan of deception. Was he the person responsible for the planning of the altitude and navigation evidence which I believed to have been false in both branches? I did not think so. He had certainly maintained a steady view, right throughout the inquiry, that the airline management was not at fault in any manner causing or contributing to the disaster. His expressed opinions on that point had been consistently pugnacious and assertive but I could not possibly envisage Mr Davis taking an active part in the preparation of all the technical evidence which formed the basis of the airline's case as to altitude and navigational procedures. The essence of the matter was, as I saw it, that the known attitude of Mr Davis was reflected in the evidence which his management and technical staff had constructed. In my opinion this was the sole extent of his influence on the case and I believed I could not fairly nominate him as an active party to the plan of deception. I therefore expressed that view in my report to the Government.

From what has gone before, it will be apparent that at the time when I came to write my report I had little doubt that the contentions of counsel opposing Air New Zealand were right in respect of both the altitude and the navigation questions.

When a company finds itself in trouble and there are legal proceedings, then it is not uncommon to find a sequence of corporate witnesses all combining to convey either a misleading impression or a false tale. This tends to occur in almost every type of case where a company has strong motives to assert that it has made no mistake of any kind. The tendency of corporate witnesses to toe the company line was indeed referred to in one of the judgments of the English Court of Appeal in recent times, and in such terms as to not indicate any degree of surprise that these practices so frequently occurred. And of course, this aspect of corporate testimony is well known to every trial lawyer.

In dealing with such situations in a courtroom, no matter whether the combination of false testimony is given on behalf of a company or on behalf of any individual, the accepted mode of deciding the conflicting issues is for the court merely to say that it prefers the evidence of one group of witnesses to the evidence of the other. Or, to use again an example of the hallowed diction used in such circumstances, a judge will say that wherever the witnesses on one side are in conflict with those on the other, then he rejects one lot of evidence and accepts the other. It is not considered a good practice in judicial proceedings to make a decisive finding that perjury has been committed.

It goes without saying that perjury is committed in the witness box in courtrooms every day of the week. Sometimes it is necessary for a judge to make a direct finding that false evidence has been given, and if necessary that false evidence has been given in concert. Sometimes the circumstances of the case leave him with no option. But, generally speaking, the convention is to merely indicate the acceptance or rejection of a particular line of evidence where the testimony is in conflict.

So what was I to do here? This was not the ordinary case of a group of witnesses drawn from company management who had combined to tell a concerted tale which was not true. This indeed, as I saw it at the time, had taken place. But it seemed to me that there were only two courses which were open to me.

These two alternatives were either to apply the ordinary judicial procedure of simply rejecting the evidence of the navigation and altitude witnesses called by the airline, and say that I preferred the views expressed by the witnesses who testified against the airline, or alternatively to brand the airline evidence in this respect as being a concerted attempt to deceive the Royal Commission. This was not ordinary litigation. It was not litigation at all. It was an inquiry into one of the world's worst aviation disasters.

I was also aware that once I had rejected the elaborate evidence given by the airline on these two topics of altitude and navigation, then I was certainly going to be the victim of a public attack by Mr Davis and his colleagues. It would not matter upon what grounds I rejected the airline's evidence. If I rejected the evidence but made no finding of credibility against the airline witnesses, then this would immediately be seized upon as demonstrating the erroneous conclusions lying behind the report. It would be pointed out that I could hardly reject explanations which I had been given without also rejecting the credibility of the witnesses who had testified. If, on the other hand, I made an explicit finding of credibility against the airline witnesses, then the public attack would be even more violent. In particular, the directors of the company, or most of them, would be deeply wounded by such a published conclusion. I was well aware of the fact that they did not know the extent to which the case for the airline had collapsed.

So in the end, there was no alternative but to make an explicit finding of credibility against the airline witnesses. I therefore reported to the Government in the following terms:

> No judicial officer ever wishes to be compelled to say that he has listened to evidence which is false. He always prefers to say, as I hope the hundreds of judgments which I have written will illustrate, that he cannot accept the relevant explanation, or that he prefers a contrary version set out in the evidence.

> But in this case, the palpably false sections of evidence which I heard could not have been the result of mistake, or faulty recollection. They originated, I am compelled to say, in a pre-determined plan of deception. They were very clearly part of an attempt to conceal a series of disastrous administrative blunders and so, in regard to the particular items of evidence to which I have referred, I am forced reluctantly to say that I had to listen to an orchestrated litany of lies.

I had chosen this phraseology with some care. It seemed to me essential that the finding of credibility be not only clear but condemnatory. Above all, I felt it essential to highlight the way in which the airline had testified so as to dispel from the public mind the false impression which had been conveyed by the Chief Inspector's report, quite bona fide though that report might have been. Perhaps it might be more correct to say that I wanted to dispel the erroneous public impression of flying in cloud, low-flying, and almost incredibly reckless conduct by the crew of the aircraft, such being the overall impression contained by the newspaper paraphrases of what the Chief Inspector had had to say. So I thought that a finding of credibility expressed in these terms might well have a salutary effect. As it appeared later, I was correct in that assumption.

The airline complained vociferously once the report was released and I was publicly attacked by the management, and by the directors, and I was also, I am sorry to say, publicly insulted by the Prime Minister.

When I had been reading over the transcript of the evidence of these witnesses whose testimony I had decided to reject, and when I remembered their almost contemptuous demeanour in the witness box (and I am here referring to the management witnesses as opposed to the navigation witnesses), I was reminded of something I had once read in a book written by Professor J.K. Galbraith. It was *The Great Crash 1929* in which he had analysed the causes and effects of the stock market crash in the United States. This of course, as everyone knows, had been a massive financial disaster, the worst that the world has ever seen before or since, and after all the dust had settled a United States Senate committee began investigations into the role of the New York Stock Exchange in relation to all the errors and malfunctions which had occurred. The leading witness was a Mr Whitney who was the Chairman of the New York Stock Exchange and who testified in his defence before the Senate committee. Here is Professor Galbraith's account:

> Whitney admitted to no serious fault in the past operations of the Exchange or even to the possibility of error. He supplied the information that was requested, but he was not unduly helpful to Senators who sought to penetrate the mysteries of short-selling, sales against the box, options, pools, and syndicates. He seemed to feel that these things were beyond the Senators' intelligence. Alternatively he implied that there were things that every intelligent

schoolboy understood and it was painful for him to have to go over the obvious.

This is not a bad description of the general way in which the management witnesses testified before the Royal Commission. It almost seemed as if they believed that I was required by law to accept without qualification everything they said.

And, as I have already indicated, the most striking thing was that the attitude of the management had not varied one iota from the first day of the hearing until the last. The management had been aware, without the slightest doubt, that their altitude defence had collapsed around their ears. They must also have been aware, and again I thought without any doubt, that the elaborate sequence of navigational mistakes which I had listened to were not believed in their entirety by anyone in the courtroom. I could not help but be impressed by the apparent lack of intelligence on the part of these management witnesses. I could only suppose, and I had to assume, that they were all intelligent men, that they were going to brazen the whole thing out to the end, and that they would treat any ultimate opinions expressed by me against the management as being erroneous and not warranting serious consideration. As Mr Davis had said so often to anxious members of ALPA who had spoken to him during the hearing, the Government stood behind the management. I think they must have thought that with the Government behind them they were immune from any criticism.

The stand taken by the airline at the inquiry was in no way different from that taken by some airlines and aircraft manufacturers in other major disasters. But whereas the 'cover-up' tactics in other major disasters had been skilful and sophisticated, one could hardly say the same about the present case. The tactics employed had been unintelligent and obtuse and I am sure did not reflect the true intelligence of the witnesses who lent their aid to the plan of deception. I could only share the attitude which I knew prevailed among the ALPA contingent and among the various counsel who had felt obliged to test and probe the attempts by the management to whitewash their own organisation, namely that if the airline had come to the inquiry and disclosed at the outset the fact that there were at least some people who knew the real altitude facts and who also knew the real location of the destination waypoint in 1978 and in 1979, then the whole inquiry would probably have been over in three or four weeks and would have terminated in the airline's being complimented for its frank disclosure of all the facts.

XXIV

THE MARTIN LETTER

I have described already the unfavourable reception by the airline management of the findings of credibility which I had made in my report. Their protestations of innocence, which were suspected by many to have been prepared well in advance of publication of the report, were vociferous in the extreme. But many months later there was released to the New Zealand press a document which had a resounding impact upon public opinion. This document was a letter sent by Mr Martin to Lloyds insurance brokers throughout the world, including their Auckland brokers.

The reader will remember Mr Martin. He had met Baragwanath and myself in London in November 1980 and I have described the anxieties which he had then expressed about the nature of the airline evidence. And the reader will remember that I had been well aware that Mr Martin would immediately pass this information on to Air New Zealand.

Mr Martin's letter to the brokers for Lloyds described this interview and it went on to recite the legal position with regard to claims for damages. The letter had been sent to New Zealand shortly after our London interview with Mr Martin and the full text of this interesting document was leaked to the New Zealand press on January 29, 1982. The vital passage in the letter, which attracted nationwide attention in New Zealand, reads as follows:

> It cannot be said that, from Air New Zealand's point of view, the evidence which has been brought out at the Royal Commission has been satisfactory. There have obviously been very considerable 'political' and personal differences and difficulties which have resulted in a rather grimmer picture being presented to the Royal Commission than was anticipated.

Some weeks ago the judge presiding over the Royal

Commission, Mr Justice Mahon, and counsel to the Commission briefly visited London principally for the purpose of discussing matters with the accident investigation branch of the Department of Trade here. Due to a lucky coincidence, Mr Martin of this firm was introduced to Judge Mahon and Mr Baragwanath and was able, after discussion of the matter with Mr Glover, to have a brief 'without prejudice' discussion with them. That 'without prejudice' discussion revealed some anxiety on the part of the court about the way evidence had been presented and might be presented in the future.

As a result, there has been further discussion of the whole matter between (here Mr Martin named the legal representatives of Lloyds in Auckland and the legal representatives of the airline), and there has been some considerable modification of certain proposals for evidence which have resulted in a far better impression of Air New Zealand having been given during recent days than previously.

The evidence of Mr Davis, the chief executive of Air New Zealand, is still to be given and it is very much to be hoped that he will come up to proof and not be damaged by hostile cross-examination.

By the time the Martin letter was released to the press, Air New Zealand had a new top management and a new Chairman of Directors. The new chairman was a well-known and highly successful New Zealand businessman with a reputation for speaking his mind. He made a public statement announcing that he had directed an inquiry as to how this letter had come to be leaked to the press. He said that he had established that a copy of the Martin letter had been received by Air New Zealand and said that at first he believed that someone in the airline had passed the letter to the press. However, it was later ascertained that the leak had come from outside the airline and it later appeared that an insurance company employee in Auckland had been responsible.

But the significant point about the Martin letter was that no one speaking on behalf of Air New Zealand ever denied the validity of Mr Martin's letter, and it has never been denied to this day. I had deliberately warned the airline, through its insurers, that the altitude and navigation evidence, in my opinion at that time, was false evidence given in concert, and the airline had immediately acted in response to that warning.

In one or two immaterial respects, the letter was not quite correct. As previously indicated, our discussion with Mr Martin in London was certainly not 'without prejudice' and, in addition, it was certainly not by chance that we had met Mr Martin. Once he had found that Baragwanath and I were in London he had made it a matter of urgency to see us before we returned to New Zealand.

No doubt it was wrong for an insurance employee — if he in fact was the culprit — to have made this letter public. But its repercussions on Air New Zealand were very severe. All their protestations about the terms of my report ceased. Even the Prime Minister was silent.

By any standards, the Martin letter must surely be, when viewed in its entirety, the most instructive document ever released to public view within the context of civil aviation disasters.

XXV

SOME UNEXPLAINED MYSTERIES

By the time the hearings of the Commission had concluded, every aspect of the disaster and its surrounding circumstances had been explored by counsel in considerable detail. But in the end, there were certain areas of inquiry which did not result in any decisive answer. What I shall do now is to set out briefly some, though not all, of the events or occurrences which were never fully explained.

What happened to the flight bags of the aircrew?

At the inquiry, counsel for ALPA and for the Collins estate were not satisfied with the information available about the recovery of the flight bags which are part of the essential equipment of each pilot. The relevant flight documents for any flight are contained in a flight bag carried by the pilot as he boards the aircraft, and the bag is kept next to him during the flight so that he is able to extract any maps, charts or flight manual which may be required.

These flight bags are rectangular in shape, about forty-five centimetres long, thirty centimetres deep and fifteen centimetres across. They are made of durable material and have handles on the top so that they may be carried like small suitcases.

When Captain Gemmell was being cross-examined, he had been asked about the flight bag of Captain Collins. He had first said that he had never seen the flight bag in question (it had the name of the pilot stamped in gold lettering on the top), but, at a later stage, he had changed his mind and said that he had in fact seen it. This altered recollection had a profound effect upon counsel present, as I was later informed, and I was surprised myself in view of the complete certainty on every point of evidence which this particular witness had displayed throughout. I was aware of the fact that the first piece of the witness's evidence on this topic was probably due to a mere slip of memory, but there were other views on the matter. One view was that he had become aware that someone might say that they had seen him examining this very flight bag, but I was not at all disposed to accept this unkind suggestion.

The flight bag, according to Captain Gemmell, had been empty when found. It had also been quite undamaged. Counsel for the Collins estate made a great point of this. He pointed out that an employee of the company had taken the trouble to deliver to Mrs Cassin the name tag which had been on her husband's flight bag, and which had obviously been attached to it after the disaster because the tag had been unbuckled and was itself intact, whereas the entirely undamaged flight bag belonging to Captain Collins had been located on the ice but had never since been seen.

The inference was that the airline had not wanted to have to explain to Mrs Collins that there were no documents in the flight bag when found, and that it had been thought better to dispose of it and not return it to her.

The questioning of Captain Gemmell about this flight bag received some prominence in the New Zealand newspapers. In a day or so I received a letter from a Mr Woodford, who has been mentioned earlier as one of the three mountaineers first dropped on to the crash site after the location of the disaster was known. In his letter Mr Woodford said that he had found the flight bag and that it was empty when found. He resented any suggestion that there had been documents in the flight bag and that Captain Gemmell had taken possession of any documents in the vicinity of the crash which had not been accounted for.

Mr Woodford's explanation for writing the letter was that he had read extracts in a Christchurch newspaper about the cross-examination on this point and he had felt it his duty to write to the Commission with this information. But I must say that when I read his letter I had the feeling that Mr Woodford might have been invited by a telephone call from Auckland to send such a letter. Perhaps I was wrong. It was just that the terminology of the letter did not quite convey an impression of unsolicited explanation. Christchurch is not much more than one hour's flight away from Auckland but the airline did not fly Mr Woodford there in order to amplify his letter by giving evidence.

I was not at all surprised that the flight bag might have been empty when found. The actual sequence of events immediately following the initial impact of the crash had been discussed with Air Marshal Sir Rochford Hughes. He had said that whether the flight bags of the pilots had been propelled forward by the impact or whether they had ejected sideways when the flight deck detached itself from the fuselage and was thrown out to the left, the flight bags — which would have been unfastened — would have ejected all the documents which they contained.

However, the fact remained that this undamaged flight bag had been seen outside the damaged flight deck but had not been returned to Mrs Collins.

Following the conclusion of the evidence given before the Commission I had given some further thought to this query about the flight bags and I had asked Harrison, one of the counsel assisting the Commission, to make suitable inquiries.

These inquiries disclosed that the helicopter pilot who flew property from the crash site to McMurdo remembered either one or two flight bags being placed aboard his helicopter, and he said that they were then flown by him to McMurdo. This had been independently confirmed by the loadmaster of the helicopter who recollected seeing the flight bags. The senior police sergeant in charge of the disaster property store at McMurdo was also interviewed, and he recollected either one or two flight bags among other property awaiting packing for return to New Zealand. He said he believed that he had given the flight bags to the Chief Inspector. The Chief Inspector, at that time in Australia, had been interviewed by Harrison by telephone, but he said that no flight bags were ever handed to him.

When the police had compiled their inventory of property in the store to be sent in police custody to New Zealand, it did not refer to the flight bags which had evidently been in the store. It will be remembered that the Collins flight bag had his name stamped clearly upon it.

The inquiries, which I had directed to be made, seemed to have petered out at this point. Since the police property sheets had not referred to any flight bag belonging either to Captain Collins or First Officer Cassin, it seemed that they may have been delivered to someone by the police at McMurdo Station after they had been taken into store, or to someone at Auckland after they had arrived. No one could say what had happened to them, and I had to leave the matter at that.

I may say, however, that a further inquiry made by me for the purpose of writing this book has established that the two flight bags did in fact arrive in Auckland on an RNZAF Hercules. They were then handed over, along with other property in the aircraft, either to the police or to Air New Zealand. The flight bag of Captain Collins was last seen at the Auckland mortuary along with other property, and it was from there that the flight bag was taken away by an unknown person and never seen again.

The gap in the passengers' photographs

When, at an early stage of the inquiry, I had surveyed the available range of passengers' photographs, I had been concerned, to some degree, that there was a sequence of photographs which seemed to me to be missing. Many hundreds of photographic prints had been developed from the cameras found on the crash site. The photographs produced at the hearing showed views to the east, west and north. But there was not a single photograph which showed a view to the south, that is to say, towards Ross Island.

If you looked at the flight path of the aircraft as it completed its two orbits, it was obvious that there had been four occasions upon which the aircraft had been side-on to Ross Island. On the two most southern aspects of the orbits the aircraft had been only five to ten miles from the ultimate impact position. Each of these turning sequences had meant that the passengers on one side of the aircraft or the other had been able to take photographs to the south from this fairly short range. Each semi-circular southern aspect of an orbit had occupied about six miles of airspace and accordingly each sequence close to Ross Island had given passengers a total of about two minutes to take photographs. Then there had been the other and more northerly turning sequences, and although they were at longer range, again, passengers on one side of the aircraft or the other had been presented with a further total of about two minutes within which to take photographs to the south.

Having regard to the hundreds of photographs which were developed at McMurdo, and to the fact that there must have been something like 200 cameras on the aircraft, it seemed to me inevitable that on the four occasions just described when the aircraft was turning on a track which presented a side-on view to the south, there must have been a total of something like forty photographs taken pointing south. In addition to that, the presence of such photographs could easily have been identified by reason of the developed pictures, for example, of Beaufort Island. It was only necessary to go back a few frames before the Beaufort Island pictures in order to pick out those photographs which had been taken to the south.

I went to the DSIR in Christchurch and examined all the available remaining photographs which they had. There were none which I could see had been taken to the south. I wrote to the Chief Inspector. I did not reveal the purpose of my inquiry, but I asked whether he could supply me with any photographic prints still remaining in his possession which had been developed from passengers' cameras. He sent me a prompt reply in which he said that all the photographs he had had in his possession had, at one time or another, been handed out to various counsel at the inquiry and he had no photographs left. I was well aware of the fact that the Chief Inspector had been very helpful to counsel in producing all manner of information and I had no doubt at all that his total supply of photographs had left his possession in the manner which he described.

But if there had been a number of photographs taken from the passengers' windows to the south, then what had those photographs disclosed? I had no doubt at all that if any had shown a low cloud base descending nearly to the foot of the ice slopes of Mount Erebus, then such photographs would have been identified and they would without question have been published as part of the Chief Inspector's report. They would have vindicated the very theory which the Chief Inspector and Civil Aviation had so consistently impressed upon me, namely that the aircraft was either flying in cloud or towards low cloud or towards impaired visibility. So, it was obvious that no photographs of that kind had ever been recovered.

Therefore I was uneasily aware of the possibility that there had been photographs which in fact depicted the whiteout to the south which the weather conditions had undoubtedly created. I could only assume that, in the course of sorting out these hundreds of photographs, someone, either at DSIR or attached to the Chief Inspector's Accident Branch, had seen them only as showing some featureless expanse of white and had not realised their significance.

After my report had been published I received a letter from Mr Charles Neider of New York, who is a leading expert on Antarctica, and he raised with me the same question. Where, he asked, were the series of photographs which must certainly have been taken by passengers with their cameras aimed to the south? It was his opinion, having studied the report closely, that such photographs must certainly have been taken.

So this was another of the unresolved mysteries of the inquiry. I would have given a great deal to have seen what the passengers had seen when they looked to the south because that would have been what the flight crew had seen. And I had the uneasy impression that, somewhere or other, during this highly complicated and difficult process of sorting through hundreds of photographs, evidence of a vital nature might have been unidentified or mislaid.

The documents on the snow

One of the most controversial questions raised with regard to the accident investigation procedures carried out on the crash site had been in relation to the recovery of documents from the crash site. Apart from the operations and flight manuals, which are carried as a matter of course on every flight, the only documents from the flight deck which had been recovered appeared to be three in number:

1. A RNC chart (not a topographical map) which contained track and distance diagrams for Qantas and for Air Force flights, but not for Air New Zealand, and which contained information as to various radio frequencies.
2. A sample flight plan printed in October 1977 which contained among the list of co-ordinates the latitude and longitude of the NDB at McMurdo.
3. The quarto-size piece of paper containing Captain Johnson's notification dated November 8, 1979 that the NDB facility was withdrawn and including a reminder that the minimum safe altitude in the McMurdo area was 6,000 feet.

It was pointed out by counsel for ALPA that if these documents were the only flight documents (apart from the manuals) recovered from the ice, then it was curious to find that each document was in favour of the case which the airline was now attempting to advance. It was pointed out that the following documents, which clearly had been carried in the flight bag of Captain Collins along with the three just specified, had not been recovered:

4. The map upon which he had been working with plotting instruments the night before the fatal flight.
5. The large map which he spread out upon the carpet of the dining room because there was not room for it on the table.
6. The group of maps which had been in the bookcase next to the atlas.
7. The *New Zealand Atlas* which he had been working on the night before the flight and which he had taken with him to the briefing session.
8. The large topographical map issued to him by Flight Despatch on the morning of the flight.
9. The briefing documents handed to him on November 9, 1979, which probably contained certain notations of his own.

10. The contents of the ring binder notebook which he had brought with him to the briefing of November 9.
11. The track and distance diagram showing the flight path to be down the centre of McMurdo Sound.
12. Another track and distance diagram also showing the flight path down the centre of McMurdo Sound.
13. The Antarctic strip chart showing the military track down the centre of McMurdo Sound.

To this list there needed to be added, in my own opinion, one more document and that was a copy of the flight plan distributed to Captain Collins and members of the other crew at the briefing of November 9. It had been said in evidence that these copies had all been retained by the briefing officer at the conclusion of that briefing. On the other hand, counsel assisting the Commission ascertained after the evidence had been closed, but before final submissions were advanced, that the Director of Flight Operations had telephoned one of the pilots who had been to the Collins home the day after the disaster, asking whether among the documents at the Collins home there had been a flight plan because, according to the Director of Flight Operations, a copy had been given to Captain Collins at the briefing of November 9 and Captain Collins had taken it away with him. The Director of Flight Operations had been advised that there was no such flight plan at the Collins home, nor any other material relevant to the flight.

It appeared from this that the Director of Flight Operations had been under a misapprehension. If the evidence of the briefing officer had been correct, then the flight plans distributed at the briefing had all been collected and retained by the briefing officer. But it had seemed to me, as I had listened to the evidence of Mrs Collins and had discussed their evidence with the two Collins girls, that Captain Collins was very unlikely indeed to have plotted any flight track on a large map without the aid of a copy of the flight plan produced at the briefing. Without a complete list of all the co-ordinates, how could he have plotted a track from Auckland to McMurdo and from McMurdo back to Christchurch? At least fourteen different sets of co-ordinates of latitude and longitude would have been required.

Even if a copy of the existing flight plan for Antarctica had not been retained by Captain Collins at the November 9 briefing, all he had to do in order to obtain one was to procure a printout from the ground computer at some time between November 9 and November 28.

If the foregoing assumption was right, as I thought it was, then the only three flight documents found on the snow had been in favour of the company's case, and that of the remaining eleven documents (if we take the collection of maps from the bookcase as being one document) at least ten had been in favour of the proposition that Captain Collins had relied upon the incorrect co-ordinates.

Captain Gemmell had been cross-examined about all this. He had been appointed by the Chief Inspector as a co-investigator. He was known to have searched the crash site for any evidence which might have given some indication of the cause of the disaster. First Officer Rhodes, who had completed previously an air accident investigation course and who had been authorised to be at the scene as a representative of ALPA, had said in evidence that he had seen Captain Gemmell with a plastic bag full of documents.

The suggested inference by ALPA therefore was that because there had been an instruction by the Chief Executive immediately after the disaster that all documents relating to Antarctic flights and to this flight in particular, were to be impounded, that one of Captain Gemmell's duties upon arrival at Antarctica had been to carry out this very task, and to carry back to Auckland all such documents which he had been able to locate or which other people might have located and handed to him.

But Captain Gemmell had denied all this. He said that any documents recovered by him or handed to him at the crash site had been handed over by him to the Chief Inspector.

It then appeared that, after giving his evidence, First Officer Rhodes had been confronted by the Director of Flight Operations in respect of his suggestion that Captain Gemmell had recovered a quantity of documents at the crash site, and at what appeared to be the associated inference that some of these documents had not since been accounted for by the airline management.

It was clear that the Director of Flight Operations had told First Officer Rhodes that he must either make a direct allegation against Captain Gemmell or else make no allegation at all. No one could say that this confrontation by the Director of Flight Operations was unwarranted. The inference which might be drawn from the evidence of First Officer Rhodes was certainly very serious. So, as a result, First Officer Rhodes was recalled as a witness by the airline. He referred to his discussion with the Director of Flight Operations. He now said that he wished to say that he had 'no reason to doubt Captain Gemmell in any way, shape or form'. This, of course, meant that First Officer Rhodes was acknowledging the obvious fact that he had no direct evidence in his possession which would indicate that Captain Gemmell had recovered any documents, including any one or more of the eleven documents which I have specified, without having accounted for all such documents to the Chief Inspector. I thought that this was a very proper concession to make, but First Officer Rhodes still maintained, in spite of his interview with the Director of Flight Operations, that Captain Gemmell had brought a quantity of documents from the crash site back to Auckland.

As may be imagined, this particular sequence of evidence — and I am here referring to the whole question of documents recovered from the site — produced a very strong atmosphere of bitterness between ALPA and the management.

The difficulty was that the only three flight documents which appeared to have been recovered all tended to support the case for the airline. Document 1 gave information about the radio frequencies; Document 2 gave the co-ordinates of the McMurdo NDB even though that document was two years old; Document 3 has been sufficiently described — not only did it remind pilots that the minimum safe altitude in the McMurdo area was 6,000 feet, but it also reminded pilots that subject to this special low altitude clearance the minimum safe altitude in general was 16,000 feet. Naturally, it did not pass without comment that the author of Document 3 had himself flown over McMurdo at 3,000 feet on one of the previous flights.

Most of the other eleven documents would all have been against the case for the airline had they been recovered. The mathematical odds against only these particular three documents having been recovered out of the total of fourteen were certainly very high.

In particular, the attitude of ALPA towards the non-recovery of Captain Collins' atlas was particularly hostile. There had been recovered from the wreckage many copies of Eliot Porter's book on Antarctica. Its cover is predominantly white, whereas the cover of the atlas had been black with two bright gold stripes, one narrow and one bronze, in a conspicuous modern design. The dry powdered snow drifting across the slope had not concealed the Porter books. How had it concealed the atlas? And, of course, the atlas must have been projected forward on impact or ejected on to the snow with the other maps and documents in the flight deck when impact took place.

Then there was the single sheet of quarto paper which I have referred to as Document 3. Wherever it was found, it must have been in approximately the same location as the atlas which I knew weighed over 1½ kilograms. How could that loose sheet of quarto have been recovered without the atlas being recovered, to say nothing of the other varied documents which I have listed?

One principal difficulty was that the Chief Inspector had not been able to say by whom or where the documents numbered 1-3 inclusive had been found. They had obviously been found by someone, and then handed to him at some unknown later time, but we did not know whether they had been given to him in Antarctica or in New Zealand.

But for my own part I could see nothing in all this which suggested any course of misconduct on the part of Captain Gemmell. Despite the long odds against such an occurrence, it may well have been that the only relevant flight documents recovered from the crash site were the Documents 1-3 inclusive. It was not probable, but it was possible. But suppose that one or more of the other eleven documents had been found. I was aware from my visit to Antarctica that not only the police but other persons searching the area had been told to hand to the Chief Inspector or Captain Gemmell any documents which appeared to have come from the flight deck. The Chief Inspector had told me in evidence that he had left it to the Air New Zealand personnel to assess the relevance of any documents found. So if any one or more of the documents listed 4-14 inclusive had been recovered and handed to Captain Gemmell, then all he had done was to carry them back to New Zealand with other articles and documentation which had been recovered from the site. No doubt he had handed all these discoveries to the airline management in Auckland. They would certainly have been entitled to see them. Once out of Captain Gemmell's custody, then he had no further responsibility as far as they were concerned.

I came to the clear conclusion that, upon the evidence available to me, there was nothing to associate Captain Gemmell with any disappearance, if it ever took place, of documentation, recovered from the crash site, which went to support the view that the crew had relied upon the Dailey Islands waypoint as exhibited to them on the flight plan produced for their inspection at the briefing of November 9. I ultimately reported in these terms to the New Zealand Government.

But the opportunity for all these accusations against Air New Zealand had arisen, without question, from the discovery that there had been an order for destruction of documents given by the Chief Executive immediately after the disaster.

With regard to this question of destruction of documents, an attempt was made to assert that it was left to the 'in-house committee' to determine which documents were to go through the company shredder. But Captain Gemmell, the dominant member of this committee, said he had no knowledge of this arrangement.

I was sure that none of these questions about recovery of flight documents from the wreckage would have arisen had it not been for the document destruction order issued by the Chief Executive. No doubt he acted in good faith, but he certainly committed an act of folly, as this chapter reveals.

The ring-binder notebook

I have referred earlier to Mrs Collins's description of the diaries habitually carried by her husband. One was a small notebook with a red cover which he used to carry in the top pocket of his jacket; the other was the ring-binder notebook, which was returned to her by Air New Zealand, but with all its pages missing.

It was the ring-binder notebook which Captain Collins used for noting down flight information which he thought it necessary to retain. He used to carry it in his flight bag because it was too large to carry in his pocket. This was the notebook which he would have taken with him to the briefing of November 9, 1979, nineteen days before the fatal flight.

At the inquiry, Mrs Collins had produced the empty ring-binder with her husband's name and initials imprinted across the top in embossed tape and some detailed questions were raised by counsel for the Collins estate as to what had happened to the missing pages.

Mrs Collins had described her husband as a dedicated note taker. It was quite evident that at the November 9 briefing he would have recorded in this ring-binder book such relevant points as were not covered by the written briefing materials and which were conveyed verbally by the briefing officer. It was also apparent, at least in my own view, that Captain Collins was almost certain to have recorded in this notebook the information that Antarctic aircrews were entitled to descend to any altitude in the McMurdo area authorised by the U.S. Air Traffic Control. This information was at variance with the written briefing material and, having regard to the note-taking propensities of Captain Collins, it seemed a certainty that he would have recorded this aspect of the briefing in his notebook.

In addition to all this, had he used his notebook to record the destination co-ordinates appearing on the flight plan which was produced? Had he also recorded the Cape Hallett co-ordinates so as to know the exact course of the last leg of the computer flight track? He had his atlas with him at this briefing. Had he marked on his atlas the approximate position of the waypoint just to the west of the Dailey Islands and noted that the flight track proceeded from Cape Hallett across the Ross Sea and then down the centre of McMurdo? Had he recorded this in his notebook?

The counsel for the Collins estate, together with senior counsel for ALPA and counsel for the passenger consortium, were all very concerned about what had happened to the pages from this ring-binder notebook, the cover of which, entirely undamaged, had been produced in evidence.

Counsel assisting the Commission located the police property sheet which had listed the items of property identified as belonging to Captain Collins. This sheet had recorded the presence in the Collins property bag of two 'diaries'. These diaries had been seen by the same pilot who had visited the Cassin home and taken away the flight documents. He had been asked about this ring-binder notebook when he gave evidence and had said that one of the two diaries which he had seen was this empty ring-binder notebook and that it had been handed over in due course to Mrs Collins. The other diary, the witness said, had been found to have belonged to a flight stewardess and it had been ultimately delivered to her family.

The person who had signed for and received the two diaries from the police on behalf of Air New Zealand had been a Mr Ian Hambly, an employee of the company. Mr Hambly had not been called as a witness, but the pilot who had returned to Mrs Collins this empty ring-binder notebook had said that he obtained it from Mr Hambly. He had also said that it was empty when given to him by Mr Hambly and that he did not know what had happened to the missing pages. But after the pilot had given this evidence, there was a further development.

Mr Hambly got in touch with counsel assisting the Commission. He had either heard of the pilot's evidence or had read it in the newspapers. He said that the ring-binder notebook had not been one of the two diaries for which he signed. As a former police officer he was fully familiar with police property sheets and was quite clear that the police would never have referred to the notebook as a 'diary' had the pages been missing. In other words, according to Mr Hambly, the pilot who handed the empty notebook to Mrs Collins had not received it from Mr Hambly and it had not been in police custody in Auckland.

Again I instructed counsel for the Commission to make further inquiries. Harrison interviewed Inspector Mitchell who had been in charge of the police property at McMurdo. The inspector believed that he had been shown the ring-binder notebook at

McMurdo and he believed that all the pages were then missing. This had seemed unusual, as it was thought unlikely that Captain Collins would have carried with him a ring-binder notebook with all the pages removed, especially if he had taken that same notebook to the briefing of November 9.

So, for the moment, the question of the ring-binder note-book remained indecisive and quite uncertain. Where had the pages gone? They had clearly been removed by someone, and if so when and why?

I must now go forward a little way in time. After my report into the disaster had been published, the pilot who had handed the empty notebook to Mrs Collins gave an explanation which was made public. He said that he himself had removed the missing pages before returning the book to Mrs Collins. He said that he had done this because the notes had no aviation significance and because they had been soaked in kerosene. He said that he had remembered this when his wife reminded him about it on the evening of the day when he had given evidence.

The pilot did not explain why he had not returned to the inquiry the next day and told me about his altered recollection. It would have been quite a simple thing to do but now, some months after he had given this evidence before me to the effect that he did not know what had happened to the missing pages, he was publicly stating that he himself had removed them, and that they contained no flight data or flight information.

However, as at the time when I came to publish the report, I could only conclude, on the evidence which had been given, that the black ring-binder notebook had not been in police custody when two 'diaries' were signed for by Mr Hambly on the police property sheet and that the notebook had been returned to New Zealand in police custody and that someone, whether at McMurdo or at Auckland, had removed the pages.

But even the belated statement of the pilot who said he had removed the pages had still not resolved the question where the notebook had been before the pages were removed. Mr Hambly was adamant that this was not one of the two diaries which he had been handed by the police.

It might have been thought that the foregoing was the final instalment in the enigma of the ring-binder notebook. But such was not the case. A long time after the inquiry had concluded and my report had been published, some new facts were revealed.

As was the case with nearly every document recovered from the crash site and produced at the inquiry, I had never been told where this ring-binder notebook had been found. The practice adopted by the Chief Inspector had simply been to produce the very few documents recovered. It was clear that the Chief Inspector had relied upon the Air New Zealand personnel present to evaluate the importance or relevance of any documents found.

But, many months after my report had been published, I at last discovered who had found the ring-binder notebook. It had been found by two police officers — one a sergeant, the other a constable — who had been among the first group of police landed at the crash site. When searching the wreckage in the vicinity of the flight deck, and in the close vicinity of the body of Captain Collins, they had seen the empty flight bag and they had also discovered near it, a ring-binder notebook with hard-back covers and with the name of Captain Collins printed on the outside. The notebook covers and the pages were undamaged. The two police officers had no difficulty in reading the contents.

They found that there were pages covered with figures and calculations which were obviously flight data. Neither police officers could follow the significance of the various groups of figures, nor the written notations, but they clearly comprised technical details relating to a particular flight, and the police officers immediately saw that the contents of the notebook would be of considerable interest to the investigating authorities. Accordingly they placed it in a plastic property bag and made sure that it was carried off to the store where recovered property was being assembled at McMurdo Base.

In due course the Chief Inspector's report was published, and then after some months the report of the Royal Commission was published and the two police officers naturally believed that the flight data in Captain Collins' notebook had been preserved and investigated.

However, some months after my report was published, the police officers watched, with great interest, a television documentary dealing with the proceedings of the Royal Commission. They followed the sequence of events in the courtroom and saw and heard various witnesses give evidence. Then there followed a piece of evidence on which they concentrated with particular attention. The witness was the Air New Zealand pilot who had handed the ring-binder notebook back to Mrs Collins. The police officers were astonished to find that the notebook had been described as being empty, and that the pilot who handed it back to Mrs Collins had no information as to where the pages had gone. The police officers knew that when they had recovered the notebook from the ice its pages had been intact and had contained the flight data.

From that time onwards the two police officers had become very concerned at what had happened to the informative pages which they themselves had seen. Where had they gone? The police officers prepared and sent to police headquarters in Auckland a report setting out what I have just described. But they were told that because the Commission of Inquiry was now concluded, there was no point in taking the matter any further.

But time went by and the more the police sergeant and his colleague thought about the incident, the less they liked it. It looked very much to them as if these pages of flight data had been improperly removed. So they decided to tell me about it. I thought that what they had to say might be of interest to readers of this book. I asked them to describe the nature of the entries which they had seen on the various pages and, from their description, it was clear that the information recorded included latitude and longitude co-ordinates together with various written notes relating to the Antarctic flight, otherwise Captain Collins would not have taken the trouble to place the notebook in his flight bag and take it with him. There had been about thirty pages in the notebook, and the only entries were the notes and flight data on the first six or seven pages. They also confirmed that the pages were undamaged and not soaked with kerosene or otherwise affected by the impact of the aircraft striking the slopes of the mountain.

I append this late discovery only as a matter of interest. I had been fully aware at the inquiry, and counsel opposing Air New Zealand had all been fully aware, that Captain Collins had without doubt taken this notebook with him to the briefing on November 9, 1979. I had always been sure that the missing pages had almost certainly contained destination co-ordinates for the fatal flight (it being remembered that these co-ordinates had been underlined in ink on the flight plan produced at the briefing), and verbal additions to the written briefing.

Until the disclosure by the two police officers, there had been no hard evidence to support this belief, held by me and by various counsel. But now the evidence was clear beyond a doubt. At some time between the finding of the notebook on the ice and the delivery of the same notebook to Mrs Collins, the pages had been removed by a person or persons unknown, and they had plainly been removed because they recorded information which, at that early stage, the airline had been anxious to conceal. The written notes of Captain Collins had proved beyond doubt, in my opinion, his reliance upon the 'false' co-ordinates produced to him at the briefing of November 9, 1979 and in all probability they had also recorded the specific authority given to him at the briefing to approach McMurdo at whatever altitude was suggested or directed by the American air traffic controllers at McMurdo Base.

Miss Keenan's diary

I have just described the delivery to Mrs Collins of her husband's ring-binder notebook, and I referred to the fact that, on the police property sheet relating to Captain Collins, there was an entry saying that the police held two diaries which had belonged to him.

But it appeared that one of the diaries belonged to a flight stewardess who died in the disaster. Her name was Diane Keenan. According to Mr Hambly, who signed for the two diaries and handed them to someone in the airline, neither diary had included the ring-binder notebook. The two diaries for which he signed were the small diary of Captain Collins and an anonymous diary later found to belong to Miss Keenan. So Mrs Collins was handed (by the airline employee) the small diary and the empty ring-binder notebook, and Miss Keenan's diary was returned by the airline to her family.

During the hearing a suggestion was put to me that someone from the airline, being anxious to obtain the ring-binder notebook, had gone to the police property store at the Auckland mortuary and had placed Miss Keenan's diary among the Collins property and had taken away the ring-binder notebook. By this means, the police property sheet would remain correct. It would refer to two diaries. Thus it was, so the theory went, that Mr Hambly had later collected and signed for 'two diaries' on the police property sheet. In the meantime, the pages in the ring-binder notebook had been torn out and destroyed by someone. Then the small diary and empty ring-binder notebook had been returned to Mrs Collins, Miss Keenan's diary to her family, and the police were never aware that the switch had taken place.

Some force was lent to this theory, so it was suggested, by the fact that Miss Keenan's name had been torn out of the top of the front page of her diary before it was placed among Captain Collin's property in the manner described. A check with the Keenan family confirmed that their daughter's diary had been returned by the airline with a top rectangular section of the top page torn away. The appearance of the Keenan diary lent some weight to the switching theory. The flight bag of Captain Collins and his ring-binder notebook had been found to the left of the flight deck section which had itself been to the left of the main

270

track of aircraft damage. Neither the flight deck, nor any articles found to its left, had been affected by fire. But Miss Keenan's diary was scorched around the edge which meant that it must have been in very close proximity to the intense fire in the main fuselage section. It must therefore have been found far away from the flight bag and the ring-binder notebook.

This 'diary-switching' allegation was feasible enough as a practical possibility. But I had neither the time nor the inclination to inquire into the matter.

What happened to the airline files?

As the inquiry progressed I had become more and more restive about the absence of any relevant documentation in the possession of the airline. An order for the production of documents had been signed and served, but the only result had been the production of a small file put together by what was termed an 'in-house committee' of Air New Zealand which had been set up just after the disaster in order to begin inquiries. But this file, if I can call it that, was of no assistance. It contained only copies of briefing documents and one or two expressions of opinion by members of the committee which were of no consequence. The question arose as to why the file had not been produced before, and a careful study of its contents provided the answer.

Evidently, there had been produced to the committee an initial explanation from the Briefing Section which had been recorded in a document marked J2 on this file. Then it appeared that some days later the members of the committee had discovered that the explanation was incorrect. They had called for what apparently was the correct explanation. Once this was received then the original document J2 was removed from the file and a new document J2 was substituted.

I had little doubt that the unsatisfactory aspect of the original J2 document had been an omission to refer to the production at the briefing of the standard Antarctica flight plan with the destination co-ordinates, as will be recalled, underlined in ink. But Captain Simpson and his crew had been present at the same briefing. The production of a flight plan with the Dailey Islands co-ordinates had undoubtedly become known. In any case, even if the original J2 explanation had been unintentionally mistaken, it now required a correction.

It was very obvious, so it seemed to me, why this 'in-house committee' file had not previously been produced. It seemed clear that the management had not wished to disclose the occurrence of an initial explanation (the exact terms of which I will never know), which the committee had been obliged to reject.

I expected to see the relevant parts of the Commercial Affairs Division files, the Flight Operations Antarctic file, the Navigation Section files dealing with Antarctic flights and so on. But not one operational file was produced. The internal memoranda referred to by Captain Grundy were not produced. Captain Johnston's briefing file, as he said, had been handed over by him to the management and he had never seen it since.

I felt obliged to confront the airline counsel with these deficiencies. They seemed to me to be as anxious about the documentary situation as I was. One of the two senior airline counsel then went to the trouble of paying a prolonged visit to the airline head office to inquire into all this, but he got a negative response from every division. There were no relevant files or documents other than documents produced already.

So where did the company's operational files go? Were the Antarctic components of company files all put through the shredder as being 'surplus copies' of documents thought to be held in some other file?

Among the documents never produced to the Commission was a copy of the minutes of a meeting of directors held only a few days before the date when the Royal Commission hearings were to begin. These minutes recorded the decision that the case for the company would be founded upon the breach by the aircrew of the 16,000 feet minimum safe altitude and that the company would further rely upon the Chief Inspector's opinion as to the cause of the accident.

The existence of these minutes was not revealed until after my report was published. The company was certainly fortunate that a person or persons in its employ had decided that these documents were not relevant to the terms of reference of the Commission and had evidently not disclosed the documents to the airline counsel. One can imagine the ensuing ordeal of the Chief Executive in the witness box.

In addition, there was not disclosed a further document which again did not come to light until after my report had been published. This was a written note of a verbal report by the Chief Executive to his Board of Directors made on December 5 1979, seven days after the disaster. The change in the flight track, and the failure to advise the aircrew of that change, had been known to the management ever since the night of the disaster. But in making his report to his Directors, the Chief Executive had indicated that the reason for the aircraft being off-track was not known.

It was not only the company directors who had been kept in the dark about the computer mistake. When Captain Cooper departed for the United States in order to be present at the readout of the flight deck recorder tapes, he was unaware of the change in the flight track. He had been sent to Washington to interpret the voice tapes without knowing this vital fact which had been known to Flight Operations Division for six days before his departure.

The burglary at the Collins house

During her evidence Mrs Collins had described how someone had broken and entered her home in Auckland on March 29, 1980. The police had been notified and they had attended the scene and verified that a burglary had been committed.

Mrs Collins had been asked to notify the police of the nature of any articles which might have been stolen. She had searched the house and discovered that the burglar had been content with taking away only one item of property — a file of documents which she had kept relating to the disaster.

The burglary had taken place on March 29, 1980 after the Chief Inspector had delivered to her solicitors his preliminary report containing a list of allegations of negligence on the part of her husband. The file to which Mrs Collins referred had been contained in a drawer of a desk. The file had been in the left-hand side of the drawer; on the right-hand side there had been various items of jewellery, including rings set with precious stones and the like. The unknown burglar had disregarded the jewellery lying openly in the drawer after he opened it. He had taken only her file of documents.

Counsel for the Collins estate had understandably dealt with this matter with some degree of circumspection, but he had obviously not liked this incident. In his view, and in the view of the ALPA representatives generally, there was a possible analogy here between this incident and what had happened with regard to the Cassin documents.

The suggestion was that the airline had been very anxious to find out what documents had been left at home by the two pilots. It will be remembered that the Director of Flight Operations had been anxious to discover, quite understandably in my opinion, whether any flight plan had been found at the Collins home by the pilot who had visited Mrs Collins on the day after the disaster but, of course, Captain Collins had taken his flight documents away with him. First Officer Cassin had not. The airline, knowing these facts, had got possession of the Cassin flight documents as soon as possible. The pilot who had visited Mrs Cassin, and who had taken the documents away, had also visited Mrs Collins. But he had made no enquiry of her as to any documents which she might hold.

With regard to the Collins burglary, the opinion was held by some of the counsel opposing Air New Zealand, and as it turned out later by a good many other people, that the occurrence was linked with the knowledge that Mrs Collins had been given a copy of the Chief Inspector's interim report some days beforehand. The newspapers had announced on March 4, 1980 that the interim report had been delivered to interested parties and some days later the newspapers reported that the representatives of the two dead pilots had been given copies of the report, which meant that the aircrew was being blamed by the Chief Inspector. The burglary itself had taken place on March 29, 1980.

Assuming the evidence of Mrs Collins and her later discussions with me to have been correct, then the unknown person who entered her house had been very selective as to what he took. Why had the documents been taken and the jewellery left alone? The burglar would know, but I doubted whether I would ever be privileged to hear his explanation.

My own impression of the incident was that someone who had lost a relative or friend in the disaster had become aware from the newspapers that the aircrew was being blamed, and by reason, probably, of emotional disturbance might have searched the Collins home for any documents relating to the disaster.

274

XXVI

A REFLECTION
ON THE ALLEGATIONS OF
'PILOT ERROR'

The circumstances of the final stage of the approach of Flight
TE901 towards Ross Island will never be fully known, and,
without the advantage of the CVR and the digital flight data
recorder (the 'black box'), would never have been known at all.
The airline witnesses who appeared before me were intent upon
establishing pilot error as the effective cause of the accident.

This is a conventional stance, adopted by airline operators and
sometimes by aircraft manufacturers, when an inquiry is
convened. In most cases the object is to persuade the tribunal that
in spite of some technical malfunction of the aircraft which
originated the chain of events, the pilot had the chance, even at the
last minute, of avoiding the accident. The types of pilot error
suggested in such cases normally include flying on a course or at
an altitude which in the circumstances was unsafe, or was not
authorised by the airline operator, or was forbidden by aviation
regulations, and in suitable cases it may be alleged that the pilot
was too slow in his response to an emergency.

When the aircrew has been killed in a flying accident,
allegations of 'pilot error' require careful consideration, for they
will depend mainly on inferential conclusions rather than direct
evidence. It is a mistake to draw conclusions or to make inferences
without assessing all the known facts, and, in this case, I think
this error was made by the Chief Inspector when he deduced that
Captain Collins was 'uncertain' of his position, and I think the
same error coloured a good deal of the evidence adduced on behalf
of Air New Zealand.

I had no doubt that the management had first intended not to
disclose to anyone that the flight crew at their November 9

275

briefing had been provided with a copy of the standard Antarctica flight plan showing the Dailey Islands waypoint. If this fact became known then the subsequent change to that flight plan would also become known; the Navigation Section had become aware, on the night of the disaster, that the alteration to the destination waypoint had not been revealed to aircrew on the fatal flight. And I also had no doubt that at that early stage, only a day or so after the crash, the Chief Executive had been assured by his technical advisers that the alteration to the standard flight plan had nothing to do with the disaster.

But the fact of that drastic alteration having been made just before the departure of the fatal flight was potentially a very dangerous disclosure if it were revealed. The Chief Executive's advisers had been adamant, no doubt, that the mere perusal of the standard flight plan of the briefing and its return to the briefing officer shortly afterwards, could not possibly have revealed to the flight crew that the computer track was different from that being described by the briefing officers. But the advisers of those who would bring claims against the airline would unquestionably seize on this information and assert that either Captain Collins or First Officer Cassin had noted the destination co-ordinates and relied upon them, and had not realised, when typing the long sequence of figures into the aircraft computer nineteen days later, that one digit had been changed. And such an allegation would be a serious matter for Lloyds because, if established in court proceedings, it would wipe out the $42,000 limit per claim which would result from a finding of pilot error, and liability for damages would be unlimited.

Hence the verbal report by Mr Davis to his board of directors on December 5, seven days after the disaster, when he said that in view of the instrumentation in the plane, he could not think 'why he (Collins) got into this position'. Mr Davis did not reveal to the directors that the standard flight track had been altered and the flight crew not told. I should repeat here that the existence of the minutes of that board meeting was never revealed to the Royal Commission, despite my formal written order for production of all documents, and one can imagine the ordeal of Mr Davis under cross-examination if counsel had been aware of what he had said in this respect, and in other respects, to his board members on December 5.

But this initial plan to conceal the flight track alteration, for that is what I thought it was, very soon collapsed, and for a simple reason. It was belatedly discovered that another flight crew had been present at the same briefing, and members of that crew had told other pilots, after the disaster, about the production of the flight plan by the briefing officers. It was no longer possible to conceal the flight track alteration, and it now became necessary to tell the Chief Inspector about it. This was done about three weeks after the disaster. But the airline management persuaded him, and I had no doubt that they were stating their real belief, that the flight crew on November 28 had not been misled by the unrevealed alteration to their computer track.

I wondered what would have happened if Captain Simpson and his crew had not been present at the briefing. The management believed that the production of the standard flight plan at the briefing had no real relevance to the disaster, but would be dangerous to the airline and its insurers if it became known. My opinion was that, in those circumstances, no one would ever have been told about the production of that flight plan or of its later alteration. The flight plan delivered to the aircraft on the morning of the flight would have been in conformity with the verbal additions to the written briefing material to which the briefing officers would testify, namely that the flight path lay over the peak of Mount Erebus. Thus the crew of the fatal flight would always have known that their computer track was on a collision course with the mountain. The disaster would have been totally inexplicable, except on the basis that the crew deliberately flew towards the mountain at low altitude and in cloud.

The principal factors relied upon by the airline witnesses were altitude, speed, heading, terrain, and weather. But a conclusion based upon those five factors alone meant the omission of perhaps the paramount factor — the skill and experience of the two pilots.

This was not the case of a top-dressing aircraft or a deer-hunting helicopter in which a degree of risk is undertaken by the pilot as part of his operational duties. Nor was it the case of an amateur pilot flying a light aircraft in a manner suggesting or establishing his folly or his ignorance of sound aviation practice. The pilot and co-pilot of the DC10 were commercial pilots of long experience. Neither Captain Collins nor First Officer Cassin would consciously take the slightest risk in the course of flying the aircraft. Once due weight is given to that factor then it becomes difficult to infer that the pilots were uncertain as to their position. But one can go further than that.

Why did Captain Collins bring the aircraft back on to its Nav track at the conclusion of the second orbit? This was the continuing obstacle to any suggestion that the crew were 'uncertain' as to their position. The rearming of the Nav mode could only mean that Captain Collins had in front of him a plotted track showing exactly where the Nav track would take him, and this wholly negated any suggestion that he or First Officer Cassin were 'uncertain' as to their position. On this basis the cornerstone of the whole allegation of pilot error begins to crumble away, because every alternative course of conduct which it is suggested the pilots ought to have adopted, and every additional monitoring precaution it is suggested they should have taken, is based upon the primary and false thesis that the crew were not sure where the aircraft was.

It is instructive to consider what might have happened had the altered co-ordinates in the flight plan not resulted in disaster. Suppose that as Flight TE901 approached Ross Island the cloud obscuring Mount Erebus had been dissipated for a moment, either by sunlight or by the wind, so as to reveal to the aircrew the presence of the mountain in their path, and the aircraft had then climbed safely away. In due course there would have been instituted in New Zealand a public inquiry into the incident. At that inquiry the persons placed on the defensive from the outset would have been the relevant personnel of the Flight Operations Division of the airline.

Captain Collins would have produced the whole of the contents of his flight bag, and they would have included his maps, his atlas, all his flight documents, and his black ring-binder notebook with all its pages intact. The crew would have testified as to the pre-descent briefing, and the pilots would have been able to say exactly what they saw on the approach to Ross Island. I doubt very much if there would have been too much heard at such an inquiry, with Captain Collins, First Officer Cassin, the two flight engineers and Peter Mulgrew present and listening, about wrongful reliance on the inertial navigation system, unlawful descent below minimum safe altitude, flying towards an area of deteriorating visibility, and the like.

On the vital question of visibility there would have been, I need hardly say, the evidence not only of the flight crew but also of large numbers of passengers who must have looked at Ross Island in the course of the orbiting turns which the aircraft made. No doubt all this is obvious enough, but I only stress the point that there were areas of fact in this investigation which will always remain unknown simply because all the occupants of the aircraft lost their lives, and that inferences of 'pilot error' should not too readily be drawn when the circumstances are equivocal, and when the tale of the aircrew themselves can never be told.

XXVII

HOW THE 'BLACK BOX' READOUT WAS MISINTERPRETED

I have described already the general function of the 'black box' and the incredible volume of data which its electronic system can retain. It had established every movement of the aircraft itself and of its controls during the last phase of the journey from Auckland. Needless to say, considerable attention had been paid by the transcribing authorities in Washington to the events of the last two or three minutes of the flight.

A readout from the 'black box' is obtained by plugging its recording apparatus into a computer printout machine. A printout can then be obtained for any particular segment of the flight. All the aircraft's operational and mechanical functions are printed out with great rapidity right across the screen, one line after another, and transcribers are able to tell exactly how the aircraft was flying and how it was being piloted, and how its controls were being operated at the particular time. The transcript thus obtained had been summarised in suitable form in Washington and from the transcript there had been prepared an appendix which explained what the printout had been saying. This appendix appeared as one of the annexes to the Chief Inspector's report.

At the hearing of the Royal Commission, little or no attention had been paid to this particular annex. I had read through it and found that its main relevance was to illustrate the course of events once Captain Collins had decided that he would fly away. The 'black box' had recorded Captain Collins as having pulled out the Heading Select knob. The aircraft had then commenced a right-hand roll in accordance with the previous selected heading. Then the roll had been corrected immediately as the Heading Select knob had been moved around to the left. Before the new heading of the aircraft had been effectively established, the GPWS system

279

had sounded and the aircraft had, within seconds, collided with the mountainside.

When I came to consider this 'black box' readout in the course of writing my report I gave it close and detailed attention, and it seemed to me, as I went through the passages word by word, that there was something wrong about the interpretation which the authorities appeared to have placed upon the readout.

As will be remembered, it was perfectly clear from the flight deck recorder tapes that no one on the flight deck had ever seen the mountainside, even at the last second. It was also established that the aircraft was flying in clear air. And there could be no doubt that the crew had been deceived by the whiteout ocular illusion, and this was why they had never seen the mountainside.

In these circumstances, what was it that the CVR and the 'black box' could tell us about the last few minutes and seconds of the fatal flight? The way in which these electronic devices are used is quite well known. The voice recorder tape and the electronic recording system of the black box are married together by synchronising the tapes. The result is to correlate the comments of the captain and the co-pilot and the flight engineer with the mode of flight of the aircraft at that particular time.

Now here the difficulty was that there appeared to be an apparent conflict between the available facts as to the weather and the voice recorder tapes on the one hand, and the 'black box' readout on the other hand. There had been extracts from the CVR which, when transcribed by the experts, had suggested that some persons on the flight were describing the weather outside as being 'thick', or were otherwise describing the visibility as being impaired. It was found, however, on re-examination of the tapes, both in Washington and in the United Kingdom, that these remarks alluding to the weather had in fact not been made and, indeed, there was nothing said between pilot and co-pilot which cast any doubt at all upon the fact that they were flying in visual meteorological conditions (VMC) right until the moment of impact.

But the conflict with the 'black box' readout was that the latter, as transcribed in Washington and as printed in the Chief Inspector's report, appeared to suggest that there had been some violent last-minute avoidance manoeuvre by the crew because they had been flying in poor visibility and had suddenly seen the mountainside before them. This was in direct conflict with the apparently clear evidence from the CVR that no one on the flight deck ever saw the mountainside. What was this conflicting evidence apparently provided by the 'black box'? What did it really say? This obviously required close attention.

In the first place, the 'black box' referred to a sudden application of left rudder appearing in the last few seconds of flight. It was said that in the last 3.5 seconds of flight there was a sudden large application of left rudder of three degrees which rapidly increased to a maximum of thirteen degrees left rudder just prior to impact. Because the 'black box' showed that rudder was only applied to a maximum of up to one degree for very short periods when the aircraft was flown by the auto-pilot, therefore the assumption was that this violent left rudder was applied manually, that is to say, by the pilot. I emphasise that this was an assumption made by the transcribers. This was the first major area in which the 'black box' was plainly in conflict with the CVR.

The next contradiction was in connection with the alteration in the attitude of the aircraft. Prior to impact, the aircraft had been flying in a clean configuration, that is to say, with no flaps extended, and this gave it a nose-up attitude of five degrees. The reason for a clean configuration being required was that if the flaps were extended to facilitate slow speed, and if for some reason they could not be retracted due to icing or some other cause, then the aircraft would have to fly 2,500 miles back to New Zealand with the flaps out. So, we have, first of all, a nose-up attitude of five degrees during the last stages of the flight.

Then the 'black box' went on to say that there had been a sudden upwards pitch of the aircraft somewhere about four seconds before impact from five degrees nose-up to a maximum of 10.9 degrees nose-up. It was recorded by the transcribers that this pitch upwards started from a sudden — seven degrees in two seconds — application of nose-up elevator, four seconds prior to impact. Then there is a cautionary observation that the data for the auto-pilot contained some doubtful information as a result of a tape break.

So there, with these two factors, you had a strong contradiction with what had been happening in the aircraft according to the comments between pilot and co-pilot. About four seconds prior to impact, there had been a sudden strong application of left rudder accompanied by a strong application of nose-up elevator, and the inference from these facts clearly was that the crew saw the mountainside something like four to five seconds before impact and attempted to fly away.

But what did the CVR tell us about these last six seconds of flight? First of all, six seconds before impact there was the sudden warning from the ground proximity system. This was followed by the flight engineer announcing the altitude as 500 feet. Then the ground proximity warning system sounded again, and the engineer announced the altitude as 400 feet. Then the pilot requested 'Go round power, please.' Then the impact took place.

Over these six seconds, where was the indication either from pilot, co-pilot or engineer of this sudden application of left-hand rudder, and the sudden nose-up elevator so violently applied? Not a word was said by anyone on the flight deck about either of these two violent manoeuvres. Nor was a word said by anyone as to seeing anything in front of the aircraft. I could not see how this sequence of events, very clearly recorded on the voice tape, could be reconciled with the readout of the electronic tapes from the 'black box' supplied by the Office of Air Accidents.

The first thing that occurred to me was that the so-called manual application of left-hand rudder might have occurred not before, but after impact. The known sequence of events, according to the 'black box', as from some twenty seconds before impact had been this. First of all, as the voice tapes told us, the flight captain had decided to turn away because he was twenty-six miles out from his destination waypoint, and obviously he and the crew could see nothing ahead of them but a flat white plain. He and the co-pilot had discussed whether they would turn left or right.

The captain had then pulled out the Heading Select knob, thus disengaging the aircraft from its Nav track. The moment he disengaged the Nav track, the aircraft began to roll to the right in obedience to the heading which had previously controlled the Heading Select dial. But the captain had then turned the Heading Select dial to the left so as to command a left turn and the aircraft had immediately responded by correcting the right-hand roll and starting to roll to the left, and it had struck the mountainside with the aircraft probably rolling just to the left of the centre line.

If the number one engine, that is to say the engine on the left side, had struck the ice first, the aircraft would have been whipped violently to the left just prior to the number three engine striking the ice, which would have made it straighten up. It seemed to me that this initial violent left swing of the aircraft might have been recorded by the 'black box' as the violent left-hand rudder to which it referred. It was only an assumption by the transcribers that the left-hand rudder had been manually applied. It could easily have been manually applied in the sense that the pilot's foot would have been jammed down on the left-hand rudder by inertial force as a result of the violent initial left-hand swing before the aircraft straightened up. But, whatever the cause, it seemed quite possible and indeed probable, that the 'black box' had recorded the violent left-hand rudder as occurring after the impact and not before.

Then, what about the sudden and equally violent nose-up elevator involving a seven degrees lift in two seconds and a total change from five degrees nose-up to a maximum of just on eleven degrees nose-up prior to the aircraft striking the mountain?

Again, this seemed capable of being explained by the fact that the mountain sloped upwards at the point of impact at an angle of thirteen degrees. There seemed to me, having regard to the variations possible in the readout, to be little reason why the five degrees should not have suddenly changed to eleven degrees because the aircraft had struck at 300 miles an hour an ice slope with a thirteen degrees upwards inclination, and the 'black box' had correctly recorded a sudden upwards change in the angle of flight.

Whereas the 'black box' had been saying impact, then left-hand violent rudder, then violent nose-up elevator, the transcribers had read it exactly the other way round. Violent left-hand rudder, violent nose-up elevator, then impact. If my own deductions were correct, the transcribers had read the 'black box' information the wrong way round.

I pondered for some time upon this theory and put it to the experts. I was assured I was right about the left-hand rudder application, and that it was simply not possible for the rudder to have been applied with that degree of violence by a pilot, and this was borne out by a further consideration which I pointed out to the experts. It was clear that the 'black box' did not record any movement of the ailerons on the alleged left-hand rudder turn of thirteen degrees. The ailerons on the DC10 are linked with the spoilers, and the left-hand spoilers had not moved either. This therefore postulated that the pilot, if the transcribers were correct, had applied violent left-hand rudder and had not touched the yoke handle of his controls so as to operate the ailerons or the spoilers, and this was confirmed to me as being an impossible construction.

The key to this mistaken readout was, of course, the theory in the mind of the transcribers that the aircraft had been flying in cloud just prior to impact, that the crew had seen the ground seconds before impact, and had tried desperately to climb away to the left.

The 'black box' readout had taken place only days after the disaster, at about the same time as the CVR readout. At that time the passengers' photographs had not been printed. The transcribers of the 'black box' were not aware that the aircraft was flying in clear air. They proceeded upon the assumption that the aircraft had been flying in cloud because it was apparently outside their aeronautical knowledge that in polar regions an aircraft flying in clear air can fly directly into the side of a mountain.

And so, in my opinion, the transcribers had made the mistake which investigators have often made in times gone by and in different circumstances. Many police inquiries have gone wrong for the same reason. The mistake they made was to first postulate what they thought had happened, and then treat all information which did not fit their theory as being not correct.

So here we had this investigatory defect revealed in startling form. The transcribers disregarded the simple facts which the 'black box' was telling them and substituted their own version of what it was trying to say. You will recall what I said about the break in the tape and the slight uncertainty about the timing of what occurred and so on. The transcriber, acting in perfectly good faith, believed that there must have been at this point a fault in the electronic readout sequence.

I must say that I was considerably perturbed to have ascertained the facts thus described. As I say, I had checked out my theory with senior jet pilots of long experience and they had all agreed entirely with what I had to say. The question was: Should I reveal in my report to the Government what had happened with regard to this 'black box' readout?

I spent some time pondering over this. I was well aware that one of the terms of reference by which my inquiry was controlled was devoted to the aspect of air accident investigation. On balance, it almost seemed as if I had a duty to reveal the way in which the 'black box' readout had been tampered with, using that phrase in no sinister sense. But on further reflection, I changed my mind.

The report which I would publish was already adorned with references to evidence which I had been unable to accept, and the disaster itself had, of course, been unique in its location and in its circumstances. I did not feel that it would be wise to alarm professional bodies like overseas air accident investigators and the International Airline Pilots' Association with this revelation. The 'black box', after all, is rightly believed to be incapable of error. But, as with every computer printout or readout, it is possible for the transcribers to interpret what they are seeing in different ways. I did not want to cause unjustifiable alarm by alluding to this very unfortunate course of behaviour involving the 'black box' readout in the present case. So I kept silent. Perhaps I was wrong. However, this book tells the story.

XXVIII

WHAT I THINK REALLY HAPPENED ON THE FATAL FLIGHT

The unique nature of this air disaster was not only founded solely upon the location of the crash in the frozen wasteland of Antarctica. It had another highly unusual feature, and that was that, from the time the aircraft left New Zealand until its wreckage was found upon the mountainside of Mount Erebus, no living person either heard or saw it.

Without the assistance of the flight deck recorder tapes and the information provided by the 'black box', the disappearance of this big modern jet with 257 people on board would have remained a mystery forever and the reason for its destruction would never have been known. But, with the aid of the two recording devices, a considerable number of relevant facts can be established, and from those facts a number of inferences can legitimately and in some cases conclusively be derived. Here is what I think really happened:

On the morning of the flight Captain Collins and First Officer Cassin reported to the Flight Despatch Office at Auckland International Airport. There they were provided with the computer flight plan for the journey and they studied, with accustomed concentration, the weather and fuel data printed into this standard Antarctica flight plan.

Not a word was said by any Flight Despatch officer during the course of the inquiry as to any conversation which took place on this occasion between the two pilots and the personnel at the Flight Despatch Office. I was being asked to accept, so it appeared, that the two pilots, about to start on this long journey to a virtually uninhabited part of the world, had not made a single inquiry about any feature of the flight. But, of course, that could

285

not have been true. They would have done what every flight crew would have done.

First of all the pilots would have questioned the Flight Despatch personnel (whoever they were) as to the details of the most recent weather forecast from Antarctica. They would have been told that Ross Island was under a low overcast with a base of between 2,000 and 3,000 feet and with cloud-free areas over the Victoria Land region. They would have been told that the forecast indicated that the overcast lying over the McMurdo area was static and likely to remain so.

The presence of a cloud base of 2,000 feet or somewhat higher would not have suggested any problem either to the Flight Despatch Office or to the two pilots because under the overcast there was reported visibility of forty miles in all directions. The pilots would have been advised that it would therefore be necessary to fly beneath the overcast in order to fly over the McMurdo region in clear air and that the normal operating altitude into McMurdo was about 1,500 feet. Subject to the possibility of snow showers or some other unfavourable weather development, the pilots would therefore have come to the conclusion that there would be no difficulty in operating the ordinary scenic flight over the McMurdo bases and the areas to the south before flying back from the south towards McMurdo and then turning towards Victoria Land so as to give passengers a view of this area from about 10,000 feet or so, and then climbing to cruising altitude and returning to New Zealand.

I am certain that either one or both of the pilots would have referred to the fact that the computer track for the aircraft would take them directly from Cape Hallett to the destination waypoint just to the west of the Dailey Islands, so that even if the overcast extended for a good many miles north of Ross Island, the aircraft need only be held in the Nav mode in order to arrive at about the centrepoint of the beginning of McMurdo Sound, and at that point they would then be either at or close to the radar range of American Air Traffic Control and their descent through the cloud into the clear air under the cloud base would be vectored by the Air Traffic Control.

The crew would have been in constant radio communication with Mac Centre as they approached McMurdo Sound and would have been kept up to date with any change in the weather conditions, particularly if the clear visibility beneath the cloud base had become impaired, because if that occurred, then the aircraft would have been required to divert back to the north-west towards the South Magnetic Pole which was the alternative viewing area. However, Flight Despatch would have warned the two pilots, and in any event I am sure that they were aware of this well before the morning of the fatal flight, that there had been a volume of complaints from passengers who had been on the recent flight which had been compelled to divert to the South Magnetic Pole. Consequently, although diversion to the alternative route might well be required if the weather conditions so demanded, the pilot in command would need to be satisfied that the weather had indeed deteriorated over McMurdo to an extent sufficiently unsatisfactory to require any diversion.

The aircraft therefore departed at 8.17 a.m. New Zealand time and set out on its journey. The flight path over New Zealand was completed when the aircraft 'overheaded' the beacon at Invercargill which is the southernmost city of the country, and the crew would have verified by reference to that beacon that the aircraft was flying exactly on track. The next leg of the computer track took the aircraft towards the Auckland Islands, and the next two waypoints were merely geographical positions out at sea with the aircraft still flying on a track heading towards the Balleny Islands.

Captain Collins had at his disposal a 'strip' topographical map displaying New Zealand at the top and the McMurdo area at the bottom, and on that map he had plotted the aircraft's track starting with the Auckland waypoint and terminating with the Dailey Islands waypoint and he had also plotted the return track to Christchurch.

In addition to that, he had with him his *New Zealand Atlas* with, on page 185, the only large scale topographical map available to him which showed the McMurdo region. This map displayed the area from just north of Beaufort Island down to a point about 100 miles south of McMurdo base. He had probably plotted on page 184 the track from the Balleny Islands down to McMurdo, but he had certainly plotted on the large scale picture on page 185 the track passing Beaufort Island fifteen miles to the west and proceeding down the approximate centre of the sound to the waypoint just to the west of the Dailey Islands. I also think it highly likely that he had marked off in segments the various distances to run on this last sector of the track and that in any event he had plotted the distance to run from the Byrd reporting point to the Dailey Islands waypoint.

As the aircraft approached the Balleny Islands it was flying at 33,000 feet and the crew would have observed without difficulty that they were flying directly on line with Buckle Island which is the centre of those three islands, and would therefore have verified that, in accordance with their expectation, the aircraft was flying on track and there was no need to make a manual alteration to the computer calculation which illustrated the track.

As the aircraft 'overheaded' Buckle Island it would have rolled to the east (i.e. to the left) and begun the next leg to Cape Hallett. Again, as the aircraft approached Cape Hallett, it would have been seen by the crew to be in line with that part of the extremity of the cape which contained the buildings which at one time were occupied by personnel who manned Hallett Station. Again, no need for any manual update of the computer flight track calculation. The aircraft was switched into Heading Select in the Cape Hallett area so as to deviate somewhat from the computer track, no doubt for the purpose of giving passengers better opportunities for photographs, and as the 'black box' showed, the aircraft was then locked back into the Nav mode and proceeded south on the final leg of the outward journey.

The crew would have been looking out for Coulman Island which is about seventy-five miles south of Cape Hallett and would have seen that the aircraft was flying over the approximate centre of Coulman Island, whereas the track plotted by Captain Collins the night before would have shown the aircraft to be flying slightly to the west of that track. But no regard would have been paid to that slight deviation because of the narrow conformation of Coulman Island as it lies north to south and the very slight deviation of two or three miles at that point would never have been observed.

As the aircraft flew on, still being held in the Nav mode, the deviation between the real track and the assumed track would gradually widen until, as the aircraft approached Franklin Island, the difference between the two tracks would have been about fifteen miles. And there can be no doubt that if the crew had seen Franklin Island just on their left when it should have been about fifteen miles to their left, there would have been an immediate question as to whether their flight path had been correctly programmed. But, as Mr Thomson had demonstrated, there were no passengers' photographs of Franklin Island, which was therefore certainly covered in cloud and thus the cross-track deviation was never revealed to the crew. The aircraft therefore flew on, still locked in the Nav mode.

Somewhere about midway between Coulman Island and Franklin Island, when the aircraft was about 200 miles from the McMurdo waypoint, Captain Collins would have initiated the normal pre-descent briefing. At that time the aircraft was flying in clear air but far below, and some distance ahead, there could be seen a solid cloud layer which, as later ascertained, had a base of about 10,000 feet. In the far distance there would have been seen the general location of the McMurdo area which would have been totally obscured by cloud, and the cloud cover had also obliterated from view Mount Erebus and the other mountains of Ross Island. On the right, extending far away to the south, would be seen the clear white mountain tops of Victoria Land.

Earlier in the flight, Captain Collins had received a McMurdo weather forecast transmitted by Auckland radio. The forecast over McMurdo was for a cloud base of 4,000 feet with visibility still at forty miles and with occasional light snow showers.

After discussion with the crew, Captain Collins decided to let the aircraft down at a gradual rate of descent until he had penetrated the high cloud below him, and he would have demonstrated on a map his plotted track running from Cape Hallett to the head of McMurdo Sound and he would also probably have indicated the track which he had plotted on page 185 of his atlas which gave a close-up of the McMurdo Sound area. He would have said that because the NDB had been withdrawn, and because the DC10 was not equipped to receive any directional aid from the TACAN, the Nav track must therefore be exactly followed until radar contact was made.

Captain Collins would have said that he would call for a radar letdown when the aircraft had arrived somewhere near the entrance to McMurdo Sound and he anticipated that this letdown would bring him out into clear air at somewhere between 2,000 and 3,000 feet at a point about midway down the sound.

The course to be then taken by the aircraft would depend upon the visibility below the McMurdo cloud base. If visibility remained clear in all directions then the aircraft would continue on down the sound, would fly over Scott Base and McMurdo Station, and after circling over the Ross Ice Shelf at about 2,000 feet would then turn north, fly over Scott Base and McMurdo Station again, and then fly towards Victoria Land before increasing altitude to the cruising height for the flight back to New Zealand.

It would have been agreed between Captain Collins and the other crew members that if, upon penetrating the cloud base north of McMurdo, the visibility was not sufficiently clear or if there were snow showers, then he would abandon any attempt to fly over the McMurdo area and would turn away towards the sunlit mountains of Victoria Land.

A decision would have been reached, again agreed between Captain Collins and the other crew members, as to the point at which the aircraft would fly away from McMurdo Sound if conditions under the cloud base were found to be unsuitable for viewing and that point was probably settled at some figure like thirty miles from the Dailey Islands waypoint. Alternatively, the departure point would have been fixed at about the vicinity of the Byrd reporting point which Captain Collins had previously calculated to have been twenty-three miles from his destination waypoint.

With the pre-descent briefing completed, a decision would be made to commence the descent at a point some distance ahead. None of this briefing was recorded on the flight deck recorder tape because it was completed outside the thirty-minute time span of that tape.

What happened thereafter need not now be repeated in detail. I have described it all in a previous chapter.

Suffice it to say that the offer of a radar letdown received from Mac Centre was first accepted by the aircrew but was ultimately abandoned when the crew saw beneath them, at about 18,000 feet, and with sixty miles to run, huge areas of clear air which meant that the cloud cover below them had become disintegrated. These large areas of clear sky displayed many square miles of ice and sea, as revealed by the passengers' photographs, and the opportunity now presented itself for the aircraft to descend in one or two orbits in clear air so as to level out at about 2,000 feet below the overcast which they knew was still in position in the McMurdo area. No radar assistance was now required. Mac Centre gave clearance for the DC10 to let down flying VMC and to proceed visually to McMurdo. The aircraft then descended to 2,000 feet and flew on under the overcast on Nav track. Captain Collins then descended to the altitude of 1,500 feet which had been recommended by Mac Centre.

In the meantime there had been identified the headlands, many miles to the left and many miles to the right, which, upon reference by Captain Collins to his plotted track, coincided with the headlands to left and right of the entrance to McMurdo Sound. Peter Mulgrew, who was observing these features and comparing them with the map which Captain Collins had in front of him, pointed out Cape Bird to the left and Captain Collins thus had a visual fix from someone familiar with the area. I also believe that he obtained a further visual fix of the headlands to the right from Peter Mulgrew who would have been leaning forward to the left of Captain Collins as he indicated the coastline far to the right, and I believe that the garbled nature of his remarks was due to his voice not being directly intercepted by the microphone. I also believe, as does Mr Thomson, that he identified further features to the right which were not picked up by the microphone at all, with Mulgrew leaning forward to the left of Captain Collins as he picked out the various features from the map.

So not only was the Nav track supposedly taking the aircraft directly between the headlands left and right of the entrance to McMurdo Sound, but also Captain Collins had obtained visual fixes to left and right confirming his Nav track position.

Then there came the decision, clearly announced by Captain Collins and recorded by the voice tapes, that he was going to fly away. He prefaced this announcement by saying that they were twenty-six miles out. Then there was the brief discussion between himself and First Officer Cassin, previously described. Captain Collins pulled out the Heading Select knob and, because the previous setting in Heading Select had been on a heading which would have taken the aircraft to the right, the aircraft commenced a right-hand roll but had rolled only about one degree or so before the Heading Select knob was turned to the left and the throttle levers were pushed forward as the preparations were made to put the aircraft into a climb.

On two occasions when travelling on international flights in DC10 aircraft I had sat in the seat behind the pilot in command and I had discussed with him and the crew whether, when Captain Collins had elected to fly away, he had selected a new heading before he pulled out the Heading Select knob, or whether he would have done this the other way round. Each of these flight crews had taken the view that Captain Collins would have pulled out the Heading Select knob and then turned it to the desired heading. These opinions confirmed what has just been said about the commencement of a right-hand roll as recorded by the 'black box', and then the immediate alteration to a left-hand roll just prior to impact.

I stress this only because when Civil Aviation officials had studied the sequence of movie film taken by a passenger through one of the right-hand windows of the DC10 in Antarctica, they had mistakenly believed that the beginning of the right-hand roll and then the correction to a left-hand roll had been evasive manoeuvres applied by Captain Collins as a result of suddenly seeing the mountainside ahead.

One of the flight captains had demonstrated to me the process in flight. He reached up and pulled out the Heading Select knob and turned it to a heading slightly to the left of our track. The aircraft rolled slightly left and then straightened up. Then he re-armed the Nav mode and turned the Heading Select knob to the right. The aircraft rolled slightly to the right and then when it had recaptured its Nav track it rolled slightly left and assumed its former course. The demonstration was repeated, and I was able to see for myself the commencement of the initial stages of the change of course. They were far less noticeable than the slight shift of the starboard wing of the DC10 as seen through the movie film to which I have already referred, as Captain Collins disengaged the Nav mode.

It was just after Captain Collins had switched into Heading Select that the GPWS sounded. I had no doubt, when writing my report, and I have no doubt now, that none of the flight crew believed that the GPWS system was functioning correctly. The aircraft was flying at 1,500 feet and everyone on the flight deck could see in front of him a perfectly flat vista of snow running many miles away into the distance. But when a GPWS warning is sounded then flight deck training asserts itself. The pilot in command calls for 'go round power' and pushes the throttle levers forward to the 'go round power' setting and at the same time he puts the aircraft into a climb. These manoeuvres are automatic. But a fraction of a second after 'go round power' was called for the aircraft struck the mountain with its engines beginning to develop the degree of high power commanded by Captain Collins.

Why did Captain Collins say, 'We'll have to climb out of this'? It will be remembered that he had been preoccupied with trying to obtain contact with the TACAN. The only information available from the TACAN was the distance to run. Successful contact with the TACAN would have resulted in a printout on the DC10 instrument panel giving the miles to run to the TACAN, and Captain Collins knew that this distance would be approximately the same as the distance to run to his plotted waypoint west of the Dailey Islands. In addition, the aircraft was failing to achieve communication with the Ice Tower. I think that what Captain Collins wanted from the Ice Tower was a report from the radar operator as to the range of the aircraft as depicted on the Ice Tower radar screen.

There can be only one answer to the question why Captain Collins decided that it was time to climb away. According to his own instruments he had now less than thirty miles to run, and despite the abnormally clear air of Antarctica he still could not see in the distance such obvious features as the buildings of Mac Centre and the unmistakable height of Mount Discovery. All he could see was this long vista of white. The visibility was clear enough. It was simply that in the far distance there was nothing to be seen. He may have believed that there was something wrong with the DME function on his aircraft. But, in particular, he may have been concerned not only at the absence of any landmarks forward of the aircraft, but also at the disappearance of any distinct horizon in the far distance.

For what follows, I am indebted to a very astute deduction made by Captain Vette. He pointed out to me, when this book was in the course of preparation, that with thirty miles to run to the destination waypoint the headlands to left and right of the aircraft had now receded from view as the aircraft flew on. At the time when they were still visible to left and right and slightly forward of the aircraft, they would have constituted two points of surface reference which the brain would connect by creating a distant forward horizon existing on the same level as the bottom of each headland. So whereas the eye would not in fact be seeing a forward horizon thirty or forty miles ahead, the brain of the observer would create one as a result of the clearly visible flat ground left and right, and the known perfectly flat terrain running miles away into the distance forward of the aircraft.

But, once the headlands left and right had receded from view, the points of reference denoting a forward flat horizon would have vanished. And immediately the impression of a forward horizon would have vanished also. There would then have been no horizon. And with the disappearance of the previously observable far distant horizon the instinct of the trained aviator would ring an alarm bell in the mind of Captain Collins. So this was yet another factor which would have induced the sudden decision to climb away, it being noted that this decision was made only a minute or two after the headlands left and right had been no longer observable. Such is the theory of Captain Vette, backed by his vast flying experience, and I can only say that it seems convincing to me.

In addition, one must go back to the pre-descent briefing which was not recorded by the voice tapes. There can be no doubt that a point had been fixed at which the aircraft would fly away if the forward observation of the known features of the head of the sound had still not come into view. And I suspect that this point had been pre-determined at either thirty miles to run or at twenty-three miles to run being the approximate position of the Byrd reporting point. Whatever point had been pre-determined, the pre-descent briefing decision had been put into effect. With the plotted track on the map before him, and with high ground more than twenty miles away on either side, the decision may well have been 'ultra-cautious' as Captain Wilson had agreed in his evidence. But Captain Collins and his crew had complied exactly with the pre-descent procedure.

How had the DC10 been operated during the last stages of the flight? Captain Collins was holding the aircraft exactly on its Nav track. He was plainly checking his position on the track plotted on the map in front of him. He could be heard on the voice tapes saying 'Up to here now', a remark accompanied by the sound of the rustling or crackling of a map. He identified in front of him the coastline to left and right as depicted by the map, and he had the identification by Peter Mulgrew, mistaken as it was, of those two coastlines. On at least thirteen occasions during the orbiting sequences he and Cassin audibly confirmed that they were flying VMC. Their flight deck drill, as demonstrated by the tapes, was impeccable. And when, with a clear white flat vista stretching out in front of him, he still could not see the buildings of the McMurdo base in front of him, he made the decision to fly away. I could not see that the aircrew had committed any act or omission which amounted to imprudence or lack of due care, a view which is shared by every flight captain with whom I have discussed the question, and I reported in those terms to the New Zealand Government.

Once the various criticisms of the flight crew, so assiduously advanced by the airline, the Chief Inspector and Civil Aviation, are set on one side as being without foundation, then what is left? The plain and obvious cause of this massive air crash originated from the concurrent effects of two different factors, the existence of which were not for even one moment suspected by the aircrew. One was the unannounced alteration to the flight track of the aircraft; the other was the presence of a classic clear air whiteout illusion as the aircraft approached the mountain.

Without the flight track alteration, the whiteout in Lewis Bay would have been of no consequence. The DC10 would not have been in Lewis Bay. But even with the flight track alteration, a cloudless sky would have nullified its effect. The aircraft would have approached Lewis Bay with the mountain ahead standing high in its path and the aircrew would have seen, at a range of not less than 100 miles, that they were flying on a computer flight path widely divergent from the track which was plotted on the map which they had before them.

Without the precise co-ordination in space and time of these two factors, there could have been no disaster.

I had had these reflections in mind as I stood with my companions on the slopes of Mount Erebus on the first anniversary of the disaster. Four thousand feet below were the ice cliffs which marked the frozen coastline of Lewis Bay, and over to the north-west, twelve miles away, the slopes of Mount Bird were enveloped in streams of pale cloud which were drifting towards us. The northern aspect of Mount Erebus was wholly concealed by cloud as from a level of about 1,000 feet above us. But, now and then, for a few seconds, the breeze would disperse the cloud and expose the wide buttress of black rock below the crater. Sometimes the drifting clouds from Mount Bird would obscure the sun and, when this happened, the bright foreground of the snow below us would lose its shape and contour and appear only as a featureless white expanse.

Towards the north, where the sunlight was sharp and clear, the flat ice shelf and pack ice stretched away into the far distance, and this had been the approach path of the aircraft towards the mountain. I could see the area about twenty-five miles to the north, where Captain Collins had re-armed the Nav mode so that the aircraft would return to its Nav track and thus fly, as he thought, down McMurdo Sound.

At that time, there had been patches of cloud above the aircraft which therefore was flying over landscape of alternate sunlight and shadow. But further on, the cloud base had been lower and unbroken and there was no sunlight on the snow. Visual contrast had entirely disappeared, and the aircrew could not discern that the white landscape ahead was sloping upward to meet the cloud. This could not have happened on the day of my inspection, but only because the cloud across Mount Erebus was drifting, not static, and its base was high enough to reveal the rock outcrop on which we were standing.

But the shifting variations of cloud and light demonstrated to us the simple fact that in Antarctica the occurrence of visual deception is not a phenomenon, as it might be in a temperate zone. It is part of the ordinary weather pattern of the region. On the day of the disaster there had been a solid and stationary low overcast over the whole of the McMurdo area, but it created visual deception only in those areas where landmarks had disappeared from view. Lewis Bay had been such an area. McMurdo Sound was not.

By a navigational error for which the aircrew was not responsible, and about which they were uninformed, an aircraft had flown not into McMurdo Sound but into Lewis Bay, and there the elements of nature had so combined, at a fatal coincidence of time and place, to translate an administrative blunder in Auckland into an awesome disaster in Antarctica.

Much has been written and said about the weather hazards of

Antarctica, and how they may combine to create a spectacular but hostile terrain, but for my purposes the most definitive illustration of these hidden perils was the wreckage which lay on the mountainside, showing how the forces of nature, if given the chance, can sometimes defeat the flawless technology of man. For the ultimate key to the tragedy lay here, in the white silence of Lewis Bay, the place to which the airliner had been unerringly guided by its micro-electronic navigation system, only to be destroyed, in clear air and without warning, by a malevolent trick of the polar light.